A LIFE'S

THE STORY B BOOK

A LIFE'S JOURNEY

THE STORY BEHIND A BOOK

Ahmed Paul Keeler

EQUILIBRA

EQUILIBRA PRESS

A LIFE'S JOURNEY
THE STORY BEHIND A BOOK

ISBN: 978-1-9161738-3-5

Equilibra Press
Cambridge
United Kingdom

Book design & typesetting:
New Andalus Productions

Cover image:
Annabel Keeler

Enquiries:
www.equilibrapress.com

ACKNOWLEDGEMENTS

A LIFE'S JOURNEY: THE STORY BEHIND A BOOK is really in itself a book of acknowledgements. In relating my story, I have endeavoured to recall the many people encountered during a long life, whose knowledge and wisdom enabled me to write *Rethinking Islam & the West: A New Narrative for the Age of Crises.*

I now have another set of acknowledgements for those who have generously given their time in helping me put together this present volume. Many of those in my story have helped me locate documents, recall events and then read through my transcript. Their comments and suggestions have been invaluable. My thanks go out to all of them.

The work was expertly copy-edited by Aziza Spiker, who noticed things that had passed us by, and beautifully designed by Abul Qasim Spiker who has also managed the publication of the book. I am deeply grateful to them both.

Finally, my deepest debt of gratitude is to my wife, Annabel, whose role in the completion of my book has been crucial. Annabel has been my astute editor, my most insightful sounding board and critic, and my partner for the greater part of my journey.

CONTENTS

PROLOGUE

THE CONVERSATION

'When will the book be ready?'
'What book?'
'Your book.'
'I'm not writing a book.'

MY FRIEND THEN set out to persuade me that I must write a book. He said that I had lived an extraordinary life; that I had passed through a unique period of history; that I had garnered along the way many interesting insights; that I owed it to the coming generations who could never enjoy the experiences that had been given to me; that I had met and received so much from the many people I had encountered along the way; that, indeed, I had a duty to pass it on in a book.

When he mentioned duty, I flinched a little as I was of that generation that prized this virtue very highly. However, I was unconvinced, considering myself to be an organizer not a writer. The incident faded from my memory. At the time of the conversation, I was directing the Golden Web Project in which I was fully engaged. Three years later my Project was terminated.

I had arrived at the age of seventy and I considered that my working life had ended in failure. Since the success of the World of Islam Festival in 1976, not one of the projects I had initiated had been realized.

I was settling into being grandfather to a bevy of little people, determined to at least make a success of this role, when a postcard arrived on my breakfast table. It consisted of four words, "How's the book going?" Now, I had been without a project for several months and was beginning to feel the strain; the periods of my life without projects that fully engaged me, were always the most difficult to bear. What was left for me to do? I realized with trepidation that writing a book was probably the only viable option left to me. Friends helped me to overcome my reservations and a dear friend, who I will introduce to you later in the story, convinced me that many people had derived benefit from my projects since the Festival, and that I should not view them as failures.

OBSTACLES

However, there were formidable obstacles that I had to overcome. The first was that I didn't like looking back. I have always lived in the present, fully occupied with and committed to the project that I was working on at the time. The second was that I was not a hoarder; the work of reconstructing the past would require quite an extensive research programme, involving family and colleagues with whom I had worked over the years, and hours spent in archives and libraries. The final problem was that I was not a writer. I had certain skills of persuasion which I had needed in order to convince funders, and to engage and motivate the teams involved in my projects. My three years at drama school had equipped me with tools that were useful in the presentation of ideas and proposals. I could talk quite convincingly, but writing was another matter. The process by which I transferred to paper what skills I had as a talker, I relate in Chapter 19.

THE PATTERNS EMERGE

My reluctance to look back into my past, however, began to disappear as I perused my life, and patterns began to emerge. I could see how my life had been defined by projects, beginning with my complete absorption in the beautiful little church we attended when I was a child. I was so engaged in the rituals that took place on Sundays, that at the age of six I set up an alter in my bedroom with cross, candlesticks and all the furnishings, and, insisting upon the attendance of my parents and very reluctant siblings, conducted communion services, using Ribena for wine, in a silver cup my sister had won in a ballet competition, and ice-cream wafers for the bread. I loved the bible stories and everything to do with the Church. My next project provided me with my refuge from the horrors of prep school. My mother kept canaries in a large aviary in the garden. I decided to breed violet budgerigars, and *The Cult of the Budgerigar* by W Watmough became my new bible. My father built me a set of aviaries, using a conservatory for the inside sections. An uncle who kept foreign birds took me under his wing, so to speak, and I accompanied him to shows where I proudly exhibited my prize birds. The holidays were dedicated to my budgerigars, and during the term, my letters home were full of instructions regarding the pairing of the birds. As I relate in Chapter 1, on arriving at Lancing College at the age of fourteen, acting and the theatre claimed me for the next seven years and the budgerigars faded away. There followed some eight or nine projects which engaged me from my graduating from Drama school at the age of twenty-one until I reached my seventieth year. I now realized that it was through these projects that I met the people and absorbed the knowledge and understanding that would end up in my book. As I went deeper into my story two powerful themes became evident.

CHANGING WORLDS

The worlds were changing and I was changing worlds. The West went through a dramatic transformation from deeply conservative global empires, to the cultural revolutions of the 1960s and the full manifestation of modernity by the 1980s. The Islamic world, having been shattered by the European Empires, went from obscurity, to becoming, with oil and religion, the big issue for the West. I was the last generation to be educated for empire, turned rebel in the 1960s, and then entered Islam in the 1970s. I experienced the different worlds both as an insider and from outside. However, on leaving school in 1960 my life also became defined by the second of the themes.

AGAINST THE TIDE

Unwittingly, I have found myself travelling against the tide throughout my working life. I went for three years to the drama school that was the first to promote the new playwrights who were tearing down the establishment that had nurtured me. I then spent five years deeply engaged in modern art, which was in its infancy in London and struggling to survive. Finally, at the end of the sixties I was swept up into the Hippie movement that had completely rejected the mainstream and wished to create a new world of love and peace. All of these worlds were revolutionary and, in different ways, were challenging a deeply entrenched establishment.

My entry into Islam provided me with the momentous insight that guided all that was to follow. I was initiated into the world of Islam through a master of traditional music. Through the perspective of tradition, I was able to see the modern arts, in which I had been immersed, from another perspective. The gulf between the traditional and the modern became clear. But the tide was now with the modern, and I would witness the revolutionaries of the 1960s conquering and becoming the establishment, first in the West and then increasingly in the Islamic world. The struggle for survival was now with the traditional, and I found myself in the thick of it.

There was, however, to be one glorious moment when a vision of the traditional world of Islam would be glimpsed, and that was with the Festival of 1976. Looking back, it appears like a miracle; everything seemed to be arranged for it to be able to happen. The timing was right, the people were there and the institutions were receptive. But after the Festival, a great change began as Islam increasingly became identified with terrorism, turning Islam into a toxic term. From the end of the Festival to my seventieth birthday I was engaged in a tremendous struggle to continue the work I had begun with the Festival.

ALL THE WORLD'S A STAGE

As I studied the trajectory of my life, it appeared to me that I was like an actor who was given his part, scene by scene, but had no idea what was going to happen next or how the play was going to end. I began to realize that perhaps there was a meaning to my journey that could only now make sense. If I was to fulfil my task in life, my projects had to fail, everything happened as it should have done. Each project had delivered a piece of a puzzle that I was now beginning to put together. However, what started as an autobiography was now changing into something else. The subject of my book would become my understanding of Islam and the West.

Professor Khaled Fahmy, when he introduced *Rethinking Islam and the West: A New Narrative for The Age of Crises* at the Cambridge University book launch, explained how this was not a usual academic work dependent upon archival sources, but the result of a life's journey. It is this journey that I have endeavoured to capture in what follows.

I

FROM 0 TO 50 YEARS

1

BORN TO SERVE

CHILDHOOD

I WAS BORN JUST outside Windsor in 1942, right in the middle of the Second World War. Windsor was a deeply conservative town, at the very heart of the British Empire, and the castle was the favourite palace of His Majesty King George VI. To grow up with a real castle of such imposing character was awe-inspiring for a child, and I needed no encouragement to accompany my mother when she went shopping in the town, for each day the military band marched up the high street for the changing of the guard. At the entrance to the castle was a statue of Queen Victoria, who had been dead 40 years when I was born but was still very much alive in Windsor.

We lived in a fine house surrounded by a beautiful garden, which was the creation of my mother. Through the gates beside the house, leading to what had been the stables, was the factory. My father was an inventor who founded a business manufacturing optical instruments, which developed into a world leader in its field. So, at the bottom of our garden, we had carpentry, machine, paint and assembly shops, producing precision instruments designed by my father and his team, and exported all over the world. However, the factory and the family haven were two quite separate realms. Whereas we could roam freely in our garden and even wander into the adjoining countryside, our visits to the factory were strictly supervised, as it was a hazardous place for children.

The family midwife Nurse Griffin, whom we called 'Griffy', was a formative influence in my life. She was a true Christian and taught me to love my Bible and Jesus. As a nursery nurse, she had taken care of us when we were babies, and then remained closely attached to the family until her death aged 97. By the age of five, I was a server in our local Parish Church and was immersed in its rituals and life. It seemed at the time I was destined to become a priest. There were five of us children; my sister was the eldest and I was the third of four brothers. We were a happy family. Our home life was full of games and activities, and we seemed to spend most of our time playing outside. For our holidays, we went camping in the West Country, where we set up our tents and parked our caravan in fields beside the sea, or next to a river in which we could swim. But for us boys, this halcyon childhood was rudely terminated when, on reaching the age of eight, one by one, we were packed off to boarding school.

PREP SCHOOL

Prep school was a terrible shock, and I spent six years incarcerated in an institution where we lived in constant fear of the headmaster and his wife. The discipline was draconian and the food was awful. However, we formed friendships, camaraderie grew amongst us, and somehow, we survived and made the best of it. At times we even enjoyed ourselves. Games were compulsory and we played them all: football, rugby, cricket, athletics, tennis, squash, fives, shooting and boxing. For some of us it was great, for others, a nightmare. To see weaker boys being beaten up in the annual compulsory boxing competition was not a pleasant sight, but we were assured it built character. We were taught to be fiercely competitive, but we also learnt teamwork and fair play. Music was another activity that brought great pleasure to some. We learnt to sing hymns and anthems tunefully, and could take up an instrument if we wanted to.

Central to our lives was the Christian year, with the festivals of Christmas and Easter devoutly observed, and we knew and loved the stories of the Old Testament prophets. However, Julius Caesar and Latin were supreme in the classroom. Gentle Jesus and the warrior Caesar were the most powerful figures in our education. They were both celebrated, but the contradiction in their messages was never addressed; they inhabited quite separate spheres.

We knew by heart the stories of the heroes of England: Alfred the Great and his burning of the cakes; Sir Francis Drake finishing the game of bowls and then defeating the Spanish Armada; General Wolf surprising the French by taking an army up an impossible mountainside and winning Canada for the British Empire; and the death of Admiral Lord Nelson, saviour of the nation against the depredations of the French. We knew little about India beyond the terrible murder of British prisoners in the 'Black Hole of Calcutta', and the burning of widows on funeral pyres. India was 'the white man's burden'. What little we knew about slavery was limited to the role of the great British reformer William Wilberforce in persuading the British parliament to abolish it.

However, our heroes were not confined to the past. We had just defeated the most evil force in history, and through the cinema we were reliving the war and the incredible stories of bravery and the sacrifices that our soldiers, sailors and airmen had endured. We had stood alone and triumphed - the Americans as usual arrived late, and we knew nothing of the Eastern Front and the millions that had died in Russia. For this education had a purpose: to prepare us to become dedicated servants of Empire and leaders of mankind. It was based upon the Spartan philosophy that if you took a child from its family when it was eight, you could turn it into a loyal servant of the state, and we were the last generation to be educated for Empire. After ten years of boarding school, away from home the greater part of the year, the child, now having become a man, could be sent to any part of the Empire upon which the sun never set, and be expected to do his duty.

'The English: the greatest and most civilized people that ever the world saw.'

We believed this statement of Lord Macaulay with our whole being. After all, the British Empire had surpassed Rome; our version of Christianity was the best; we had produced the greatest scientists and were the creators of the Industrial Revolution. Our mission in life was to civilize, Christianize and modernize.

I was ten when the King died. His image had been cast upon our minds through the stamps, coins and pictures that were entwined with our lives. He was greatly respected and loved. The headmaster's announcement of his death took place while we were having lunch and is still crystal clear in my memory; I can see the plate of spam fritters, boiled potatoes and cabbage before me. The nation joined with the three Queens, his mother, his wife and his daughter, in mourning his untimely death at the age of 56, exhausted by the burden of office which he had carried with great courage throughout the war. A year later, the young and beautiful Princess Elizabeth was crowned Queen Elizabeth II. A new era had begun. Millions of families, including our own, bought television sets to watch the coronation. Within a short time 'the box' was in the corner of most living rooms, and we were being fed a diet of films and shows from America, where the TV was already well established. I was part of that last generation whose early childhood was lived in the pre-television age.

PUBLIC SCHOOL

I was fourteen when I joined my two elder brothers at Lancing College. I had needed to spend an extra year at my prep school in order to pass the entrance examination. However, it was well worth the wait. It enabled me to enter a world far removed from the fearful prep-school regime that had broken into my childhood. Lancing College is in a stunning setting high up on the South Downs, surrounded by countryside and overlooking the sea. In my day it was a haven of peace, yet to be spoiled by the thundering road that now links Brighton and Worthing, and the hideous additions to the school since the sixties. The College was founded in the nineteenth century, and was part of the revival of Christianity which saw the rebirth of Gothic architecture. Lancing College with its chapel was one of the finest examples of this Renaissance. I spent four happy years in this beautiful, humane, Christian environment, where the study and practice of art, music and drama were seriously cultivated, and were considered to be an important part of school life.

The Chapel was the tallest in England and stood like a colossus above the school, dominating its surroundings. It was at the centre of our daily lives. The school came together for morning prayers after breakfast, and was gathered once more for evensong at the end of the day. On Sundays and during the festive seasons, the Chapel came into its full glory, with the beauty of the architecture providing the setting for a musical feast, served up by one of the finest school choirs in England. When I was at Lancing, the Chapel was still being built and the west end was sealed off with sheets of corrugated iron. A temporary covered walkway linked the Chapel to the School.

Our housemaster, Patrick Halsey, was a remarkable, cultured, deeply eccentric and greatly loved character whom we knew as 'Tiger'. With humour and wisdom, he presided over a community where children matured into young men and the Christian virtues of kindness and compassion were cultivated through his example. In our last year, he would take a group of us on a grand tour of Italy. The year I went we visited Florence, Sienna, Assisi and Venice. With this remarkable journey my time at Lancing came to an end.

My next port of call should have been two years' National Service in the army, where, coming from a public school, one would automatically be selected for officer training and then be given a platoon. However, National Service was abolished in 1960 and I missed having to do it by a month. The normal trajectory after National Service was to take up your place at university, where the education of a gentleman was completed, and then join a London club where male members of the establishment continued their public-school existence. However, these were not normal times. England was in the throes of a cultural revolution, which, during the sixties, brought about momentous and lasting change. Our generation had been educated to take up our place in a world that no longer existed. The British Empire was over.

THE THEATRE

On arriving at Lancing I had found a new enthusiasm, which began to replace the priesthood as my goal in life. Auditions were taking place for the school play, which was to be *Hamlet* by William Shakespeare. I auditioned and landed a part. The standard of acting and production values for a school dramatic society were exemplary. The master in charge, Donald Bancroft, was a brilliant producer who was well known for his adaptations of the classics for radio. As in Shakespeare's day, in our all-male environment, the younger boys played the girls' parts, and I was chosen for the role of Ophelia. I immersed myself in the play, attending every rehearsal, drinking in the discussions surrounding the plot. By the time we were finished, I knew the whole of *Hamlet* by heart. This profound and troubling play was the beginning of my real education. The formal education in the classroom had left me cold and continued to do so throughout my time at Lancing. I had found my niche and my passion. Nobody from my prep school came to Lancing, so I had to make new friends, which I did in my house and through the school plays, which took place annually. I played Sir Patrick Cullen in *The Doctor's Dilemma* by Bernard Shaw, Dogberry in Shakespeare's *Much Ado about Nothing*, and Moses in *The Firstborn* by Christopher Fry.

I formed my own dramatic society at home, so my love of theatre carried over to the holidays. The company was made up of friends from Lancing, my old prep school and the church. We produced *Rope* by Patrick Hamilton, *The Diary of a Scoundrel* by Alexander Ostrovsky, and our own production of *The First Born* by Christopher Fry. As well as acting in them, I made the sets in my father's carpentry shop and managed the company. All profits from our performances, which were held in church halls, went to the Guide Dogs for the Blind.

The height of my dramatic career at Lancing was reached when I played Dr Faustus in Christopher Marlowe's prescient play, which envisions the birth of modern man. By my last year at Lancing, the theatre had become my life to the exclusion of practically everything else. My heroes were the great classical actors of the day, above whom towered Sir Laurence Olivier, whose films of Shakespeare's *Henry V*, *Hamlet* and *Richard III*, I saw many times.

And so it was decided that, as my academic qualifications were negligible and fell far short of getting me into any university, I should be allowed to indulge my passion and audition for drama school. But little did I know what lay in store for me. At the age of eighteen, I stepped out into the world and landed, unwittingly, right in the middle of the cauldron of rebellion that was engulfing the arts, where I would swim, flounder and nearly drown during the first nine years of my adulthood.

2

INTO THE MAELSTROM

DRAMA SCHOOL

IN 1960 THE TWO leading drama schools in London were the Royal Academy of Dramatic Art (RADA) and the Central School of Speech and Drama. I auditioned for the Central School and was accepted. I did not go on and try for RADA as Central School seemed keen to have me. If I had gone to RADA, my life could have been very different. RADA was a drama school in the traditional mould where the classics still held sway. However, Central School had just undergone a radical change. It had linked up with the Royal Court Theatre where the young anti-establishment playwrights were being incubated. Their production of John Osborne's *Look Back in Anger* had been ground breaking. At Central School, a new regime was being established and I was part of its initial intake.

During my first year I had a room in a boarding house in Golders Green and travelled each day to the school in Swiss Cottage. For the first time in my life, I suffered intense and aching loneliness, separated as I was from my Lancing community and friends. However, steeled in prep school to make the best of it, I threw myself into the work.

We were fed a diet of unremitting angst. Our classics were the 20th century works of Samuel Becket and Bertolt Brecht, and our staple became the new British playwrights such as Harold Pinter, Arnold Wesker and, of course, John Osborne. Through their plays, they were undermining the world that had nurtured me and the values that had informed my life. The establishment, the family, the church, the army and the world of business were all targets for their brilliant, cruel, insightful, dramatic constructions. In compelling language, they laid bare the wasteland of broken relationships, exploitation, disconnection, and alienation that were festering in our modern society. There seemed to be no solutions, only bitterness, anger and unremitting suffering. After three years, I had learnt the basics of my craft, but something had drained out of me. I was no longer in love with the theatre. My enthusiasm to become an actor had died. I was marooned in unfamiliar territory. Nothing engaged my whole being. And then I met an artist.

SIGNALS GALLERY

My new friend, the Philippine artist and poet David Medalla, introduced me to modern art, and this strange world became my next total obsession. I began by holding exhibitions in the family home. In the early sixties, support for modern art and the avant-garde was still in its infancy. Sir Roland Penrose, whose house was filled with works of the modern masters, was a founder of the Institute of Contemporary Arts and one of its few patrons. In order to keep the Institute going, every so often he would sell a work of art and replace it with a copy. When I met him, his house was already half full of copies. The avant-garde was only just surviving. The Institute was located in a terraced house in Dover Street and one of the floors provided a modest space for its temporary exhibition gallery.

I convinced my father to let me have one of his shops in the West End of London, on the corner of Wigmore Street and Welbeck Street. There I opened my gallery, which we named Signals, after a series of works by the Greek artist Takis. With its four floors of exhibition space, it became one of the largest galleries of its kind in London. In the early sixties, Pop Art was the rage and the Americans dominated the scene. My gallery specialized in Kinetic Art. This is the art of movement, where the artist creates change within the object, or between the object and the viewer. The gallery represented a number of artists, who mostly lived in Paris, Rio de Janeiro and Caracas. There was a strong Latin-American representation. The gallery with its artists, surrounded by all those involved in their promotion, presentation and support, became my new community. My engagement with the artists was exhilarating; visiting their studios, planning their exhibitions, acquiring their works and sometimes even selling a piece. We held individual and group exhibitions, and there was a tremendous sense of achievement and satisfaction when, after all the planning and preparation, an exhibition finally opened and the public who appreciated our kind of art was admitted. The gallery produced a newspaper, *Signals*, which, besides promoting and recording the exhibitions, brought together on its pages diverse articles, poems and pictures that explored the relationship between art, science and technology, for it was their symbiosis that was at the heart of the gallery's philosophy.

However, the gallery was not financially viable. The sales hardly made a dent in the massive costs of shipping and mounting the exhibitions, producing the newspaper, and the sums spent on buying works from the artists and building a collection. Debts were mounting and the gallery was beginning to endanger the family business, so my father pulled the plug. I had to sell the collection, and the gallery went into bankruptcy. I was devastated. I was 25 and I thought my life was over. The gallery had only been open two and a half years but it had been an incredibly intense experience in which my whole being had been engaged. In the heat of the crisis, I had broken with my father, and as I waited for my train on Windsor station after leaving the family home to return to London, I seriously contemplated suicide, for the only time in my life.

The gallery closed in 1967, at the time when across the Atlantic an extraordinary rebellion of the youth of America was taking place. When it arrived in England, it was to sweep me up and take me on a strange and dangerous journey, one which encompassed my life for the next year and a half.

THE EXPLODING GALAXY

Opposition to the Vietnam War had fermented a movement which united the youth of America. The massive protests that took place had played an important part in bringing the war to an end. A section of this rebellion was inhabited by those who came to be known as Hippies. Their disillusion with the established order was total. Their mantra was to 'turn on', meaning come alive, 'tune in' to the 'life force' and 'drop out' of the corrupt, moribund existing order. They wished to create an alternative world of peace and love. It was through music that the hippie tribes gathered to celebrate their newfound liberation. Sound, made possible by loud speakers that could boom out to reach a million ears, in an environment of flashing, melting, strobing lights, and with the addition of mind-enhancing substances, brought this strange congregation to a state of collective ecstasy. Having rejected their Christian heritage, they sought spiritual solace in India and amongst the Native Americans. The gurus and maharishis flocked to America and set up their ashrams, now and then appearing at great gatherings of the faithful, where the peace they promised mingled with the frenzied music of the bands. In England, the Beatles were transformed into a band whose music perfectly encapsulated the psychedelic, and their song 'All you need is love' became the anthem of the movement.

My home in London, which was all that I had left after the collapse of the Gallery, became the residence for a hippie commune we called the Exploding Galaxy. The house was a hive of activity where the members of the group planned and rehearsed the latest 'Galactic' offerings. The mission of the Galaxy was to turn all of life into art. Happenings took place in parks, on buses and at gatherings of the faithful. The Galaxy included poets, musicians, artists, writers and dancers, and our productions, though they meant a great deal to us, were incomprehensible to the uninitiated. People would stand around in states of bemusement, amusement and sometimes hostility when confronted with our uninvited offerings.

The arrival of the Kathakali dance troupe from India and their performance at the Sadler's Wells Theatre made a huge impression on us. Their artistry and power of storytelling through the movement of their hands, faces and eyes was remarkable. Accompanied by hypnotic rhythmic music, it was a mesmerising experience, and was the catalyst for the high point of the Galaxy's short existence. 'The Bird Ballet', loosely based on the Persian poet Attar's *Conference of the Birds*, brought together all the members of the Galaxy. Rehearsals took place in a church hall and it was staged at the Roundhouse, a large converted Victorian railway building. The Galaxy put its heart and soul into the production, which lasted over three hours. However, the response from the Guardian critic was that, although he could see that the cast were enjoying themselves, he had never been so bored in his life.

But time was running out. Our self-obsessed, happy community was oblivious to the misery we caused to our neighbours living in the adjoining terraced houses. Hippies were not popular. Our impromptu happenings had upset members of the public, and articles appeared in the tabloid press attacking our way of life. The police moved in and planted drugs in the church hall where we were rehearsing, and then in the house. Meanwhile, a young incredibly rich French heiress appeared and started showering money in all directions, some of which fell upon members of the Galaxy. This money was the catalyst that set-in motion the gradual dispersion of members of the Galaxy: some joined the hippie trail to India; others wanted to set up a commune in Scotland. Meanwhile, I was taken up with organizing our legal defence, for the police had brought charges for possession of the drugs that they had planted. Preparing our court case turned into a campaign which involved the support of prominent people and the press. After months of court appearances, most of the charges were thrown out. In the end, the eldest member of our community was made the sacrificial victim and fined. The spell had been broken and the community was scattering.

It was at this low point that I met two people who would completely transform my life. The first was Annabel, the woman who was to become my wife, and then, together, we were invited by an Indian friend to a private concert of North Indian classical music.

3

USTAD MAHMUD MIRZA

WE WERE TO MEET Ustad Mahmud Mirza, who would become the keystone for my life's work. However, our first encounter could well have been our last. Before the private concert began, our Indian friend said he would like to introduce us to the musician who was a friend of his. We joined the queue, and when our turn came shook hands and gazed upon him with eyes that saw wonder in everything that came from India. Mahmud was due to perform in the second half of the concert; the first half was taken up by a pair of singers. During the interval a very aggressive gentleman, who was something to do with the organization, confronted us and because of our hippie attire, saw to it that we were evicted. We told our friend that we would wait for him in the pub around the corner, and left. After the concert Mahmud asked our friend what had happened to the two young people he had met before the concert. On being told what transpired he insisted on meeting us and our friend went and fetched us.

Thus began our association. The first time we heard Mahmud play was a few days later in the Chelsea home of the folksinger and artist Rory

McEwan. Mahmud chose to play Darbari, one of the most powerful *ragas*, created by Mia Tansen. As he unfolded the *raga*, stage by stage, we were taken to a place of peace and beauty, the like of which we had never experienced before. Here, at last, was an art form that was wholly alive and complete. We became inseparable from him. Within a short time, he had brought me back into a world of normality. It was as though he had plucked me out of a stormy sea in which I had been drowning, shaken me off, and placed me on dry land. We had all wanted to go to India, but India had come to us. However, it was a very different India from the one we had been expecting. Over the winter of 1968–69, I showed Mahmud the sights of London and he began to introduce me to the world from which he came. Mahmud and his music became the guiding light which we now followed. Annabel, who was more musical than me, studied the *ragas*, whilst I organized his concerts. We were also introduced to curries and she learnt to cook from Mahmud, who excelled in this art as well!

Mahmud's disarming modesty covered a formidable presence. He had been initiated into music at the age of six by his maternal uncle, the sitarist Ustad Haidar Hussein Khan, who was the doyen of one of the greatest of the *gharanas*, or lineages of music, which went back 500 years to the great court musician, Mia Tansen. Mahmud was a child prodigy and gave his first public performance at the age of eleven. After the untimely death of his uncle and teacher, when Mahmud was only twelve, he was taken under the wing of Pandit Jiwan Lal Matoo, who was the disciple of arguably the greatest master of the 20th century, Ustad Abdul Wahid Khan. The Pandit was unusual amongst musicians. He was both musicologist and performer, and his understanding and knowledge of the *raga* system and the history of the music was unrivalled. Mahmud was entirely receptive to what the Pandit was able to transmit, and he became the complete traditional musician, both in practice and theory. With this background he was perfectly prepared to recognize, resist and challenge the onslaught of the modern which, from the 1960s, would engulf Indian classical music.

Over the years Mahmud has given a number of interviews for Indian newspapers in which he has tackled every aspect regarding the changes that were taking place. He decried the association of the sitar with the hippies and pop music in the West, warning of the danger of attaching it to a fad, for once the fad was over, the interest in the music would fade, and this is what happened. He railed against the fusion of Western music and Indian music, stating that they were each complete systems and their fusion made a nonsense of them both. He championed the cause of the traditional lineages of music (*gharanas*), asserting that the schools of music being introduced in imitation of Western music academies were incapable of producing master musicians. He bewailed the transformation of the music from a serious contemplative form to light entertainment, and the emergence of the cult of celebrity. All the while, his own music retained its integrity and remained true to the tradition.

His cause became mine, and I seem to have been perfectly prepared to play the role of championing his music. My childhood was steeped in the architecture and environment of the Gothic tradition. I had grown up in a world in which the Gothic revival of the 19th century had fully flowered. The order, beauty and rituals of the lovely church of my childhood and the glorious chapel at Lancing had nourished and formed me. Then, from the age of 18 to 26, I had been whisked away, and without any volition on my part, tossed into the deep ends of the worlds of modern theatre, art and the counter-culture, long enough to be fully immersed but not long enough to become established within those worlds. My meeting with Mahmud drew me back into the world of tradition, and I could see and experience the chasm that existed between the chaos and angst of the modern and the order and beauty epitomized by his music.

In early 1969, Mahmud and I were standing on the platform at Marylebone underground station, waiting for a train and discussing our plans for the future. I expressed my desire to visit India, but he suggested instead that I should go to America. Now, my grandfather had come from Philadelphia and moved to England in 1906, so the Keelers had both business and family links in the USA. We were expecting our first born to arrive in the spring, and everything was calling for a new beginning. I was ready for a challenge that would fully engage me. My house was sold after the last remaining members of the community had gone, and after charges, debts and repairs to a much-abused dwelling, there was enough left over to ferry me across the water and set up home for a few months. In early May, my parents and parents-in-law, together with Annabel and our new-born son, came to the airport to see me off. Annabel would join me when I had organized a place for us to live.

The day after my arrival in New York, I was invited to dinner by an art critic I had known in my previous life. On arrival I stepped straight back into the world Mahmud had rescued me from. The hash was circulating, and I joined the party. Now during my year and a half as a hippie I had never had a bad experience with drugs. I was now to experience a terror that nearly unhinged me. I left the party stating that I was going back to London. Somehow, I believed that I could arrive there instantly. By some miracle I was able to find the hotel I was staying in and reach my room. I had a work by the philosopher Schopenhauer with me, and I read it through the night, believing that a man of his intellect must have experienced what I was going through, that of being confronted by the terror of eternity. As the sun rose the terror began to lift. I had experienced the fear of God, and recording the event as I write this passage, I realize it was a warning to completely break from my former life, which is what I did.

I threw myself into a whirlwind of activity. I began by travelling between Washington and Boston on Greyhound buses, mostly at night so that I could save on hotels. I met with concert promoters, journalists and academics at the universities. By the summer I had organized a series of concerts for March of 1970 that would start in Boston, take in Washington and Baltimore and end at the Lincoln Centre in New York. I found an apartment in Dover Delaware which was midway between the various venues and Annabel and the little one joined me. However, the money was fast running out, and after only three months Annabel and baby had to return to London. It was a sad day when the truck arrived to carry away the furniture which we had lovingly purchased a few weeks before, and I had to return the keys to the landlord. I went back to my life on Greyhound buses, staying in very cheap hotels, or relying on the kind hospitality of relatives and a growing network of friends that was forming between Washington and Boston.

During the year I spent in America I went through an intense education. I was discovering a new world. There were several museums and libraries that contained material on India and the Mughal Empire, and I devoured their collections. I attended lectures in New York and at Harvard. I met with scholars who specialized in my area of interest. I spent hours in the Museum of Fine Arts in Boston, contemplating the glorious miniatures that had belonged to Ananda Coomaraswamy. I could begin to imagine the cultural world to which Mahmud's music belonged. I decided to organize a special event that would show the music in its context of the Mughal court; it was to be entitled 'The Arts of Mughal India'. Brandeis University agreed to host the event and I set about inviting the scholars who would present the various aspects. I secured the participation of Prof Annemarie Schimmel, the world expert on the poetry of Rumi and a specialist in Urdu and Persian poetry, Stuart Cary Welch, an authority on Mughal miniature painting, Dr Daud Rahbar, a poet and scholar of Urdu literature, and a well-known Kathak dancer who was visiting Harvard University at the time. With this event my plans for Mahmud's tour were complete.

I found an apartment in the Boston area where I had formed a circle that included scholars and critics eagerly anticipating the arrival of Mahmud and his drummer. Annabel arrived with our now ten-month-old son and together we prepared the apartment which would be our base camp for the tour. When all was ready, Mahmud arrived from India with his tabla player. The tour took place, and the concerts were well received with glowing reviews. The critics recognized that they were witnessing something special. Prof Annemarie Schimmel, who was enthralled by Mahmud's knowledge and mastery of the music, proposed that he come to Harvard for a year as a musician-in-residence. I was able to arrange a grant from the Rockefeller III Foundation to cover the cost of the appointment. However, it never happened. It appears that an Indian government official stepped in and suggested to the foundation another 'more appropriate' musician. This was my introduction to the politics that was endemic in the world of Indian music and that dogged Mahmud's career.

But the tour had been a great success, and the event at Brandeis University had opened for me the door into Muslim India which I was eager to pursue further. Mahmud and his accompanist returned to India, and Annabel and the little one to London. I remained to tie up the loose ends. Although the concerts had been quite well attended, after the costs and management fees were covered, little was left over. I could not see any future for me in America. I was keen to delve deeper into the world that had been opened up for me. I wanted to present the Arts of Mughal India event in London. The year in America had been incredibly valuable; I had made a clean break with my past, entered a new cultural field, and regained my enthusiasm for life.

But before we leave America, I want to introduce a painting that captivated me and a book that shattered me. The painting hangs in the National Museum of Art, and is a Madonna and Child by Giotto. Every time I went to Washington, I spent time in the gallery, absorbed, sometimes for up to an hour, gazing at this glorious painting. I was experiencing the miracle of fatherhood, but it was the relationship between mother and child that was beyond words. This wonder was expressed in the painting.

The book that shocked and shattered me was *The Case for India* by Will Durant, which was given to me by an Indian professor from Boston University. I was already familiar with Will Durant's magnus opus on world history. During the 1920s he had visited India, at a time when the West was being regaled with the vision of the white man's burden and images of widows burning on funeral pyres. He wanted to discover for himself the reality of the situation. Although my knowledge of India had vastly improved, I still retained a deep sense of the fundamental virtue of the British. This book shattered me. Durant was a fair man and his judgement that the British had committed the greatest crime in history with its rape of Bengal and further subjugation of the sub-continent, seared my soul. I read the book in one sitting and phoned the professor in the middle of the night, berating him for having given me the book. But my eyes had been opened and it was the beginning of my serious study of the European empires and their impact on the traditional worlds they encountered.

I arrived back in London in early summer 1970 and immediately approached the Institute of Contemporary Arts with the idea of hosting the Arts of Mughal India. Modern art was on the rise and the ICA had moved into palatial accommodation in a Nash terrace facing St James Park. I made the case that the traditional arts of India were contemporary. The idea was warmly accepted, and the event duly took place later that year in November. This time the participants were Bamber Gascoigne, who had just completed his book on the Moghul Empire, and gave an illustrated lecture on the development of Moghul architecture, Robert Skelton from the Victoria and Albert Museum, whose talk was entitled 'The Grand Moghul', and Ralph Russell, Reader in Urdu at the School of Oriental and African Studies, who spoke on the *ghazal* in Mughal poetry, with readings by Dr Khurshidul Islam, Reader in Urdu at Aligarh Muslim University. The two evenings of lectures provided the setting for the music, and on the third evening Mahmud gave his recital. The event was a great success and the director invited me to set up an Oriental programme of lectures and events.

The first event I organized was to take music lovers more deeply into Mahmud's music. Indian Ragas relate to the cycle of the day and night and to the seasons. In the modern concert scheduling, only afternoon or evening ragas were being performed, and the length of concerts were limited in duration. During February 1971 five concerts at different times of the day, including an all-night concert, took place in intimate settings which did not require microphones. The concerts were a tremendous success, and a circle of devoted listeners began to form. There followed a series of lectures on many aspects of Indian and increasingly Islamic subjects. My horizon was extending, and I was on the brink of the great vision that would set my course for life and lead to my conversion to Islam.

4

THE WORLD OF ISLAM FESTIVAL 1971

ON RETURNING TO London, I had continued the study I had begun in America. Whilst engaging with the ICA, I spent all the time I could in the British Museum reading room and the Victoria and Albert Museum library. To read about the cultures and civilizations of the world and then walk around the galleries looking at their artifacts was an incredible education. This period was an intense learning experience, and it was during an afternoon at the British Museum in early March 1971 that I had a vision of the unity of Islamic civilization. Mahmud had introduced me to Mughal India, and several of the kinetic artists of my gallery had been inspired by the geometric patterning of the Alhambra, so I knew something about Moorish Spain. These two cultures, thousands of miles apart, belonged to the same world; the principles that governed their arts were the same, and yet they were ethnically and linguistically totally different and had completely separate histories. The only thing that connected them was Islam. With great excitement I approached

David Thompson, the director of the ICA, with the proposal to hold an event that would celebrate the arts of the 'World of Islam'. The idea was accepted, and I set to work organizing what would be the first of the World of Islam Festivals. Two and a half years had elapsed since my meeting with Ustad Mahmud Mirza. I had been immersed in his music, learnt about his tradition, been introduced to Mughal India and been given a vision of the wonder and unity of the world of Islam.

The Festival was set to take place in November 1971, which gave us nine months to put it together. The first consideration was the exhibition that would be mounted in the ICA's main gallery. We settled on geometric pattern as being the most appropriate theme, one which expressed the unity of Islam and would also be readily accessible to the Western visitor. I invited Keith Albarn, a young, highly imaginative artist and designer to undertake the task. He put together a team and set to work analysing the patterns. He consulted with several of the museum curators responsible for the Islamic collections, who were already engaged with the Festival, preparing their lectures. A remarkable research project ensued which resulted in a beautiful and thought-provoking exhibition. The centre piece was the analysis of a paradise garden carpet from Iran. Included in the exhibition were architectural elements, photographs and a display of carpets. The exhibition was critically acclaimed, with Terence Mullaly of the Telegraph stating that it could change the course of the arts. Keith and his team's research culminated in his book *The Language of Pattern* published by Thames and Hudson in 1974.

The other high point of the Festival was the focus on the poet Rumi. Mahmud and I set to work planning a programme around this seminal figure. Rumi was famous for his poetry and for the Sufi order that he founded. The Mevlevi, known for their whirling dance, had been suppressed under Ataturk, the founder of modern Turkey. However, after World War II they had been resurrected in Konya as a heritage ensemble. This ensemble gathered together the remaining classical musicians, who could perform the music that accompanied the whirling dance and included settings by the greatest Turkish composers. With the rush to modernize and westernize, the traditional forms of classical music had all but disappeared. We invited the ensemble to the Festival and were able to witness the last generation of musicians who had grown up in the traditional system. Twenty-three musicians and fifteen whirlers gave nine performances of the liturgy to full houses at the Friends' House auditorium in Euston.

Afterwards, a concert was held at the Queen Elizabeth Hall, with the Turkish musicians performing in the first half, and Mahmud after the interval. The concert demonstrated the relationship between the Maqam system in Turkish classical music and the *raga* system in Indian classical music. Supporting the appearance of the Mevlevi were two memorable lectures. Prof Annemarie Schimmel joined us again from Harvard, and gave her lecture entitled 'Pilgrimage to Maulana Rumi', and Dr James Dickie from Lancaster University spoke about Mevlevi architecture and ritual.

The Festival also included: readings from *The Thousand and One Nights*, by the actor Michael Hordern; an evening of Arab and Persian poetry; a seminar attended by thirty scholars entitled 'The Islamic City and its Role in Art'; a series of fifteen lectures; a schools programme; an evening devoted to the Holy Qur'an and the life of the Prophet; and a cycle of *ragas* for the different times of day given by Mahmud. There were so many memorable moments, but one of the lectures that made a deep impression on me was Dr Oleg Grabar's 'The Muslim Achievement in the Minor Arts'. He demonstrated how, what we considered minor arts, such as pottery, glasswork and metal work, were in Islam the means by which the ordinary activities of life, such as eating, drinking and washing, were sacralized. Our search in the sixties for all of life to become art was to be found here in Islam.

The Festival had been a great success. From the opening by HRH Princess Margaret on November 7 to the final event seventeen days later, an enthusiastic public had enjoyed an extraordinary programme that for many was their first introduction to Islam and its civilization.

The project had been successfully delivered. However, far from being able to enjoy this moment, I was staring disaster in the face. Three months before the Festival opened, owing to a shortfall in the ICA funding, the underpinning of the Festival was withdrawn. I was given the option of taking full responsibility for the event myself and raising the required funds, or the Festival would have to be cancelled. Of course, there was no question of cancelling the Festival, so I set about fundraising. When the receipts from the paying events and the money I had been able to raise were totted up, there was a gap of some ten thousand pounds that I personally owed to creditors.

Once again it was a catastrophe that catapulted me into my next project, which I would never have even considered if my back had not been up against the wall. In January 1972 my eldest brother was getting married to a Swiss lady. I flew out to Switzerland a week before the wedding and, staying in a chalet in the mountains, contemplated my dire situation. After much soul-searching, I asked myself the simple question, 'Was the World of Islam Festival a good idea?', and the answer that came back was, 'Yes, but it has to be done at the highest level, involving all the major institutions and engaging all the possible modes of presentation, and it must be opened by Her Majesty the Queen. The outstanding debt of the 1971 Festival will then be seen as part of the preparatory costs for the main event.' By the time I returned to London, I had the whole scheme for the great Festival of 1976 sketched out.

5

THE WORLD OF ISLAM FESTIVAL 1976

THE PLAN

THE FOCAL POINT of the Festival would be three major international loan exhibitions; these would be devoted to the Holy Qur'an, the Arts of Islam, and Islamic Science and Technology. Once these were in place, museums and galleries would be encouraged to mount other exhibitions on different aspects of Islamic art and culture. A major event would be an evening devoted to the recitation of the Holy Qur'an by one of the masters of this most glorious of Islamic arts. A series of lectures would draw together the main themes of the Festival. There would also be numerous lectures and seminars accompanying the exhibitions in the museums and galleries, and arranged by the learned societies and universities. A series of concerts covering the important musical traditions would be supported by a major exhibition of music and musical instruments and an album of recordings. A documentary film series for television and ideas for books to be put to publishers completed the plan.

MUSEUMS, GALLERIES, AND THE ARTS COUNCIL OF GREAT BRITAIN

My first port of call was the Arts Council of Great Britain. The Festival needed an anchor institution and the Arts Council was perfect for this role. They were one of only two institutions that could organize and mount blockbuster international loan exhibitions, the other being the Royal Academy. However, the Arts Council had the advantage of being the enabler of arts across the country, and could act as a clearing house for the loans coming from abroad. They could organize and present at the Haywood Gallery 'The Arts of Islam', which would be the largest and most comprehensive of the exhibitions. With this in place, venues for the other exhibitions would naturally follow.

I approached the director of exhibitions, Norbert Linton, and outlined my plan. He discussed it with his colleagues and several days later we met and he laid before me a major problem. Whilst his colleagues supported the proposal, he did not want to present it to the Exhibitions Committee at this time. The Chair of the committee was John Pope-Hennessy, who specialized in the Renaissance, did not like Islamic art, and would be likely to turn it down. However, Pope-Hennessy was to retire in a year's time, and they were confident that the new chairman would be happy to go ahead with it.

I was now faced with keeping my creditors at bay. I outlined to them my plan and the positive response from the Arts Council, and set to work building further institutional support. I approached the British Library with the proposal for the Holy Qur'an exhibition, and the Science Museum with the idea of presenting the sciences of Islam. I discussed with the Museum of Mankind an exhibition based on the theme of nomad and city, and with the Horniman Museum the subject of music and musical instruments. I approached the British Museum and the Victoria and Albert Museum, suggesting that they could mount special displays from their vast collections of Islamic artifacts. By the time the year was up, I had the support in principle of the key institutions in London that were capable of mounting exhibitions relating to Islamic themes. However, everything depended on the response of the Arts Council. In early 1973 the new chair was installed and the exhibition adopted, with a budget of £200,000 agreed. The Arts Council invited Her Majesty the Queen to open the Arts of Islam Exhibition and inaugurate the Festival. Her Majesty graciously agreed and the date of April 8th 1976 was placed in the calendar.

THE TRUST

The next task was to set up a Trust that would coordinate the Festival and raise the funds required for its realization. On leaving school I had departed from the establishment and had little aptitude or experience in dealing with the world of those who inhabited the London clubs and ran the country. We would require the participation of Muslim states and the support of our government and for this we needed trustees who could provide access. I was fortunate to meet a person who had the background and contacts to enable me to establish the Trust so that I could finally share the responsibility for the realization of my vision.

Alistair Duncan was born in India in 1927. Like many Brits stationed in India, his parents sent him to England when he was a child. Though he was from an older generation, we shared a past, as we had both been incarcerated in the same prep school; however, he had the misfortune to be the nephew of the headmaster, and was marooned at the school during the holidays, as his parents were away in India. He first became involved with the Arab world when he was in the army. He was a keen photographer and in 1961 was commissioned to take colour photographs for an edition of the RSV Bible. From this evolved other photographic engagements, and he decided to give up his career as an insurance broker to become a professional photographer. I met him in 1972 at the launch of his beautiful book *The Noble Sanctuary*, a history of Al-Haram Al-Sharif in Jerusalem. I expressed my delight on glancing through his book and we agreed to meet to discuss my project. I showed him my plans for the Festival and he enthusiastically offered to help me with introductions to diplomats who had been ambassadors in the Arab world and were now retired. They were, he said, the kind of people who enjoyed serving on trusts and advancing causes that were close to their hearts.

In creating the Trust, we needed to start with the chairman. Our first choice was Lord Trevelyan who had been ambassador in Egypt, Iraq and the Soviet Union, and ended his career as the last High Commissioner in Aden, responsible for Great Britain's withdrawal. We met at his home. I outlined the plan and our progress in gaining the support of the Arts Council and the other institutions. He turned down our offer, stating that we would never raise the money from the Arabs for such an ambitious undertaking. The response from our second choice for chairman was very different.

Sir Harold Beeley was born in 1909, the son of a London merchant. He went to Highgate School and then on to Oxford University gaining a First in Modern History. He spent the years up until the war in academia. The outbreak of war found him at Chatham House working with the great historian Arnold Toynbee, and from there he went to the Foreign Office Research Department. In 1945, as war was ending, he was sent to San Francisco to work on the Preparatory Commission of the United Nations, where he helped to design the UN Trusteeship Council along with Ralph Bunche. It was after this that he entered the Diplomatic Service. Over the next twenty years, until his retirement in 1969, he served in a number of posts, including Deputy Head of the British Mission to the UN, UK Representative to the Disarmament Conference in Geneva, and British Ambassador to both Saudi Arabia and Egypt.

Sir Harold listened carefully as we outlined the plan, every so often asking pertinent questions. When we had finished, he graciously accepted our invitation, saying that he would be honoured to serve as chairman. We were incredibly fortunate that Lord Trevelyan had turned us down. Sir Harold was far better equipped to steer the Trust through the rapids that lay ahead. After the meeting, on the steps of the Reform Club, Sir Harold said to me that everything about the project appealed to him and made sense, the only problem for him was that he could not see where the money would come from. I answered that if the project was right and the time was right, the money would follow.

October 1973 was a tremendously important month for the Festival. Three major events took place. The first was that the Trust was set up and registered. With Sir Harold as Chair, it now included Lord Caradon, Sir John Richmond, Sir Anthony Nutting, and two trustees whom I had nominated, Francis Clive-Ross, the editor of Studies in Comparative Religion and John Knight-Smith, owner of Luzac bookshop and publishing house. Alistair

Duncan had accepted my invitation to become the Festival's administrator.

The second event was that the price of oil shot up, the Gulf States overnight became super rich, and the funds required for the Festival would become available.

The third event was a terrible tragedy and a massive loss for me. It was the death of the Raja of Mahmudabad, a beautiful man and true Muslim, who had become my wise counsellor and dearest friend. It was through the difficult years between the end of the first Festival and the setting up of the Trust that I had come to depend on his moral support and encouragement. It is difficult for me to describe this wonderful man and the debt I owe him. Born into the wealth of an Indian princely family, he lost everything with the partition of the Subcontinent. His wisdom, generosity and humility in his support of the Muslims of India, during the years leading up to the trauma of partition, were legendary. I met him when he was the director of the London Central Mosque and Cultural Centre in Regents Park. He had attended a showing of the film, *In the Name of Allah* by Roger Graf, which was part of the programme at the ICA leading up to the Festival of 1971. At the end of the programme, he stood up to congratulate the film-maker, and as he was leaving, I went over to introduce myself. I invited him to a private concert that Mahmud was giving the following evening at the house of the playwright Ben Levy, and he agreed to come along. So, our relationship began with music and continued with poetry, because the Raja was a poet in both Urdu and Persian and translated his compositions into beautiful English, of which he had a greater command than myself. I was a regular visitor to the handsome Edwardian mansion that housed the embryonic Cultural Centre beside the building site that would become the London Central Mosque. In his flat I basked in his presence, for on reflection I now realize he represented the perfection of *adab*, that singular quality which contains the essence of what it is to be a Muslim. Often *adab* is translated as manners, but I have taken Nicholson's translation, 'spiritual culture' as closer to its meaning. He used to cook lunch for those who were visiting him, and guests at the table could include high officials from government, myself and his cockney cleaning lady, and all were made to feel at home, at ease and important. I was having tea with him when he had a heart attack and by the evening he had died. I have never seen such grief as was expressed by his family and friends; we were all inconsolable.

He was only 56 years old and his death came as a terrible shock. A great soul had departed who was a formidable influence on my journey to Islam.

By the beginning of 1974 the Trust was fully engaged in fundraising. Over the next year, delegations visited Saudi Arabia, Iran, Iraq, Kuwait, Bahrain, Qatar and Oman. However, it was an early meeting in London at the United Arab Emirates Embassy that garnered the largest contribution which underpinned the Festival. Alistair and I met the Foreign Minister, HE Ahmed Khalifa Al Suwaidi and the Ambassador, HE Mahdi Al Tajir. I had prepared a presentation in a large album showing the participating institutions and their projects. After they had listened to the presentation and looked through the album, they thanked us and we left. A week later I was in Luzac bookshop and a call came through from the ambassador wishing to speak to me. He said that they liked our project and would contribute half a million pounds and guarantee a further half a million pounds. This was one of the moments of pure joy that remains with me – for now my vision was secured. Sir Harold Beeley then invited the ambassador to join the Trust, and with Sabih Shukri, the manager of the Arab Bank, becoming the treasurer, we had an organization that was strong enough to deliver the Festival. With the institutions in play and the Trust formed, we were now ready to engage the librarians, curators and scholars who would create the substance of the Festival.

GUIDING PRINCIPLES

There were two guiding principles that would determine the content of the Festival. The first was the unity of Islam and Islamic Civilization. Back in the 1970s Islam was perceived as a religion like Christianity, and the world of Islam was broken up into Arabs, Turks, Persians, Malays, Indonesians etc, each with their own cultures. India was seen as a quite separate realm, dominated by the Hindus and their long history. This was the result of the Western academic process of specialization; few of them seem to have had any sense of the whole. The second idea relates to the first. It was to understand Islamic civilization in terms of its own criteria. An example of the Western approach to Islamic art is that the absence of paintings and sculptures of the human form was seen as a disadvantage and the result of a prohibition. It was clear to me that calligraphy and geometric pattern expressed a very different world-view from that of the West, and there was nothing lacking. Western academics, whilst enjoying brilliant insights into aspects of the civilization, were no help when it came to comprehending how everything fitted together. The two scholars who were essential in helping us realize this task were Seyyed Hossein Nasr and Titus Burckhardt.

SEYYED HOSSEIN NASR & TITUS BURCKHARDT

I met Dr Nasr during the last days of the first Festival. He happened to be in London and we invited him to give a lecture. His lecture, entitled 'Islam: Knowledge and Action', was electrifying. The power of his oration and the clarity with which he unfolded his subject totally captivated me. I realized I was in the presence of a powerful thinker who understood Islamic civilization as a unity. I read his work *Science and Civilization in Islam*, which provided the approach that I wanted to adopt for the Sciences of Islam exhibition. He suggested I should meet Titus Burckhardt, who could deliver the framework for the Arts of Islam Exhibition.

At this time Titus Burckhardt was the UNESCO advisor for the preservation of the city of Fez in Morocco. I flew out to Fez to meet him. At the airport I was greeted by a tall imposing figure who would become my guide, taking me deep into the appreciation of Islamic art, architecture and the environment. He combined strength, gentleness, subtlety and humour with profound scholarship, and he was a joy to be with. During my visits to Fez over the next months we worked on the plan for the Arts of Islam exhibition. I had already decided that, accompanying the exhibitions devoted to the Qur'an, the Arts and the Sciences, there should be beautifully prepared, large format, illustrated books. I had difficulty in recruiting him to act as a consultant to the Festival, because of his heavy work load with UNESCO, however, I now went about trying to convince him to write the book on Islamic art. It was more his humility in the face of the challenge than his work load that was the obstacle to his accepting my invitation, but I would not take no for an answer, and he finally agreed.

Titus Burckhardt gave me a wonderful introduction to the mysteries of the Islamic city. He would take me around the labyrinthine lanes, entering craft shops, houses and mosques, where he was welcomed and entertained.

I was introduced to the open-hearted nature of Muslim hospitality. Titus Burckhardt knew the city intimately, and was clearly a greatly loved and respected figure. Taking me to the various craft workshops, he would all the while impart his knowledge regarding the significance of what was before us. In one studio, the master craftsman was putting the finishing touches to a huge bronze candelabra. Burckhardt asked if it was for the palace, the master replied that it was for the mosque. Here, I experienced one of the most important aspects of Islamic civilization: the palace and the mosque belonged to the same culture; there was no division between sacred and secular. Another moment that remains with me was when he took me onto the roof of a house and we surveyed the city. The assembly of houses with their courtyards had the appearance of a honeycomb, the lanes and market streets were the arteries of the city and the green roofs of the mosques with their minarets the focal points. Everything was connected and it would be possible to walk from end to end of the city on the roofs. After contemplating this extraordinary world for several minutes in silence, Burckhardt said, 'The Islamic city is like a family monastery'. Burkhardt ended up advising on the Arts of Islam Exhibition and the Film series, writing the book on Islamic Art, and producing the audio-visual presentation for the City of Fez display in the Nomad & City Exhibition. I was intimately involved in all of these and privileged to be his devoted student.

EXHIBITIONS PROGRAMME

The challenge that I faced in setting up the three major exhibitions, was to marry the Islamic perspective, represented by Burckhardt and Nasr, with the particular knowledge and expertise of the Western curators and librarians. I had to bridge the chasm that separated these two perspectives.

We were very fortunate with the Qur'an Exhibition in having Martin Lings, the British Library's Emeritus Curator of Arabic Manuscripts, and his deputy Dr Yasin Safadi. They both approached the subject from an Islamic perspective and with Martin Lings' profound knowledge and Yasin Safadi's efficient organization, we were able to gather together, from collections around the world, the finest display of Qur'ans ever seen, which illustrated every period and region of the world of Islam, and was captured for posterity in the catalogue and the magnificent book that was produced. The Trust provided the funding for new showcases so that the manuscripts could be displayed to their best advantage. The British Library was yet to move into its new premises, so the exhibition took place in the magnificent King's Library in the British Museum. Muslims came from all over the country to experience the blessing or *baraka* of this supreme manifestation of Islamic art. On the final Sunday of the exhibition, I encountered an elderly man who was standing in front of one of the great Mamluk Qur'ans weeping. He had travelled up from Manchester every weekend to spend time in the gallery with the Qur'ans. He told me how much he would miss them, and what a tremendous blessing their presence in London had been.

The normal way of presenting the arts of Islam would have been either to arrange the exhibits according to type, for example, metalwork, pottery, calligraphy etc, or on the basis of region or historical period. To give credit to the curators on the selection committee, once the criteria had been established, they wholeheartedly dedicated themselves to making it work. It is worth quoting from the catalogue to show the spirit in which the exhibition was assembled:

> '...it was agreed to attempt to define the essential character of Islamic art, to trace out the elements that are present in it, separately or more generally together, by which we try to identify the Islamic creative spirit. These characteristic elements were taken to be calligraphy, geometry, the arabesque and the treatment of figuration. Thus, the galleries of the Hayward are arranged to display the unity in Islamic art as well as its diversity.'

The Arts Council invited Basil Gray, Keeper Emeritus of the British Museum Oriental Department, to chair the selection committee. The committee also included from the Victoria & Albert Museum, Basil Robinson, Keeper Emeritus, Donald King, Keeper of the Department of Textiles, and Robert Skelton, Deputy Keeper of the Indian Section; from the British Museum, Ralph Pinder-Wilson, Deputy Keeper of Oriental Antiquities; and from the British Library, Martin Lings. Also included were Edmund de Unger, a prominent collector of Islamic Art, Titus Burckhardt and myself. The secretary to the committee was Joanna Drew, who had succeeded Norbert Linton as Director of Exhibitions. The exhibition designer was Michael Brawne.

The Arts of Islam Exhibition included 669 exhibits that came from 126 collections in 27 different countries. I witnessed the process of their selection, and travelled with members of the committee to various museums, engaging, on behalf of the Trust, in negotiations for the loans. To see the artifacts through the eyes of these experts, who had devoted their working lives to their study, was incredible. In the Cairo Museum, Basil Gray explained to me why we must have a particular ceramic bowl in the Exhibition, and Martin Lings showed me the great Mameluke Qur'ans that were being selected for his exhibition; these encounters deepened my understanding of the beauty of Islamic art and increased my appreciation for the knowledge and insight of the curators and librarians in whose company I was fortunate to find myself.

It was considered that architecture was central to any understanding of Islamic art, not only as the setting for the other arts, but also because it is in Islamic architecture that the dominant themes have found their fullest expression. It was therefore considered crucial that architecture should be represented in the exhibition in such a way that its critical role could be understood, and that sufficient examples should be seen in detail to convey its use of both space and decoration. The method that was chosen was to use colour slides, back-projected onto nine screens in order to build up a mosaic of images. The result was spectacular.

Roland Michaud, the renowned French photographer, was commissioned to undertake the assignment. He already had a large photographic collection of various parts of the Islamic world, and augmented this with a year's commission, funded by the Trust, taking in Morocco, Tunisia, Egypt, Syria, Turkey, Iran and India. Roland Michaud also provided the pictures for Burckhardt's book on the arts of Islam, and Nasr's book on Islamic science. Working with him, opened for me an amazing window on the world of Islam. He, his wife and young son were like nomads. They did not just visit a place, they spent months living with the people in the environment he was photographing. He captured many sites which have since been destroyed by the terrible wars that have raged across the Middle East over the last 40 years. His collection is priceless. He and his photographic collection were inspiring and provided me with a great education.

In terms of the Islamic perspective, our biggest challenge had to be the Science and Technology of Islam Exhibition, which was to take place in the bastion of modern science, the Science Museum. The exhibition was paid for by the Trust, and the director accepted Dr Nasr's scheme for the exhibition. Whilst the designer entered into the spirit of the exhibition, a number of the curators were very unhappy. They considered the display had nothing to do with modern science and did not belong in the museum. The only valid approach would be to show the Islamic contribution to modern science. FR Maddison, Curator of the Museum of the History of Science in Oxford was invited to select the exhibits and, assisted by AJ Turner, gathered together a splendid display drawn from 26 collections. However, he shared the curators' views about the inappropriateness of holding the exhibition in the context of a museum of modern science, and became increasingly detached as time went on. The catalogue which he was preparing was never finished, and we had to quickly put together a simplified catalogue or guide to the exhibition in time for the opening.

The Nomad and City Exhibition turned out to be the most popular exhibition ever mounted by the Museum of Mankind and a highlight of the Festival. The nomad section featured the Bedouin of Arabia. With funding from the Trust, Shelagh Weir, Assistant Keeper, collected in the field a number of exhibits to augment the museum's collection, and produced a splendid display with, at its centre, a large Bedouin tent. Sanaa in the Yemen and Fez in Morocco represented the city section. Fez was depicted through a slide presentation arranged by Titus Burckhardt, as mentioned above. Sanaa was represented through an environmental exhibition that brilliantly evoked the atmosphere of the city. Organized by Professor Robert Serjeant, Professor of Arabic at Cambridge University, and his team of researchers, it included a souk with the smells of the spices wafting around the gallery, and the beautifully decorated and furnished interior of the upper room of a house. Tim Mackintosh-Smith, the travel writer and scholar, was so moved by the exhibition, that he took a year out from his studies at Oxford University to visit Sanaa. He has been living there ever since. A fully comprehensive illustrated book on the city of Sanaa, containing the findings of Professor Bob Serjeant and his research group, was published by the Trust after the Festival.

Music was clearly going to be an important ingredient in the Festival and we had the opportunity of presenting the music of the four great classical traditions: Arab, Turkish, Persian and North Indian. We had already made the link between Turkish and North Indian in the first festival. Now Mahmud Mirza set about meeting and selecting the musicians and musical groups that would represent all four traditions. After months of research and travel, the final list of those who would appear at the South Bank Auditoria, was confirmed: the Royal Andalusian Orchestra from Morocco, Iraqi oud player Salman Shukur; Saddedin Heper and his orchestra from Turkey; a group of the most famous classical musicians from Iran; and joining Mahmud, the singer Ustad Nisar Hussain Khan from India.

We were fortunate in that the Horniman Museum already had a collection of musical instruments from around the world. Jean Jenkins, the ethnomusicologist in charge of the collection, had in her career covered many areas of the world of Islam, recording both the classical and folk music, collecting instruments and taking photographs. The Trust now set up a budget so that she could put together a research and collecting programme that would deliver a comprehensive exhibition and set of recordings. Working with Poul Rovsing Olsen, the Danish composer and ethnomusicologist, and drawing in a wide circle of collaborators, more than twenty countries were visited and a magnificent exhibition assembled, accompanied by a series of records released by Tangent Records. With the concerts, the exhibition and its catalogue, and the series of recordings, my dream that the music from the world of Islam should be fully represented in the Festival was realized.

The exhibition programme also included: 'Paintings from the Muslim Courts of India' at the British Museum, organized by Ralph Pinder-Wilson, which drew together the finest examples of manuscripts from various collections, both public and private, across the UK; a wonderful exhibition devoted to the textiles and arts of the Hausa of Northern Nigeria at the Commonwealth Institute, which was the brainchild of the scholar and artist David Heathcote; 'Islamic Metalwork from Iranian Lands' at the V&A, selected by AS Melikian-Chirvani; and 'The City of Isfahan' at the British Museum. Exhibitions outside London comprised a beautifully presented exhibition of the textiles of the Qashqai nomads at the Whitworth Art Gallery in Manchester, put together by Joan Allgrove; an authoritative display entitled 'Carpets of Central Persia' arranged by May H Beattie at the Mappin Art Gallery, Sheffield, which then travelled to several cities in the UK; and finally, 'Islamic Themes in European Art' at the Ashmolean Museum, Oxford.

LECTURES AND SEMINARS

At this point I wish to introduce another figure who played an important role in the Festival and became a greatly valued friend. Yusuf Ibish was a fine scholar in the traditional sense. He was brought up in one of the most powerful families in Syria and was moulded by the Ottoman milieu and aesthetic. As well as being a scholar who had a remarkably broad vision of Islamic civilization and its history, he was an excellent calligrapher and a truly brilliant conversationalist, with an inexhaustible collection of stories. He had been a student at Harvard University when the Syrian government nationalized the land, and his family was ruined. This riches-to-rags experience gave him a profound insight into life, and he had an incredible presence, as though nothing could phase him. Seyyed Hossein Nasr, who had known Yusuf since they were students together at Harvard, suggested I should contact him to advise on the selection of subjects and speakers for the main lecture series. I met him in Beirut in the coffee lounge of the St George Hotel. He was at the time a Professor at the American University of Beirut. He immediately grasped the scope of the Festival, and his encyclopaedic mind began to range across the subjects and people who could deliver the lectures. He suggested we should hold a major international colloquium on the City as this was such a key aspect of Islamic civilization. So, we set to work to put these two pillars of the academic programme in place: the lecture series and the colloquium. However, Yusuf's contribution went far beyond this programme; he was also a key consultant on the Film series, and, as you will see later, a wise counsellor when the Festival entered the rapids.

The Festival lecture series was held in the auditorium of the Commonwealth Institute. The opening lecture was given by His Eminence Dr Abdul Halim Mahmud, Shaykh Al-Azhar, who earlier in the day of the 2nd April 1976, had inaugurated the Holy Qur'an Exhibition. There followed sixteen weekly lectures throughout the three months of the Festival, which covered the main themes and regions of the world of Islam. Notable among these were: a lecture delivered by M Naguib Al-Attas, which was the only item in the Festival to address Islam in the Malay world; a visit and talk on traditional medicine given by Hakim Muhammad Said of the Hamdard Institute in Pakistan; and my first encounter with Hasan Fathy, who gave a lecture on traditional Islamic architecture.

We wanted the colloquium on the Islamic City to stand out, and to have the funds to invite a number of architects, archaeologists and art historians to participate, alongside scholars in the field of Islamic studies. We primarily had in mind the problem of conservation of the Islamic architectural heritage, and the need to impress the powers that be of its inestimable value at a time when the destruction of the Islamic environment was gathering momentum. Thus, we hoped to involve UNESCO to help fund the colloquium. Titus Burckhardt's position gave us access to UNESCO, and we met Najmuddin Bammate, a senior member of the organization, who agreed to progress our proposal. I made a number of visits to Paris, meeting with the various committee members and delegates whose agreement was required. It was not plain sailing. There was an influential East German delegate who opposed the project and had named me Mr Barnum, after the circus impresario! But Bammate, who was a brilliant scholar, linguist and diplomat, and had become a passionate supporter of the Festival, guided the proposal through the Byzantine structures of UNESCO and the funds were finally allocated. Professor Serjeant agreed to host the symposium at Cambridge University, and he and Yusuf Ibish set to work drawing up the list of participants. The symposium nicely complimented the Nomad and City exhibition, and Sanaa and Fez featured prominently in the papers and discussions. After the Festival, several of the papers were published by UNESCO in a book edited by Bob Serjeant.

The Festival inspired museums, galleries, universities, institutions, learned societies and publishers around the country that had an interest in Arabic and Islamic studies to organize and produce a number of other exhibitions, a score of seminars, over a hundred lectures, and more than fifty books, in the wake of the official Festival programme.

THE FILM SERIES

Back at the beginning of 1972, immediately after my meeting with the Arts Council and their positive response to the idea of the Festival, I approached the BBC. They were basking in the international success of their first major colour documentary series, Kenneth Clark's 'Civilization', and were looking for the next subject to tackle. I met with Norman Swallow, who was in charge of the BBC flagship arts and culture programme 'Omnibus', and outlined my ideas for the Festival and the Arts Council's potential involvement. I suggested that the World of Islam would provide a rich canvas for their next venture. Norman greeted my proposal with enthusiasm, and there followed a series of meetings and lunches as the idea was floated and discussed in the various departments that had to be got on board for the project to be accepted and for substantial sums to be allocated for its realization. After months had passed, the proposal went before the committee that would make the final decision. Meanwhile, I had engaged the support of Stephen Cross, a film producer/director suggested by Norman Swallow, and with the help of James Dickie worked up a summary of what the series would include.

I first met James Dickie when he gave a brilliant lecture on the Alhambra and its gardens in the run up to the first Festival. He was a lecturer in Islamic studies at Lancaster University and had a wide knowledge and interest across a number of disciplines. When the Trust was established and the funding secured, he left his university post and joined the Festival as a full-time researcher working on the film series and aspects of the academic programme.

However, the film series would not be a BBC production. Norman Swallow, who had done his best to convince his colleagues, reported that the consensus of opinion was that the TV audience hardly knew or cared about the world of Islam and there would not be sufficient interest to justify a series. They chose to follow up 'Civilization' with the history of British architecture.

'The Traditional World of Islam', a series of six half-hour films, became a World of Islam Festival Trust production, which I co-produced with Stephen Cross, who directed the series. The films carried the Festival's message of the unity and diversity of Islamic civilization, and the episodes were entitled 'Unity', 'Nomad and City', 'Man and Nature', 'The Pattern of Beauty', 'Knowledge', and 'The Inner Life'. The BBC returned to the fray when they realized the scope of the Festival, and Arabs and oil became headline news. They bought the series for broadcasting during the Festival and made two one-hour films on the Festival itself.

A FORMIDABLE CHALLENGE

When planning the Festival I had developed the strategy of placing the various projects with institutions that were capable of realizing them and leaving the Trust as a fundraiser and coordinator. However, it did not work out like that. By the time the Festival opened, the Trust had organized a major lecture series, an international colloquium, a series of concerts at the South Bank, the production of a series of six films for television, and the publication of eight exhibition catalogues, three illustrated books on the Qur'an, Arts and Sciences, and two further illustrated books, one on the city of Sanaa and the other on geometric pattern. The Trust had also part-funded nine exhibitions, coordinated a UK wide programme of lectures and seminars, organized a highly successful press and publicity campaign, coordinated the openings of the exhibitions, and managed a host of VIPs and visitors from abroad. All this was taking place whilst the fundraising programme was still going on.

In a little over two years the Trust had developed into an organization that was able to deliver this huge programme. As director, I was in overall charge of the contents of the Festival and I was fortunate in having a highly efficient American secretary, who returned to the US after the Festival to join Henry Kissinger's research team. I dealt directly with the exhibitions, meeting regularly with the different organizers, and serving on the Arts Council committee. I also, as co-producer with Stephen Cross, dealt directly with the film series. I oversaw the highly successful educational programme of lectures and seminars, which was organized and coordinated by Anthony Hutt, who had played a valuable role in the first Festival. I also oversaw the music programme, which was run by experienced organizer Rosalind Ross, who had also worked on the Festival of 1971. The music programme was responsible for the concerts at the

South Bank and the numerous recordings that were made, which are now in the National Sound Archive. The Trust set up a separate publishing company for the production and marketing of the books and catalogues, which was headed by John Knight-Smith. However, I worked closely with the authors. Alistair Duncan took care of the trustees and chaired the management committee which met monthly to review progress. He also looked after our PR programme, which involved: organizing the inauguration of the Festival by Her Majesty the Queen; the many VIP visits and functions, including a dinner for the Shah Banu of Iran held following her opening of the Science Museum exhibition; and a meeting between the Archbishop of Canterbury and the Shaykh Al-Azhar, after he had opened the Qur'an exhibition.

We were particularly fortunate in the person who organized our press campaign. Her appointment is an interesting lesson in taking a chance. Sarah Harding had applied for the role of my secretary and, being the most interesting of the candidates, she got the job. Coming into the office after everyone had left on the first day of her employment, I found her struggling at the typewriter with two fingers. I spoke to Alistair, and our immediate thought was that she would have to go. I then thought, hang on a minute, she has come through a top secretarial agency, she clearly has an amazing capacity to convince people. We were looking for someone to look after the press, so I suggested that she might be good in this role. I wanted to be closely involved with the campaign, as I had in the past engaged with the press in a number of ways. We set to work and built up an impressive list of journalists and writers who were able to produce articles on the different aspects of the Festival. Sarah worked closely with the press officers in the participating museums and formed a coordinating committee of their members. I think it is fair to say our press campaign was quite brilliant and in itself carried a substantial body of knowledge into the public arena. Aramco Magazine devoted an issue to the Festival which covered in some detail all the events. This is what they had to say about the press response:

> Unquestionably, the full intellectual effect of the Festival will be delayed. Yet even as it opened it was clear that it would certainly have an impact. The prestige newspapers – *The Times, The Guardian, The Financial Times, The Observer, The Sunday Times* – were offering features

> and special supplements on Islam, television was giving Festival events wide coverage, the international art reviews *Apollo* and *Connoisseur,* published in Britain, had devoted whole issues to the Islamic arts, publications as far apart as *Vogue, Readers Digest* and the left-wing *Time Out* were coming out with feature stories, and it was a rare publisher's book list that didn't contain at least one title this season touching on the Islamic world.

Aramco Magazine also covered the commercial impact of the Festival:

> Islamic art, already big business in England, registered a measurable upturn. April art magazines showed 24 fine art galleries advertising Islamic wares and the two major art auctioneers in Britain—Sotheby's and Christie's—held week-long sales devoted to Islamic art. At one of them a bidder paid a record $130,000 for a north Persian 'shrub' carpet. Still further afield, designers of textiles and wallpapers were ferreting through the exhibitions for fresh patterns and colours, and one large department store clocked in with a line of spring neckties in Islamic designs—a far cry, no doubt, from the intellectual goals of Paul Keeler and the Festival Trust, yet a natural part of their more basic aim: the furtherance of knowledge of the World of Islam.

After her achievement with the Festival, Sarah Harding was recruited by the British Museum to work on their major exhibition 'Wealth of the Roman World'.

TENSIONS AND CRISES

It can truly be said that the Festival was a triumph, with an incredible programme of events successfully delivered in the space of a little over two years. And yet, when Her Majesty came to the Queen Elizabeth Hall for the inauguration on April 8th 1976, the management that had been at the heart of this achievement was in disarray and its members barely speaking to each other. Tensions had begun to appear in mid-1975. By that time the Festival had developed its own momentum. I worked out that I was engaged with over a hundred individuals. Programmes were expanding, budgets were increasing and time was disappearing. I was busy supporting the growth that was taking place. The trustees were attempting to apply the brakes. I was presenting them with one fait accompli after another, and the myriad projects progressed unabated.

At this juncture the trustees brought in a high-powered expert who specialized in sorting out management problems within organizations, with the intention of wresting control from me. The expert, whom we knew as Ziggy, did his survey and reported back to the trustees. He stated that the Festival was an extraordinary and highly complex project, and the only person who knew what was going on was Paul Keeler, who had all the strings in his hand, and that if anything happened to him the project would be in trouble. The solution that the trustees came up with was to invite Ziggy to work beside me, in the hope that this would stabilize the situation.

By the winter of 1975, we had reached crisis point. We did not have sufficient funds to complete the Festival. All the promised contributions, excepting that of Saudi Arabia, had been received, and the UAE guarantee already spent. The £200,000 from Saudi Arabia had arrived at the Embassy several times, but had been returned by the ambassador, who, we were told, was jealous that the UAE ambassador was on the Trust and not himself. However, the trustees had allowed the UAE ambassador to become detached from what was happening, and the only course of action was to approach him for a further guarantee to see us through to the finishing line. We worked out that we needed £500,000 (the equivalent of £4m today). The treasurer drew up the paperwork and prepared a letter outlining the financial situation. We found out that the ambassador was accompanying Shaykh Zaid on a state visit to Iran. I met with Sir Harold who suggested that I should go alone and present our case. Ziggy was to stand by and if I failed to secure the guarantee I was to call him immediately and the process of shutting down the Festival would begin. Fortunately, Seyyed Hossein Nasr was in Tehran and accompanied me to the hotel where the ambassador was staying. He called up to his room saying that he had a message from the Shah Banu. On arriving in the lobby, the ambassador was clearly surprised to see me. Dr Nasr informed the ambassador that the Shah Banu was looking forward to the Festival in London, and then left me with him.

We sat in the coffee lounge and I launched into my appeal. I began by informing him of the progress we had made, and the magnificent event that would be opened by her Majesty the Queen in a few months' time. I then painted as vivid a picture as I could conjure up of the catastrophe that would ensue if we had to shut the project down. Announcing the sum we required, I handed him the form to be signed and the treasurer's letter. He read the letter and signed the form. I called Ziggy who relayed the message to a very relieved Sir Harold. The tension I had been under was so great that I had hardly slept for a month. But the Festival would now be completed, and nothing would stop the realization of my vision.

The final months leading up to the opening were frenetic. The press was beginning to report on the coming event. Rumblings were emanating from an influential evangelical Christian academic who claimed that the Festival was the initiative of the Arab lobby, and the Jewish Chronicle was encouraging its readers to keep a vigilant eye on events. The PLO wanted the Palestinian cause to be featured, and this is where Yusuf Ibish played an important role in diffusing what could have developed into a serious situation. He made it clear to them that the Festival was about Islamic culture and civilization and must not be dragged into the political arena. A further crisis arose when the Egyptian authorities disputed the British Government's insurance assessment. This was only resolved when the president, Anwar Sadat, stepped in. Then there was a moment of panic when it was thought that the Iranian artefacts, which were in the sky on their way to London, had not been insured.

Another potential disaster loomed over the Isfahan Exhibition which was coming from Iran. This was of particular interest to the Shah Banu, who had made the offer to the British Museum, and it had been enthusiastically accepted by the curator in charge of the Persian collection. Enter the new director of the museum, John Pope-Hennessey, the gentleman who had caused me a year's delay with the Arts Council because of his dislike of Islamic art! He decided to cancel the exhibition because he had not been consulted, and did not consider a mainly architectural display appropriate for the museum. As far as he was concerned, the curator had no business agreeing to it. The curator immediately contacted me, deeply concerned that this would not be well received in Iran, and could affect Iran's participation in the Festival. I met Joanna Drew at the Arts Council to see if they could exert pressure. She recognized the dire situation we were in, but said that once 'the Pope' had made up his mind it was impossible to change it. She suggested we try the chairman of the trustees, Lord Trevelyan. This was, of course, the noble Lord who turned down our invitation to become chairman of the Trust, stating that we would never raise the money from the Arabs. I discussed the situation with Sir Harold; he at once telephoned Lord Trevelyan and a meeting was arranged.

We met him in his London town house and after Harold and Lord Trevelyan had chatted a while, Sir Harold began to lay before him the grave situation that had arisen. Lord Trevelyan's response was that this was a matter for the director, and he could not possibly interfere. He said it was not his concern. I could see that Sir Harold had had no response and was not going to pursue the matter. I was livid, and was not going to leave without releasing my wrath. I told Lord Trevelyan that it certainly *was* his concern. The British Museum had agreed to host the exhibition. Who gave permission was an internal matter. The cancelling of the exhibition would be seen as an insult to the Shah Banu and a very undiplomatic way of behaving. It could endanger Iran's participation in the Festival which was to be inaugurated by Her Majesty on April 8th. The British Museum would be seen to have behaved outrageously. He as chairman would be primarily held responsible for the debacle. After a stunned silence, he mumbled that he would look into it.

A few days later I was summoned to the British Museum to meet the director. I entered his office and stood in front of his desk. He neither rose to greet me nor offered me a seat. He simply announced that the Museum had decided to hold the exhibition, but they would choose their own designer, and that was that. He was white with rage, and the office was like a deep freeze. He had to have a sacrificial victim, and it was a pity that it was the designer, who happened to be Keith Critchlow, a person who had a remarkable knowledge and insight regarding Isfahan and its buildings.

It was in the final build-up to the opening of the Festival that an event occurred that led to the breach between myself and Alistair and with him the establishment trustees. It so happened that Alistair had authorized a company to promote the Festival within the tourism sector. They had produced a leaflet announcing the principal events of the Festival, on the reverse of which were advertisements, including one for the Mecca gambling company. Letters of outrage came from as far away as South Africa, and concern spread through the Muslim community in the UK. I found myself addressing, on a Sunday morning, a large auditorium full of Muslim elders from around the country. Fortunately, we had developed good relations with the Muslim associations and student organizations, all of which had been recently established by the first generation of Muslims to gather in the UK.

They were a remarkable group of deeply-committed and talented individuals. One of the pioneers was Ibrahimsa Mohamed who arrived in London as a student from Malaysia in 1962 to study law. Almost immediately he became involved in setting up the Federation of Students Islamic Societies (FOSIS), which gave the disparate student bodies establishing themselves throughout the UK a central platform. He formed a close friendship with Abdul Wahid Hamid, who came from Trinidad, and who later produced the bestselling *Islam the Natural Way.* Hamid's two-volume *Companions of the Prophet* has been a constant source of refreshment for me. Ibrahimsa and Abdul Wahid were responsible for the birth of several magazines and in 1970 launched *Impact International.* I first encountered them both during the 1971 World of Islam Festival. They were incredibly supportive and Abdul Wahid interviewed me for *Impact International*, which published a comprehensive article on the Festival. Ibrahimsa went on to work with Salem Azzam, who, in 1970, was the key mover in the setting up of the Islamic Council of Europe.

Salam Azzam was an Egyptian who worked in a senior position in the Saudi Embassy in London. He was quietly spoken and always supportive of my work, and with Ibrahimsa, organized a major conference at the Albert Hall alongside the Festival. Recognizing that the Festival was focussed on the traditional world of Islam and its culture, they wished to show that Islam was a 'living socio-political reality.' Other important figures of the time were Professor Khurshid Ahmad, an economist from Pakistan, who founded the Islamic Foundation, Leicester, in 1973, and Dr Syed Aziz Pasha from India, who was the founder of the Union of Muslim Organizations of the United Kingdom and Ireland, in 1970.

Since the 1971 Festival, I had engaged with these pioneers who established the organizations that supported the newly arrived Muslims from the Commonwealth. They helped me to understand the fears that the Muslims would naturally have towards Westerners presenting their culture and religion, and in the run-up to the Festival, they helped to alleviate those fears. None more so than on the morning I had to address the elders, outraged by the Mecca gambling advertisement. I apologized for what was a mistake on our part and explained the vision and aims of the Festival. With the support of my Muslim friends who weighed in and spoke positively about the Festival and its tremendous benefits, the crisis was diffused.

On the Monday morning Ziggy came into my office. He said Alistair was out of his depth and making mistakes. His secretary was shielding him and she must go. This really troubled me. Apart from the fact that I owed Alistair so much in the setting up of the Trust and the relationships we had formed with governments, and that he had played a crucial role in looking after the trustees, I knew that if I got rid of his secretary, I might complete the Festival, but after that I would be finished, my future in the Festival organization would be over. The trustees would never forgive me for humiliating Alistair, and I could see their point. They belonged to the establishment, and although I shared the same upbringing, I was an outsider, not a member of the club.

I remonstrated with Ziggy. I explained to him what a disaster it would be for me if I sacked Alistair's secretary. He told me that the Festival had entered a very dangerous period when there were many forces at work, he was there to advise me; if I was not prepared to take his advice, he would leave. The irony of the situation was that it was the trustees who had appointed Ziggy as my advisor. It was one of the most horrible things I have ever had to do, but it was done, and within a week I was asked to attend a hastily arranged meeting of the trustees.

The meeting took place in a hotel. All the trustees were present, except for the ambassador. Alistair sat silently, clearly deeply upset. I was then harangued by Sir Anthony Nutting who asked me how Alistair could possibly do his work without a secretary. I was told that she had to be reinstated. Ziggy sat silently waiting for my response. I made it clear that if she was reinstated, I would resign. I then got up and left the meeting.

It so happened that I had arranged to meet Dr Abdullah Naseef in the lobby of the hotel after the meeting. Dr Naseef had been a student at Leeds University in 1971, and we had met during the first Festival. He came from a very influential family of scholars, and was now Secretary General of King Abdul Aziz University in Jeddah. We will meet him again in the following chapter, where I relate how he played an important role in my next adventure. At this juncture, Dr Naseef had performed a singular service in personally delivering the Saudi cheque that had been yo-yoing between London and Riyad. He departed as the meeting of the trustees broke up. Our treasurer approached me to say that I was not to resign, and I handed him the cheque. Alistair was laid low for a couple of weeks before joining us for the final days of preparation. Despite the crises that buffeted us in the build-up to the opening, the organization we had created worked perfectly and all the programmes were delivered on time.

THE END OF MY FESTIVAL

On the morning of the inauguration of the Festival by the Queen, I went alone to the Queen Elizabeth Hall, having arranged to meet members of my family at the venue. I walked across from Waterloo Station and, finding a bench to sit on, rested awhile to ponder. All of a sudden, I experienced the most wonderful feeling of well-being. For a few moments I felt I was enveloped in perfect peace, and then it disappeared. It was as though God had given me a little pat on the back. I had delivered the vision that had been entrusted to me, and for all my shortcomings, it was well done.

I arrived at the Queen Elizabeth Hall to join the throngs assembling for the opening of this unique event that had engaged so many people and organizations in its realization. We were now sharing the fruits of our work with scholars who had gathered from around the world, VIPs, ambassadors and journalists from Islamic countries, our own scholars, journalists and members of the art, academic and political establishments, and members of the Royal family. However, this celebration was not sufficient to heal the rift that had opened up between myself, Alistair and members of our board of trustees. In a numbed state, I attended the many openings and events during the first ten days, which culminated in a memorable evening at the Royal Festival Hall, when several thousand Muslims attended the recitation of the Holy Qur'an by the great master from Egypt, Shaykh Mahmud Khalil Al-Husary. I remained as director until all the programmes were in place and then resigned, leaving the Festival and its aftermath to Alistair and the trustees, who went on to wrap it up successfully.

After the Festival, the Trust continued with Alistair as director. The UAE ambassador, Mahdi Al-Tajir, a wealthy businessman in his own right, stepped in and funded the Trust so that it could continue supporting the aims of the Festival. In time, the World of Islam Festival Trust became the Al-Tajir Trust which to this day continues to function. Alistair remained director until his death in 2007. He was responsible for the publication of a series of major works on Jerusalem, which had always remained his great love. As well as supporting exhibitions in the museums, the Al-Tajir Trust also provides grants and scholarships which have helped a number of young students in Islamic studies. Alistair and I met by chance at a conference shortly before he died. Many years had passed since our last meeting. He invited me to his office and gave me some books. I am glad this reconciliation took place. Our beginning together had been very special.

ANOTHER PATH

By the time the Festival was over, I had already been taken on another path. Six months before the Festival opened, I had embraced Islam. It took seven years from my meeting with Ustad Mahmud Mirza to the moment I recited the Shahadah. I had not been seeking a religion, I had simply found myself surrounded by the beauty, truth and goodness of Islam. When asked how I became a Muslim I reply that it was through music, food and friendship.

It is difficult to assess the impact of the Festival, but it undoubtedly affected many lives and, as in my case, led some to Islam. The Festival also acted as a catalyst for many cultural initiatives across the Muslim world, including the first conference on Islamic education, which was held in Mecca in 1977, and the formation of several museums and collections of Islamic art. But the euphoria surrounding the Festival was short-lived. Within three years, the Iranian Revolution, the Siege of Mecca and the emergence of political Islam totally changed the West's perception of Islam, and the Festival was virtually forgotten.

Decades later a young librarian at the British Library kept on coming across references to the World of Islam Festival in his researches, and started digging. He began to realize he was uncovering an extraordinary event. As it was coming up to the 40th anniversary of the Festival, he set about getting in touch with people who could help him put together an event of some kind. He contacted Sadiya Ahmed, the founder and director of Everyday Muslim, a charity engaged in promoting understanding of

Islam in Britain. They discovered that I was still alive and approached me. After they had contacted a few others who had been involved in various ways and were available to participate, they organized an evening of talks followed by a discussion in the Brunei Gallery lecture theatre at SOAS on the 27th April 2016. Everyday Muslim filmed the event and several articles appeared. The event has generated a revival of interest in the Festival. The comprehensive collection of press cuttings, which I presented to the library of Cambridge University's Faculty of Asian and Middle Eastern Studies, was in itself beginning to evoke interest among researchers, as the press coverage provides a unique window into our relations with the world of Islam, just before the descent into our present nightmare.

I have dealt with the Festival in some detail as I felt compelled to capture my memory of the event at a time when those who were not present are attempting to describe what happened. If there was not this new interest in the Festival, I would not have engaged with what happened behind the scenes. The seven years of my encounter first with Ustad Mahmud Mirza and then with Islam and its civilization through the Festivals, are the most intense in the story of how I derived the knowledge and understanding that would eventually result in my book *Rethinking Islam & T*
he West.

It was during the final days of the Festival that I was introduced to Sami Angawi, who was the director of the Hajj Research Centre in Jeddah. He invited me to attend a conference on the Hajj, which was to take place in Jeddah at the end of 1976, and which would also include taking part in the Pilgrimage. With this invitation I stepped out of the Festival and entered into my new life as a Muslim.

6

THE HAJJ & THE INVITATION

SAMI ANGAWI

SAMI ANGAWI CAME from a family of *mutawwifs*. These were the traditional guides who took care of the pilgrims. Sami belonged to the last generation that inherited this tradition, which provided him with the insiders' knowledge of the sacred cities of Mecca and Medina. The *mutawwifs* knew where the important places associated with the Prophet and his companions were located. But during the last seventy years all traces of these historic cities have been erased, and they now stand as modern concrete jungles with no past. The *mutawwifs* have been replaced by government appointees, and the new guides derive their knowledge from official brochures. The twin forces of Wahhabism and modernism ensured that nothing would remain of the cities of the Prophet, excepting their sacred centres.

Sami Angawi has been almost alone in attempting to save the cities from destruction, but although the forces he encountered were unassailable, his life's work has resulted in the preservation of precious knowledge amassed over the years. After receiving his BA and MA in architecture from the University of Texas, Sami returned to Jeddah in 1975, and at the age of 27 established The Hajj Research Centre (HRC) at King Abdul Aziz University in Jeddah. By the time we arrived in Jeddah for the conference at the end of 1976, the HRC was buzzing with activity. Sami had gathered together a number of specialists and researchers who were engaged in the documentation and study of every aspect of the Hajj, and were beginning to develop proposals on how to respond sensitively to the massive changes that were taking place.

THE HAJJ

Sami had the charisma of a young man who was totally in love with the object of his mission, and since it was a sacred mission, he was surrounded by *baraka* or blessing. He had also invited to the conference Yusuf Ibish and Martin Lings from the Festival, and the conference party that made the Hajj together also included Mahmoud Bodo Rasch, Ziauddin Sardar, Dr Zaki Badawi and Dr Kalim Siddiqui. Our Hajj was beautifully organized and Sami guided us so that we were able to fully connect with and experience this unchanging pillar of Islam.

There were two important understandings that I derived from my Hajj. The first was when we approached the Kaaba. Nothing had prepared me for this moment. It was as if I had never seen it before, and yet I had seen it in hundreds of photographs and films. As the pilgrimage unfolded so the presence of the Kaaba increased. The culmination of our visit was reached when we were allowed to enter the sacred edifice and pray in any direction. I felt certain then that this was the sacred centre of our world.

The other understanding related to the universality of Islamic civilization. Growing up as I did in a society that was deeply riven by class, racial and nationalistic prejudices, I had inherited the characteristics of my background. During the sixties and then with the Festival I had overcome these prejudices in my mind. However, it is one thing to know something intellectually, but quite another for it to inform one's entire being. I had to police myself in order to control my responses to people and situations. When facing the Kaaba, standing in the serried ranks of the worshipping pilgrims, who came from every nation, race and class, my embedded prejudices began to melt, and they have been melting ever since.

Martin Lings had made the Hajj in 1949, before the modern changes began to take place. He had been able to walk in the footsteps of the Prophet, so to speak. He was able to describe to us the changes that had taken place, so at least we were able to imagine how it must have been. Nonetheless, we were fortunate because the greater part of Mecca was still intact, although the first expansion of the great mosque had resulted in the sanctuary being cut off from the body of the town by a wide road. Medina was another story. The greater part of the city had already been erased, with only one of the traditional quarters left. But the baraka of the Prophet remained.

The Hajj, with its promise of forgiveness and renewal, was a balm for one who had recently become a Muslim. I had no idea what would happen to me next, but I was happy to bask for a short while in the heart of this glorious world of Islam.

THE CONFERENCE

I remember very little of the conference. I have, however, a vivid memory of a wonderful lecture. We were divided into groups and the chairman of ours was Hasan Fathy whom I had first met at the Festival in London. Instead of chairing a discussion, he just spoke, without notes or pauses for nearly two hours. We will encounter this great man again in the next chapter.

The Holy Kaaba has witnessed the most powerful confrontation between the traditional and the modern. When Sinan, the master architect of Suleiman the Magnificent, was sent to Mecca to build the arcade surrounding the Kaaba, he designed it so that it was lower than the sacred cube, out of respect. Now the Kaaba is dwarfed by skyscrapers containing shopping malls that are indistinguishable from any Western shopping centres, and hotel rooms whose occupants can look down upon the Haram. All the traditional occupations that served the pilgrims have disappeared. In the late 1980s, when making an Umrah, I was moved to buy an amphora from one of the water masters who served the Zamzam water to pilgrims. The next time I entered the Haram, the water masters had gone and so had the amphoras. They had been replaced by self-service plastic water dispensers and plastic disposable cups.

A beautiful water container made from unglazed earthenware and shaped so that it could rest in the sand, which allowed the water to remain cool, had been replaced by an ugly plastic object made in China. The amphora was made locally, and when its life was finished, returned to the earth from whence it came. This perfect creation, belonging to a tradition going back thousands of years to the beginning of pottery, was exchanged for a plastic container condemned to pollute the environment for thousands of years into the future. Nothing could represent better for me the truth of tradition and the insanity of the modern. My amphora, which marks the Qibla wall where I pray in my home, is a constant reminder of the Holy Kaaba and the sanity of the world that once surrounded it.

THE PROPOSAL

After the conference Sami took me to see Dr Abdullah Naseef, whom we briefly met in the last chapter when he delivered the Saudi contribution to the Festival. He and Sami told me that they wanted to initiate something bigger and better than the Festival to mark the advent of the new Islamic century that was three years away. They asked me if I could come up with a proposal.

My first reaction to their wish to do something bigger and better than the Festival was good luck to you! I was still in recovery from seven years of intense activity. However, Sami and Dr Naseef were clearly remarkable people, and already I had begun to experience the magnet of the Hejaz. This is the region that covers the western coastal area of Saudi Arabia, and includes Jeddah, the port to the Holy Cities. Through the pilgrimage, all the cultures of Dar al Islam have left their mark, and the population contains the genes of every race and nation. It is the living reality of the unity and diversity of Islam.

I told them that I would discuss the proposal with colleagues, and returned to London. In fact, there was only one person I wanted to consult. I had met Peter Hobson during the final year of the Festival. In conversation with Martin Lings, I had expressed a wish to try to include something about the Malay world in the Festival programme. He suggested

I should meet Peter, who had recently retired from the Foreign Office and had spent many years in Indonesia. Although it was too late for all but a lecture on the Malay world to be included, we became great friends, and he was a tremendous help during the final traumatic months of the Festival.

SIDI ISMAIL

Peter, whom I will now refer to as Sidi Ismail, was a recent convert to Islam. He was a brilliant linguist. Towards the end of the Second World War, he was selected from Leeds Grammar School and placed in SOAS to do a crash course in Japanese. He was sent out to the Pacific, and was present at the Japanese surrender. He then acted as a translator during the interrogation of high-level prisoners. He fell in love with Japan, and, when his task was completed, joined a translation agency and went native. After several years he realized that he must return to the UK and complete his education. Once he was back at SOAS it quickly became evident that his Japanese was better than that of his tutors, so he switched to Chinese. Although his tutor hardly saw him – he largely taught himself – he got the highest first that had ever been achieved at SOAS. On graduating, he decided on a career in the Foreign Office. He was interviewed by an old China hand who had spent many years in the country. Speaking only in Chinese, the interviewer asked Sidi Ismail if he could tell from his speech where in China he had been posted. 'No', said Sidi Ismail, 'but I can tell you are from Liverpool'. This story gives an idea of the phenomenal gift that Sidi Ismail was given. He could completely disappear into the world of the language. I experienced this when he invited me to lunch with some Japanese visitors in a Japanese restaurant. We sat on the floor around the low table, and the only way I can describe it is that Sidi Ismail became Japanese. Everything about him was transformed. I was told by a Japanese friend that Sidi Ismail was so fluent that if he spoke behind a curtain, you would be convinced you were speaking to another Japanese person.

In the Foreign Service he spent many years in Japan and South East Asia, and ended up as head of the China Research Department in London, directly responsible to the Foreign Secretary. After the withdrawal from Aden, the Commonwealth Office was absorbed into the Foreign

Office. Early retirement was on offer and Sidi Ismail availed himself of the opportunity. He was not the calibre of person they wanted to filter out, but their loss was my gain.

By the time I met him, he spoke more than twenty languages, and over the next ten years I witnessed him absorbing Sanskrit, Tamil and Singhalese. Arabic held a special place for him, and he taught my wife and myself the Qur'an. Annabel derived great joy from the classes and made steady progress, I struggled and continue to struggle, having absolutely no talent for languages.

I acquainted Sidi Ismail with my dilemma of whether to accept or decline the proposition that had been made to me in Jeddah. He responded that as a Muslim, I should accept such an invitation. Now Sidi Ismail had once said to me that the only reason I had been able to carry off the Festival was that I was completely ignorant. At first, I was rather hurt by his remark. However, on reflection I realized he was completely right. I was driven by a vision that everyone had to join in. I had no idea of the intricacies of the worlds I was engaging with and bringing together. If I had known the political, religious and cultural problems that could rear their ugly heads, would I have ever had the courage to dive in? Now things were different. I was no longer an innocent! I made it clear to Sidi Ismail that if he agreed to join me, I was happy to go ahead. He responded positively and a few days later we set off for Jeddah, the first of many trips together to that city.

7

THE TRAVELLING EXHIBITION

SAMI AND DR NASEEF took us to meet Prince Mohammad Al-Faisal, the son of the former King. He had inherited his father's devotion to Islam and had participated in the World of Islam Festival, giving the keynote lecture in the conference entitled *Islam and our World*, which had been organized by the Islamic Council of Europe and held at the Albert Hall. Prince Mohammad was engaged with a number of Islamic projects, and the top of his list was the establishment of the first Islamic bank, which he set up in Cairo. At the time we met him, he was also deeply involved in the problems surrounding water, having just retired from his governmental position in charge of desalination. He had commissioned a French company to look into the idea of dragging an iceberg into the Red Sea. It was clear that he already knew about the plan for an event to celebrate the new Islamic century, and we were there to secure the funding for a feasibility study. These were exciting times for the Gulf Arabs, and anything seemed possible. Prince Mohammad waxed lyrical about his projects and was happy to add ours to his growing list.

The first thing to be done was to create a vehicle that would be responsible for the organization of the feasibility study and the realization of the project, if that was to follow. We established the Islamic Environment Research Centre, and Sami Angawi and Yusuf Ibish joined Sidi Ismail and myself on the board. I was to direct the project and Sidi Ismail would be the Research Director. We then had the good fortune to encounter David Lake, who will feature in several roles during this stage of my journey, and he joined us as Research Coordinator. Sarah Harding, who had executed the press campaign for the Festival so brilliantly, was recruited from the British Museum and a secretary was also employed. Offices were rented in South Kensington and, with the team in place, we were ready to start our work.

One thought struck me very clearly. The Festival events had been scattered across London and the UK, taking place in many different institutions. If we could bring the whole story together in one location, that would result in a project that could certainly be better than the Festival. We could organize a really great exhibition that benefited from the experience we had gained through the Festival. From the response of the audiences to the various exhibitions, we had a good idea of what worked when presenting Islamic art, architecture and the Islamic environment. We had a network of contacts who could be engaged in such a venture. This could, indeed, provide the opportunity to complete the work of the Festival with an act of crystallization.

Our next task was to find a suitable location. We wanted a traditional Islamic environment that was accessible to the world and had a government that would be supportive. The closest we could find that fitted these requirements was the city of Fez in Morocco. We made a survey of the city and found a disused warehouse that, if restored, would be large enough to house the exhibition. However, we were having difficulty in envisioning this location as having the global attraction that we were seeking.

And then the second part of our plan fell into place. Why not make it a travelling exhibition? Not just any travelling exhibition, but a huge exhibition that, like the Great Exhibition of 1851, could be contained in its own building. Most cities around the world had parks and gardens, and these would provide perfect settings for the project. We made a preliminary study of the kind of structures that could answer our needs, and were assured that our proposal was perfectly sound. Our Travelling Exhibition was entirely feasible and, if realized, would command the attention of the world.

Our board met with Dr Naseef and Prince Mohammad in Jeddah at the beginning of September 1977. The feasibility study was enthusiastically received, and the next stage of our funding agreed. This would cover the costs through to the detailed plan of the exhibition, and its containing structure.

I was now totally committed to this new endeavour and had a clear idea of how to proceed. The first task was to create the story, the journey along which we wanted to take the visitor. Once this was established then everything else would follow. We would need a first-class exhibition design practice, architects to provide the temporary building, locations where the exhibition could be held, and transport specialists to ferry the exhibition from location to location. We would require researchers and curators to select the exhibits, as well as film makers, model makers and graphic designers. The exhibition would also engage a number of traditional artists and craftsmen in recreating the historic interior environments that would be a special feature of the exhibition.

My experience with the Festival had prepared me for the task of telling the story of Dar al-Islam through the exhibition medium. I had connected with the designers of the principal exhibitions, and studied carefully what seemed to have worked for the visitors and what had been less successful. The Arts of Islam exhibition at the Hayward Gallery could not compete with the success of the Tutankhamun Exhibition with its golden mask of the pharaoh; figurative art can be viewed in isolation and tells a story. Islamic art, apart from the arts of the book, is best appreciated in its context. This was why the Nomad and City Exhibition had been such a success. People could experience the art as it related to the Muslim way of life.

I am a talker. My imagination works best in company. I needed a companion to work with if I was to produce the story of the exhibition, and Sidi Ismail was perfect for this role. He had the scholarship that I lacked and he could write. He was a great listener and incredibly receptive, and I felt liberated in his company; my imagination could soar. He once said that he could see the ideas coming out of my head! The months through to the early part of 1978 were amongst the happiest and most fulfilling of my working life. I would talk, and Sidi Ismail would take notes, after which he would go home and write them up. By the spring we had our story with a description of how it was to be realized.

The next step was to find an exhibition designer. We researched the field and finally settled on Jasper Jacob who headed the exhibition design unit of the architectural firm, Higgins, Ney and Partners. He had designed the Libyan National Museum and had just completed the Museum of London. We had been very impressed with the Museum of London and its use of interior environments, models and films. The museum told the story of London well, and provided a very visitor-friendly experience. It was clear from our interview that Jasper was the most dynamic and interesting of the designers we had seen.

We then increased our in-house research team which included Dalu Jones, who had co-founded AARP (Art and Archaeological Research Papers) and had worked on the catalogue for the Arts of Islam Exhibition at the Hayward Gallery. We also had our wide network of research consultants from the festival which included Titus Burkhardt, and were ready to enter the next stage of the project.

The heart of our exhibition was to be the juxtaposition between the mosque and the home. Early on we decided that we would recreate in full size that part of the Sultan Hasan Mosque in Cairo which contained the mihrab and minbar. The scene would be depicted at night with replicas of the lamps that were designed for the mosque, flickering to simulate the original oil lamps. We then researched the mosque and house interiors that would complete the section, taking into account the different types and regional variations, and working out which were best represented in full size replicas, models or graphics. This high point of the exhibition would show Islamic art in its context, and would provide a splendid demonstration of the skill of the calligraphers, and the many different types of craftsmen and women that would be required for its realization. We also believed that the exhibition could make a significant contribution to the conservation of the crafts, which, with the wholesale adoption of modern architecture, were under dire threat of extinction.

By the Autumn of 1978, the outline design of the exhibition was complete, and David Lake and Jasper Jacob set out on a trip to measure and study in detail the mosque and home interiors that had been selected. Their journey took them to Spain, Morocco, Tunisia, Egypt, Yemen, Syria, Turkey and Iran. They had to make a rapid departure from Iran as they happened to be there when the revolution was reaching a critical point with the exit of the Shah. Little did we realize at the time, the significance that this event was to have on our project.

Meanwhile, Sarah Harding went to the USA to research venues, as we were beginning to consider launching the event in the States. Sarah would leave us in early 1979 to get married. Her husband, Dr Ricky Richardson was a young paediatrician at Great Ormand Street hospital, and was seconded to Brunei to set up a paediatric service for His Majesty the Sultan of Brunei. Ricky will appear again later in my story.

We were fortunate in finding a brilliant specialist in architectural model making. Kim Allen had a lifetime of experience behind him. He had been making models in the army during the war, part of which was spent in the Middle East, and had then, when peace was declared, set up his practice which specialized in historic buildings. He had just completed a beautiful model of the Dome of the Rock. Part of the model was a cut-away, revealing the building's inner structure. Kim had written an essay which explained how in the process of constructing the model of the Dome of the Rock, the pure geometry of the building was revealed. He contrasted this with the circular Byzantine buildings in which he showed how the geometry was approximated or fudged. He was prepared to clear the decks to accommodate our programme.

The outline plan of the exhibition told the story beautifully, but the way the galleries were linked created a somewhat haphazard arrangement. We had commissioned a specialist in air structures, and when he brought all the disparate galleries under one covering, he produced an organic series of bubble; it looked as though some ghastly alien creature had landed from outer space. By this time, I knew the exhibition and its layout like the back of my hand. I decided it had to be rationalized. It needed to be a modular structure that could be easily built, taken down and transported. So, I decided to build it in Lego. I bought up all the Lego in the Croydon area, separating out the white pieces. Then I cleared our front room and set to work. The different galleries fitted together beautifully, creating just off a square in its outer dimensions. I invited Jasper and Hal Higgins, his architectural partner, to view my handiwork. I wish I could have captured the look of surprise on their faces as they entered our front room. The model had to be cut in half to get it out of our house so that it could be transported to their offices.

By the summer of 1979, our plan was complete. The report, including the cost of the project, was accompanied by an album with text, plans and photographs, and a Perspex model that could be assembled, gallery by gallery. What our team had produced certainly constituted a project that would be 'bigger and better' than the Festival. The exhibition covering 5644 sq. meters was more than twice all the Festival exhibitions put together, and the visitor experience of Islam and its civilization would be better, more profound, and far more comprehensive than what we had been able to achieve with the Festival. The exhibition consisted of ten thematic areas which were devoted to ***The Holy Qur'an, the Islamic City, Knowledge and Science, Form and Design, the Mosque and the Home, Technology and the Crafts, the Way of the Nomads, Trade and Commerce, East (the Malay World) and West (West Africa)***, and finally ***the Pilgrimage and the Kaaba.*** Everything was now in place for us to start building the exhibition.

But the times were changing. 1979 began with the seismic event of the Iranian Revolution, and in November the Siege of Mecca ushered in the new Islamic century of 1400 Hijri, when a group of young Bedouin took the Haram by force. It was now that the term 'Islamic terrorism' began to be used. By the end of the year, Prince Mohammad had bowed out of the project and it appeared that our exhibition was finished. However, there was to be another extraordinary act before this particular drama came to an end.

THE UNIVERSITY CULTURAL COMPLEX

Dr Abdullah Naseef, who had followed my progress from the first World of Islam Festival in 1971, had become the Vice Chancellor of King Abdul Aziz University, in Jeddah. Saudi Arabia was engaged in a massive building programme, and one of the principal projects was the creation of a new campus for Dr Naseef's university. He was now responsible for a huge building budget, and invited us to design a cultural complex, which would be at the heart of the university. The complex would include the university mosque and our exhibition. To realize this, we needed an architect who could design and build the complex in the Islamic tradition. Dr Naseef's home had been designed by the great Egyptian architect, Hassan Fathy.

Hassan Fathy had single-handedly revived the traditional architecture of Egypt. He discovered it in villages in Nubia, about to be destroyed by the building of the Aswan High Dam. He rescued it by employing stonemasons who could build perfect domes and vaults, without scaffolding, in mud brick. His book *Architecture for the Poor* had become hugely influential. As well as the inspiring lecture at the Hajj conference, I was privileged to be in a group that Hasan Fathy took around Cairo. He gave us a memorable introduction to the courtyard house, showing us the places where the peace and unity of the building could be experienced. However, Hassan Fathy was in his eighties and not in a position to engage in a major project.

ABDEL-WAHED EL-WAKIL

After an exhaustive search for other possible architects, the only one we were happy with was Abdel-Wahed El-Wakil, who happened to be the foremost student of Hasan Fathy, and had recently been awarded the first Agha Khan Prize for Architecture. On receiving the award, he insisted in sharing it with his master mason, recognizing the part the master masons of Nubia had played in Hasan Fathy's revival of the tradition. I was to embark on a journey with a truly remarkable person who taught me how to see Islamic architecture, and whose friendship, teaching and support has continued through to the present.

In the 1960s, Abdel-Wahed El-Wakil had gone to Ain Shams University in Cairo, first to study and then teach architecture. They taught classical and modern architecture, but Islamic architecture, which he wanted to study, was not in the curriculum. It was then that a friend introduced him to Hassan Fathy, and El-Wakil became his disciple, and was taught the fundamental principles of traditional architecture, and how working within the tolerance of the natural building materials, such as wood, brick, and stone, forms can be naturally created which resonate with the human soul. These principles inform all of El-Wakil's work.

In the early 1980s he embarked upon designing and building a truly astonishing series of mosques in Saudi Arabia. Between the Holy Cities of Mecca and Medina, a dozen buildings rose up in which he drew references from across the Islamic world integrating them into a perfect harmony. The first of these was a small mosque, built on an island off the Corniche in Jeddah. The series included the rebuilding of Quba Mosque, the first mosque of Islam, and the rebuilding of Qiblatain, (the mosque of the 'two Qiblas'). The culmination of this series was the Miqaat Al-Medina Mosque Complex, where the pilgrims prepare for their entry into Medina; a majestic complex of surpassing beauty with the most memorable of minarets; the sophistication of its design is truly remarkable. During this inspirational unfolding of creativity, he gathered together master craftsmen from many places, and even revived crafts where necessary. The work of stonemasons, bricklayers, metal workers, tile makers, carpenters, carpet weavers and calligraphers, was brought together into a harmonious celebration of beauty. How this miracle was achieved, in the face of the rampant modernization that was taking place, is still a mystery to me. But part of the answer has to be the profound and steadfast commitment to the tradition of Islamic Architecture that is Abdel-Wahed El-Wakil. This was the man we were able to work with on our cultural complex for two amazing years.

In September 1980 we moved into new offices in Bedford Square, next to the British Museum, and increased our staff. We were given another exhibition to design and develop which would complement the Heritage of Islam. This was inspired by the Qur'anic verse;

> *'To Him belongs what is in the heavens and on earth, and all between them, and all beneath the soil.'* (Qur'an 20:6)

This 'Created World' exhibition would be housed in a round structure with a basement gallery devoted to geology and the study of the earth's core, a ground floor gallery dealing with living forms of animals and plants, a first-floor gallery focused on the atmosphere, weather and climate, and a top floor exploring the universe. The idea was to utilize the capacity of the modern sciences to see deep into the world of matter and far into the universe in order to celebrate and wonder at the majesty, wisdom and unity of Almighty God's creation.

The entrance to the University Centre would be through a traditional gateway leading onto a courtyard garden. At the end of the courtyard would be the great mosque, with the two exhibitions to the left and right of the courtyard. In the upper rooms, overlooking the courtyard would be a library, archive and documentation centre supporting the exhibitions. The Centre would also include an auditorium, an avenue of the living crafts, and the Hajj Research Centre. By the summer of 1982 we had completed the design of the Centre and both exhibitions were ready to be built. A full presentation with costings, including models of both the exhibitions and the Centre were submitted to the University.

It is an irony that whereas the rise in the price of oil in 1973 facilitated the World of Islam Festival, it was a slump in the oil price that sounded the death knell for the Cultural Complex and our great exhibition. Between 1980 and 1985 the price of oil more than halved, and by 1983 the Saudi government was slashing their budgets. Work on the University campus slowed down, and our project went into limbo. The final blow came at the end of 1983 when Dr Naseef left the university to become the Secretary General of the Muslim World League. A considerable sum was left owing to us by the university, which placed us in a critical situation. Over the next two years, with the support of Dr Naseef, and a group of friends that he had formed, we attempted to find a new home for the exhibition and raise the money to cover the backlog and somehow keep the project alive. But the times were against us; as the acts of terrorism in the name of Islam increased, the interest in our project diminished.

1984 was a pivotal year. My financial situation was becoming very serious. In February we went to Dar al-Islam Village in Abiquiu, New Mexico. It seemed a promising location for some elements of our project. Hasan Fathy had built the mosque there and our group of Saudis had supported the Village. But this project was also at a standstill. In May we received the sad news that Titus Burckhardt had died. However, the spirits were lifted for a short while in the Spring, when Mahmud Mirza gave a wonderful series of concerts for the different times of day, which were held in London and which we recorded and released as a box set of CDs.

By the end of 1985, Dr Naseef's group had raised the funds necessary to pay off the creditors and the Islamic Environment Research Centre was closed. I was now on my own, and only a skeleton staff remained to support my increasingly desperate attempts to find new patronage for my beloved exhibition. I had lived inside the exhibition for eight long years and could not let it go. In November 1986, I received an inheritance when the family business was sold, and we moved from our rented accommodation and bought our own house in Tonbridge. The inheritance also enabled me to settle debts that had accumulated since I had stopped receiving a salary from the project since 1983.

By the Spring of 1987, ten years after my invitation to create something 'bigger and better than the Festival', I had to finally accept that the project was finished. I made one final trip to Jeddah, to see if there was any possible avenue that remained, but it was clear that the end had come. I arrived back in England just in time to attend the final concert in a series that Mahmud was giving at the Aldeburgh Festival. It was a night concert, and he played the awe-inspiring Rag Darbari.

8
MEANWHILE

DURING THE TEN YEARS I was working on the Exhibition, other significant things were happening in our lives, which contributed massively to my understanding.

THE MARYAMIYYA TARIQA

It was through the group of Muslims I had been working with on the Festival, and who had become my friends, that my wife and I entered Islam. They belonged to the Maryamiyya Sufi tariqa whose Shaykh was the writer Frithjof Schuon, who resided in Lausanne, Switzerland. Shaykh Isa, as he was known, had developed his own method of meditation which was accompanied by texts that he specially prepared. We attended regular meetings of the group and every two or three months visited Martin Lings at his cottage in the beech woods close to the town of Westerham. Martin Lings was writing his magnus opus *Muhammad: His Life Based on the Earliest Sources*. I had already experienced the profound scholarship of

Seyyed Hossein Nasr, Titus Burckhardt, Yusuf Ibish and Sidi Ismail. It was highly stimulating to be able to practice our Islam in their company. Over a period of ten years, we formed friendships and were very much at home in our association.

In the summer of 1987, a terrible scandal at the heart of our tariqa was exposed. In 1980 Frithjof Schuon had emigrated from Switzerland to the USA and settled in Bloomington, Indiana. In England, we had been protected from what had developed in America. It transpired that the Maryamiyya had an inner core around the Shaykh whose practices were hidden from the main body of disciples. All through that summer we wrestled with the dilemma, as more was revealed to us of the immorality, weird visions, and syncretic practices that were taking place in Bloomington. A group of close friends, among whom were Sidi Ismail and David Lake, met in our house around the kitchen table, for what transpired to be the catalyst for our leaving. My friends were all intellectuals, and were attempting to separate the Shaykh as a person from his doctrine. I had never fully entered into, or understood the intellectual aspect of his method, but the immorality frightened the life out of me. Finally, I remonstrated that I didn't know about the doctrine, that was far beyond me, above the clouds, but the moral aspect was quite clear. If the moral aspect was wrong, then I could not trust in the doctrine, and I was out. We all joined hands and jumped clear of what we had come to realize was a cult.

On October 15th that year, Mahmud gave a sublime concert at the Wigmore Hall in London. After the concert we drove back to Tonbridge. That night the great storm hit, toppling thousands of trees in a swath across the country. A few days later we went to visit Martin Lings in his cottage in the woods. Around the cottage was a scene of desolation; all the trees had been flattened. We said our goodbyes and left the cottage, surrounded by the devastation wreaked by the great storm.

USTAD MAHMUD MIRZA

Meanwhile, there had been important developments in how we were beginning to present Mahmud and his music. The 1960's fad for Indian music had by now evaporated, but had left in its wake a change in the relationship between sitarist and tabla player. Instead of the drum being an accompaniment to the main instrument, through which the melody was unfolded, it had become a duet in which the rhythm had become ever more frenzied and dominant. Mahmud wished to attract a classical audience in the West, which was used to concentrated listening. In order to do this, he decided to focus on the unaccompanied form of the music. This was contained in the most sublime framework in which the melody was carried through three movements to its resolution. Mahmud gave his first solo concert in New York in November 1981, and over the years that followed he continued to present this form of the music in the West. Fortunately, we have captured some of these rare events, and David Lake began to put together an archive of the recordings. David was deeply affected by Mahmud's music, and being a musician himself, took the opportunity to study with Mahmud so that he was able to write about the music for the literature that accompanied his concerts and recordings. David became an invaluable ambassador in introducing the music to the classical music world. David Lake also became an important collaborator in the family project that Annabel and I were engaged with during this time.

POLEBROOK FARM

One of the features that distinguishes the English urban house is the back garden. Perhaps the way we were so violently uprooted by the enclosures and the Industrial Revolution has left us with a deep longing to return to the countryside. There have been several back-to-the-land movements, the most recent of which was during the sixties. Annabel and I shared in this longing and nostalgia. We grew fruit and vegetables in our own back garden and read voraciously all the books we could lay our hands on which described how to live self-sufficiently off the land. John Seymour was a great influence at this time. His book *The Fat of the Land*, inspired us to seek him out in his farm in Wales. By this time, he had become something of a cult figure and when we met him, he bemoaned the fact that he was invaded by young people from the cities who encamped on his farm; they were full of ideas and talk, he said, but incapable of solid work, whilst eating him out of house and home. Shortly after our visit, he escaped the hordes by moving to Ireland.

With our project going so well, we decided now was the time to realize our dream. We wanted to create a realm for our family, where our, by this time, four boys could grow up surrounded by all that the domesticated and wild countryside had to offer. On October 17th 1979 we bought Polebrook Farm in the Weald of Kent. Then in early 1980 we sold our house in London and moved to rented accommodation near the farm. The farmhouse had been demolished some hundred years before, but the nine fields that made up the thirty-acre property were completely intact. We had found a rare treasure. How rare only became evident when David Lake began researching the history and present condition of the farm. We needed a compelling case if we were to obtain planning permission to build our house. David produced a brilliant report which proved to be critical in our getting our planning permission in February 1982. Our report was also submitted to the Nature Conservancy Council, and Polebrook Farm was designated a Site of Special Scientific Interest. We entered into an agreement which bound us, and our successors in the property, to manage the farm in a manner that preserved its unique features.

It transpired that the farm was a pre-Norman Conquest settlement that had been cut out of the Wealden Oak Forest, with remaining strips of the forest, called 'shores', separating the fields. It was untouched by fertilizers, weedkillers and insecticides. More than 200 species of flora were recorded and it was home to a multitude of insects and birds. The fields that surrounded Polebrook had been modernized and most of the shores and many of the hedgerows removed. On passing into Polebrook from this arid landscape, the air became alive with the hum of bees and insects, and the songs of the many kinds of birds that made their homes in the trees and hedgerows. It was a hidden paradise, and it was to be our home. I took my mother to Polebrook. She was a great nature lover and grew up in the beautiful county of Dorset. After she had absorbed the serenity of the place, she said 'You know, when I was a child, everywhere was like this.' As we were to discover, Polebrook Farm comprised the only completely intact group of Medieval fields in Kent and probably South-East England.

But the farm was landlocked. It was many years since the lane that led to the property had been absorbed into the adjoining fields. We had to negotiate a new route into our farm with our neighbours. The original direct route was controlled by a farmer who wanted to charge us for access nearly as much as we had paid for the land! Another farmer kindly provided us with a much longer way in, but at a reasonable price. We then set to work hiring contractors to build the road and to bring in all the services under the road, so that there were no pylons to spoil the views. Summers were spent in tents, with the family clearing the ponds and tending to the hedgerows. An architect had been commissioned to design the house and restore the Medieval barn, which was the only building still standing.

However, our dream was not to be realized. During the pivotal year 1984, when our funds were running out, we had to sell Polebrook Farm.

9

END GAME

BY THE SUMMER OF 1987 our exhibition project was finished and we had left the Maryamiyya, which had been our spiritual home for ten years. Once again, our funds were dwindling; we had somehow to recover our situation.

ANNABEL AT SOAS

Annabel's response was to go to university. On leaving school, she had been registered to go to Bristol University to study English, German and Philosophy, but deferred her place for a year, as she decided she preferred to change philosophy for music, for which she needed to gain an extra qualification. During that year, she met me and became involved with the Exploding Galaxy, and so gave up the idea of university. In time we married and one by one our four sons arrived. By 1989, our youngest son was now nine, and at preparatory school in Tonbridge. All the boys had been blessed with Annabel's full attention during their childhoods. Now she wanted to further her study of Arabic, which she had begun informally during lessons on the Qur'an that she had followed over the years with Sidi Ismail. She applied to the School of Oriental and African Studies (SOAS) and was accepted as a mature student. However, she could not take Arabic as her first language, as she would have had to spend a year in Alexandria, and for family reasons that was impossible. So instead, she selected to read for a BA in Persian with Arabic as a secondary subject. In the Winter Term of 1988 Annabel began her three-year degree course.

THE TURKISH PROJECT

I needed a project in which I could immerse myself. I had become interested in the Turkish contribution to the world of Islam. It had struck me how, during the life of the Prophet, blessings and peace be upon him, the Turks had unified the Eurasian Steppes from Mongolia to the borders of Hungary, in an empire which lasted some hundred years. This empire remained confined to the grasslands, and all the various tribes under the Turks became part of a Turkish world. Hidden from history, a people was being forged who would later serve and protect the message being delivered at the time, by the last of the prophets. I then followed the story of the Turks through to their dominance across Dar al-Islam from India to Egypt and beyond. The Turks had received a very bad press in the West, and the scholars had viewed them as a major contributor to the stagnation and decline of Islam after the so-called Arab 'Golden Age'. I wanted to show the falsehood of this idea.

In Spring 1988, a friend secured the seed money for me to do a feasibility study, and by the autumn I had completed my proposal. However, it was very weak. I had attempted a replay of the Festival. Instead of the Hayward Gallery, I had approached the Royal Academy. They had shown mild interest in the idea, but it would take time for the proposal to work its way through their system. I had devised an initial treatment for a film series, and identified institutions that could participate in the project. But I had failed to make a convincing case, and my failure was clear to everyone who had become involved in the study. The project would not fly, and I had nowhere to go. All that I could see ahead of me was a blank wall.

BREAKDOWN

Years of stress culminated in my having a massive 'manic attack'. I hardly slept for a month and was acting ever more strangely, until one day I was called downstairs to find my sister, my wife and the doctor in the hall. They gently coaxed me into a waiting car, and I was taken to a clinic deep in the Sussex countryside. Most of my fellow patients were women suffering from depression. I remember pondering the cruelty of the modern world, that has turned the human being inside out, and crushed the feminine within us. A Jewish woman taught me how to make chicken soup. One day, by accident I wandered into the wing of the clinic where the old people resided. They sat in rows looking up at a screen with vacant stares. At meals we sat at tables each with our egg cup in which our pills were placed. The medication I was taking numbed me, but my limbs could not find a position of rest. My brother-in-law visited me and in a state of repressed anger railed at me for what I was doing to Annabel and the family. In the wreckage that my life had become, the only thing that preserved me were the prayers, which I performed on time. This was all that I had left, but it sustained me and gave me comfort. In time, my manic state was dissipated, and depression settled in. When I began to communicate this to the doctor, he sat up and became alert. I realized that he was about to change my pills. The thought struck me that he only had two kinds of pills, one to bring me down and the other to take me up. If he put me onto the uppers, I could spend the rest of my life yo-yoing up and down, and I would never get out of the place. I rowed back and made light of it. I was by now desperate to get home.

I became acutely aware of the incredibly narrow band of normality allowed in our modern secular world. When the reality of the spiritual realm is nullified, the soul is severely restricted and terrible suffering ensues. The vastness of the soul that can encompass the ecstasy of inspiration and illumination, and suffer the terrors of the dark night of the soul, is denied, and such experiences are turned into pathologies. Although still in a fragile state, I put on a brave front and convinced the doctor that I was ready for release. Before departing he told me that my attack had been brought on by extreme stress, and it was a kind of attack that was unlikely to recur.

Two weeks later, when I was at home in my garden, it began again; but I now knew what it was, and managed it. In time it settled down, and although I have experienced difficult times, equal to what led to my breakdown, I have been able to cope with them. It was the breakdown and my recovery from it, that gave me the strength to deal with the tribulations that lay ahead.

REFLECTION

When I look back and reflect upon the ten years that followed the Festival, I realize that although the Exhibition Project and Polebrook Farm failed to materialize, they contributed hugely to my understanding. Our engagement with Polebrook Farm allowed us to delve deep into our traditional countryside and placed us in contact with scholars and specialists who opened up so much that would have remained closed to us. We had meetings to discuss the management of Polebrook Farm with the director of the Weald and Downland Open Air Museum which is situated just outside Chichester. We came to know that wonderful place very well, taking the family on a number of visits. The museum has rescued many dwellings that were about to be demolished and rebuilt them in their original form. Included were two buildings from a valley close to Polebrook Farm that had been flooded to create a reservoir. These dwellings are beautifully arranged in the grounds of the museum, where one can experience a thousand years of the history of rural settlements in the weald and downland of Kent and Sussex. The new owner of Polebrook Farm built the house and continued the restoration of the property. A few years later we visited the farm. It was wonderful to see it flourishing.

But what of the Exhibition that held me in thrall for so long? This glorious project crystallized my understanding of the unity of Islam and Islamic civilization. It allowed me to contemplate the various aspects of this flawless manifestation. I was able to enter the pure architectural realm of Abdel-Wahed El-Wakil, and it enabled me to visit the sacred centre of Islam on many occasions. In retrospect, I realize it protected me from what evolved at the heart of the Maryamiyya.

It took a long time to untangle and come to an understanding of the Maryamiyya. A group of brilliant intellectuals, Islam, tradition, modernity and the 'perennial philosophy' had to be teased apart. As the scandal was brewing, a friend who had been admitted into the inner circle came back from Bloomington, and announced to me, in my kitchen, that the Shaykh had told them that he was not a Muslim; he was a Perennialist. My immediate reaction was to say, 'But Sidi, Islam *is* the perennial religion. Once Almighty Allah revealed His unity, what else is there?' He gave me a sorrowful look. 'How could a foot soldier be expected to understand?' he seemed to be saying.

I came to see that the Maryamiyya itself exposed the falsehood of the perennial philosophy. When the attempt was made to practise it as a religion, very dark forces were released. The syncretic practices had to remain secret. After all, this was the esoterism of all the religions; like other forms of Gnosticism, it had to be wrapped around by an orthodoxy to protect the inner secret. In the case of the Maryamiyya this orthodoxy was Islam. Those who had not been initiated into the centre were dismissed by the adepts as 'Muslim Muslims'.

To explain their philosophy, the perennialists use the Native American symbol of the feathered sun, which is in the form of a wheel. Each spoke of the wheel represents a religion. The religions meet at the centre, wherein resides the perennial philosophy. This philosophy is a direct challenge to Islam; the unfolding of the religions in time is nullified, and Islam becomes just another option amongst equals. Pride of place is taken up by the perennial philosophy, which usurps the unity and universality properly manifested in Islam and Islamic civilization. The perennial philosophy is a fabrication of the mind that cannot be practised or lived, but can only remain in the mind.

I began to see the Maryamiyya as the white man's equivalent of the Nation of Islam. The Afro-Americans had been so traumatized and broken by slavery, that they needed to recover their self-respect. This the Nation of Islam gave them in the guise of a distorted Islam. However, the link was there, and when Malcolm X went to Mecca, the great crossing into mainstream Islam began and continues. We Europeans and Americans are so steeped in arrogance that for many of us it is difficult to enter the mainstream of Islam directly; we have to be top dogs. The Maryamiyya provided a bridge where our vast inheritance of intellectual arrogance could exist side by side with Islam, until the reality of the one over the falsehood of the other could prevail, and the crossing into mainstream

Islam be realized. These bridge phenomena, which enable westerners to make the crossing into Islam, are a mercy from God. This is how I have come to understand the perennial religion and philosophy.

However, the scholars attached to the Maryamiya and their intellectual gifts were harnessed to draw attention to the reality of tradition for our time, and in this they delivered a great service. But the power of this reality has been deeply compromised by the attempt to elide the traditional with the perennial philosophy. What is tradition? I understand tradition to be the means by which Almighty God's revelations become manifested and unfolded in the form of cultures and civilizations. It is the masters of art, craft, knowledge and spirituality who embody and transmit the traditions. These 'traditionalist authors' have simply been telling us about the existence of these worlds. Before the advent of the modern world, all the worlds were traditional. Over time, traditional worlds can become corrupt and develop aberrations. Islam brought the final revelation to humanity into a world of decaying traditions, with the promise that it would remain pristine until the end of time.

My experience of tradition came through my meeting Ustad Mahmud Mirza. His music entered my heart. My eyes were opened through my engagement with Abdel-Wahed El-Wakil. In what follows, we shall meet other traditional practitioners, who further enriched my soul. The 'traditionalist authors' increased my knowledge and understanding. Their contribution to the Festival was immense; but it was the traditional world of Islam they were helping to elucidate. The perennial philosophy played no part in their contributions.

These authors were also important for their critique of modernity. Once the reality of tradition had broken through, the nature of modernity became clear. René Guénon, the pioneer of the traditionalist authors, laid bare the modern world in his seminal work, *The Reign of Quantity and the Signs of the Times*. René Guénon is generally cited by the perennialists as being the father of their movement, but he eschewed the Maryamiyya and Frithjof Schuon's claim to be a shaykh. Guénon passed from theosophy to Islam, went to live in Cairo and became the disciple of a revered Sufi shaykh. His practice was Islam. His intellectual journey went from the spiritual wasteland that had descended upon Europe by the beginning of the 20th century, to illuminating our understanding of the traditions of the world. He cleared the way for the 'traditionalist authors' who followed in his wake. These authors simply opened a window into the world of Islam; it is inside this world that the ocean of knowledge and wisdom is to be found.

10

CONVALESENCE & RECOVERY

THE FIRE

ON A SATURDAY morning in September 1988, Tonbridge School Chapel was gutted by fire. We witnessed the whole event, as our house overlooked the grounds of the school. This conflagration happened shortly before my breakdown. Over the months that followed my return home from the clinic, I formed a deep attachment to the burnt-out shell of the building. Somehow it represented my state; I felt emptied, hollowed out, and yet cleansed. I used to take long walks through the town and into the countryside, circling the chapel at a distance, but always aware of its presence. I little realized that the restoration of the Chapel would be my next project.

1989 was my year of convalescence. Nothing bound me. The friends and colleagues from my work and tariqa had either ceased their association with me or been scattered. I was alone with my family. I had spent years travelling out to the Middle East and had been wedded to my work. Being fully engaged with the family was the best mode for my recovery.

DRAX & YORK MINSTER

Mahmud was spending a year as musician-in-residence at York University. This had been arranged by David Lake, before he entered a monastery and began his life as a Christian Orthodox monk. In early summer, our son Ali and I travelled to York to attend a series of concerts that Mahmud was giving. We drove past Drax, the largest generator of electricity in the country. It was an incredible sight with steam pouring out of twelve huge cooling towers, with massive pylons, striding away across the land, distributing the force that was being generated; a manifestation of raw power. We arrived in York as the sun was setting and stayed the night next to the cathedral in a hotel that had once been Guy Fawkes' home. Early next morning we entered the great Minster. It was empty, except for the cleaners. I mused that when it was fully functioning some five hundred years ago it would have been brimming with life. It would have been the generator of the spirit that would have coursed through the body politic. Now it was nearly dead and it was Drax that was fully alive.

Mahmud gave three short recitals during the day at the University. In the evening we had dinner. It was clear that he was not happy. He was like a fish out of water. When he first came to England, young musicians would ask him to teach them. After a few months they would leave. I asked Mahmud what was happening, and he replied, 'They are always asking me questions, endless questions, the answers to which they could not possibly understand.' They were trying to breach the ramparts of a traditional system through their minds, which is how they were taught to approach knowledge from childhood.

Mahmud had imbibed the music from his uncle from the age of six. His uncle taught him the craft, and for the first years of his training he was only permitted to play a single raga. Once this had reached every part of him, his uncle began introducing him to other ragas. He was in awe of his teacher and followed religiously what he was told to do. He was schooled in humility and reverence. By the time he reached his teens, his craft was established, the music had fully entered his being and his soul was open to inspiration. Arriving at the age of maturity, everything had grown naturally so that his individual character could flower. Along the way, his reasoning mind had developed and could now play its role recognizing and enhancing the patterns he received through his receptive imagination, and subject to his inspiration.

In contrast, the students he was surrounded by wanted to grasp everything at once. They had been taught to think for themselves and to try to be original and innovative from an early age. The traditional mode of education and the modern had no point of connection. They saw the human being from completely different perspectives. In the traditional system the craft grew with the growth of the individual and was fully integrated in the person. A person's individuality only blossomed when they reached maturity. In the modern system, the young are expected to demonstrate their individuality from the outset. The result is the confusion and angst of the modern artist.

An example of this was related to me by a teacher at the Prince's School of Traditional Arts. He told me that when students were sent to work with master craftsmen, after a few months they got bored. The repetitive activity of craft did not engage their minds. They had been stimulated and excited by the brilliant exposition of sacred geometry by Keith Critchlow; they were intoxicated by the theory, but ended up wanting to do their own thing. This is why the Prince's School has been unable to produce any traditional masters. Once, when I was informing one of the students from the school about the work of Warwick Pethers, the last of the masters of Gothic architecture in England, whom we shall meet later in this chapter, the young man looked at me in a rather supercilious way and asked, 'Yes, but does he understand sacred geometry?' The attempt to teach traditional arts through the Western school system ends up with the student knowing facts about tradition, but being incapable of truly entering and mastering it.

ENVIRONMENTAL CRISIS

It was in 1989 that the environmental crisis was breaking into the news and becoming a major issue. During that year the climatologist James Hansen's increasingly urgent warnings regarding global warming were beginning to filter through to the public. In January the Montreal Protocol was signed banning substances that were destroying the ozone layer. In March the oil tanker Exxon Valdez on its way to California, struck Prince William Sound's Bligh Reef and 10.8 million gallons of crude oil was spilled into the ocean. It is considered the worst oil spill that has ever taken place in terms of the damage to wildlife and the environment. In May the last golden toad was sighted; the species is now classed as extinct. In October the Langkawi Declaration on the Environment was made by the assembled heads of government of the Commonwealth of Nations on the issue of environmental sustainability. It seemed that every night there were pictures of the cutting down and burning of vast areas of the Amazon rain forest.

I wanted to know more about what was actually happening. I began attending lectures and seminars and reading books. I remember asking an activist, who was part of an initiative to save the tribes of the Amazon forest, 'With all the publicity and government proclamations to save the rain forests, surely the destruction must be slowing down?' 'No', he said, 'Its increasing. They want to clear as much as they can before legislation is passed.' I attended the 'Faith and the Environment Conference' held at Canterbury Cathedral. Leaders from the different faith traditions were demonstrating how their religions valued the environment and had taken care of God's creation. I met David Bellamy, who at the time was a towering figure in the movement. I began corresponding with him, and we shall meet him again in Part 2 of my story.

Whilst we were queuing for our food during a lunch break, I had a memorable conversation with a pair of Jesuit priests. I told them about my trip to York and my thoughts regarding the power station and the cathedral, how the one generated physical power and the other spiritual power, and how the dynamism of the power station contrasted with the emptiness of the cathedral. One of them sagely nodded and said, 'Yes, we need them both.' This appeared to those who were listening to our conversation the reasonable response; but not to me. Somehow it was too much like having your cake and eating it. The power station and the cathedral belonged to completely different worlds, and the one was destroying the other – hence the environmental crisis. Such an idea could not be considered by the Conference; Christianity and modernity had fused and were indivisible, and the other traditional civilizations were following down the same path. The idea that modernity could be an alien aberration was impossible to countenance.

11

THE CHAPEL CAMPAIGN

THE CAMPAIGN

TOWARDS THE END of 1989, I had an infection of the inner ear which affected my balance. Annabel had left for SOAS and I was in the house alone. After breakfast, I went upstairs to my bedroom and it hit me. I fell down, and every time I tried to stand up, I landed on the floor. I was just able to make it to my bed and spent the day lying on my back, waiting for Annabel to come home. I thought I was dying. This was before the days of mobile phones, and there was no way that I could make it downstairs to the telephone. The doctor came and put me on medication, and I had to be grounded for a while. I began to take short walks with a stick, and was on the way to recovery when the bombshell landed.

On the front page of the local newspaper was the Tonbridge School announcement of an outrageous plan for the building of a new chapel on a greenfield site, which overlooked the cricket field, and the conversion of the old chapel into a theatre. Masters we knew in the school expressed to me their horror at what was being proposed, but made it clear they could not do anything about it. Could I do something they asked? Well, I had no project at the time, but I was loath to get involved in planning disputes as I knew how nasty they could get. Annabel finally persuaded me that we must act, and for the next two and a half years we were totally engaged in the Campaign for the Restoration of Tonbridge School Chapel.

Throughout history, fires have occurred in Gothic cathedrals, churches and chapels and, because of the massive masonry and durability of their walls, invariably their restoration took place. The walls of Tonbridge School Chapel stood proud and were hardly damaged by the fire. However, the governors of the school pleaded that the cost of restoring the chapel would be excessive, and its restoration difficult to achieve. We decided to seek the advice of the Surveyor of the Fabric of Westminster Abbey. As it was, we met the assistant surveyor, Warwick Pethers, who offered to take us to see Stephen Dykes Bower, who was the Emeritus Surveyor to the Abbey. Warwick had been his student for several years.

We met Dykes Bower in his home at Quendon, Essex. We were in the presence of the last of the masters of Gothic architecture. He had experienced the full brunt of the change when the modernists took over control of our built environment. At the time he had been Surveyor for Queens College, Cambridge. In the early 1950s the College was expanding, and he was commissioned to design a new hall of residence for the students, which was to be named the 'Erasmus Building'. The completion of his design coincided with the arrival of a new professor of architecture, who was also the Director of the School of Architecture. Leslie Martin was a leading advocate and evangelist of the International Style and made it his mission to introduce modern architecture into the fabric of the university. The Erasmus Building was chosen for his first target. The students and staff of the School of Architecture mounted an aggressive campaign. This culminated in students stealing Dykes Bower's drawings and models and throwing them into the River Cam the night before the final presentation to the Fellows of the College. Intimidated by the vociferous nature of the campaign, which had drawn support from other faculties in the university, the Fellows capitulated, Dykes Bower was sacked and Basil Spence, the architect of Coventry Cathedral, was appointed.

Dykes Bower went from being a respected and honoured member of the architectural establishment, to being an outcast, derided by the new establishment. However, he stuck to his guns, and with his few remaining projects, was able to keep the tradition alive. He retired from Westminster Abbey in 1973 where he had been responsible for the cleaning and restoration that took place after the Second World War. His work can be seen in many cathedrals, churches and chapels throughout the country. He died in 1994, at the age of 93, mourned by those who knew him and ignored by the establishment that had displaced him. There is an irony regarding the student campaign that led to the Erasmus Building becoming the first modernist structure in the university. The campaign was named the 'Society against Ugly Architecture'. Thirty years later, when every college had its modernist offering, the students talked about the UMBs: Ugly Modern Bits!

There was already a link that connected me to Dykes Bower. He had been Architect Surveyor of Lancing Chapel, and during the 1960s, he had transformed the vast expanse of corrugated iron, that had sealed the West End during my time at Lancing, into the most beautiful rose window, one of the finest in England. Dykes Bower urged us to go to Salford to one of the poorest parishes in the country, and meet a remarkable priest who could help us.

Canon Wyatt arrived to take up his position as vicar of St Paul's, Salford, to find that his church was due to be demolished. It was to be replaced by a modern structure, more in keeping with the tower blocks being erected as part of the sixties slum clearance. He at once set about garnering the opinion of the parishioners and found that they did not want the new church that was on offer, they wanted their old church to be restored. He then set about organizing its restoration in the teeth of fearful opposition from both the Church and civil authorities, who wanted to buy wholly into the sparkling new vision of modernity. But, against all odds, our hero priest won the battle.

Dykes Bower, who supervised the restoration of the church, also designed the clergy house and parish hall to come out at right angles from the church, and completed the square with a walled garden. In the middle of what became a bleak and hostile environment of tower blocks, is this haven of peace, where the priest, his wife and family have been faithfully looking after the spiritual and material needs of a traumatized community for nearly fifty years.

In order to achieve the restoration of the church, Canon Wyatt had mobilized the community. Each night a van would go out from the church to the Asian shops collecting cardboard for recycling, which in the 1970s and 80s fetched good money. With this and other local fundraising initiatives, thousands of pounds were raised which enabled the interior of the church to be finished, with its beautifully painted ceiling, its fine crafted wood and metalwork, and its magnificent alter furnishings. Here in the midst of the direst poverty and deprivation that can be found in our country, through its own efforts and ingenuity, the community created a sanctuary of serene beauty. I felt shame for Tonbridge School, one of the wealthiest public schools in England, for its pathetic response to the challenge of restoring its much-loved chapel.

Back in Tonbridge we started a petition, which in a short time gathered ten thousand signatures from the community. The campaign was undoubtedly helped by Prince Charles's documentary 'A Vision of Britain', that had recently appeared on television. The film expressed what most people were feeling about modern architecture, and gave people the courage to speak out against the ugliness that was springing up around them. Richard Williams, the Oscar-winning cartoonist, who had just finished making 'Who Framed Roger Rabbit', had been with us for dinner in our house the day of the fire, and was able to view the wreckage. He drew for the Campaign a brilliant cartoon in which Roger Rabbit's brother, James Rabbit, is seen being kicked out of the new chapel for the umpteenth time, having mistaken it for the theatre. A billboard in front of the new chapel, carries the chilling message, 'You too can learn to love ugliness.' After a year of intense engagement with local councillors, planning officers, the local community, the school and its governors, and the local and national press, the planning application was rejected. The battle had been won and the green field saved, but we were then presented with another challenge.

When the plans for the restoration of the chapel were published, it was quite clear that they had absolutely nothing to do with restoration. The architect was simply using the shell of the building to create his own modernist take on tradition. We had no choice but to continue the campaign. After months of engagement with the planning authority and the school's governors, we were able to insist that the exterior of the building was returned to its original form, with one glaring exception: the windows. Once, on a memorable walk around Cambridge, Dykes Bower pointed out to me that the windows of a building are like the eyes; if the eyes are damaged or ugly it ruins the whole face. The original windows of Tonbridge School Chapel had beautiful tracery, which was damaged by the fire, but some windows were still largely intact. The architects produced a new design for the windows which meant knocking out the remaining tracery and replacing it with vertical bars without the original cusping. To mirror the rhythm in the original design, the central bar was removed in alternate windows. The eyes of the building were to be defaced. The Campaign did everything possible to save those windows. A firm of stonemasons was commissioned to assess the cost of repairing the tracery as against removing the existing tracery and installing the new design. They found there was little difference between them, and the restoration could even be less expensive. The report was submitted to the school, but it made no difference; the tracery was hammered out and the vertical bars installed. As for the interior of the building, it owes more to IKEA than to Gothic. At the time, warehouse ceilings with exposed steel beams were in vogue with architects, and this found its way into the design at Tonbridge. The language of Gothic architecture is incredibly rich, and there was nothing to stop the chapel from being once again a fine, coherent edifice, as was so clearly demonstrated at St Paul's, Salford. But the architect had to do something different, to leave his mark on the building.

My companion throughout this battle was Warwick Pethers, who explained at every step the options available within the Gothic language. The lessons learnt from what to expect when dealing with a traditional building would place him in a good position when a formidable challenge was presented to him: the building of the Millennium Tower to complete St Edmundsbury Cathedral.

THE TOWER

Dykes Bower had been appointed in 1944 to turn the large parish church of Bury St Edmunds into what became St Edmundsbury Cathedral. During the 1960s, with very little money available, but with consummate skill, Dykes Bower created the new choir and crossing. This was to be the last great work of Gothic in England, as the modernist movement was taking over the church – or so it was thought at the time.

For thirty years, work on the Cathedral stopped. However, with the new millennium approaching it was decided that an appropriate way for the Church to mark the occasion was to complete St Edmundsbury Cathedral by building a Millennium Tower. With the death of Dykes Bower in 1993, Warwick Pethers was recognized as his successor and took on his mantle. As this was to be a Millennium project, Warwick wished to ensure that the tower would last for a thousand years. In order to achieve this, he had to return to the traditional methods of building. He had to practically reinvent load-bearing structures; the walls would be four feet thick with inner brickwork knitted into the outer facing stonework. The modern solution would have been to erect a reinforced concrete frame from which stone panels would be hung, with steel brackets tying them together. Apart from looking and feeling artificial, such structures are not built to last. Instead of cement, which is brittle and in time breaks down, Warwick used lime mortar, which takes longer to set but remains supple and lasts. Lime mortar had not been used in the erection of new buildings for many decades, and Warwick brought together a team of experts who, again, had to recover this knowledge. Warwick assembled the finest stonemasons, bricklayers, flint-knappers, carpenters and metalworkers and produced a masterpiece in design and craftsmanship. After ten years from conception to completion, Bury St Edmunds had become a cathedral city with a magnificent tower that could compare favourably with any tower in England. The citizens were proud of their new landmark, and visitors to the city imagined that it had always been there.

But the victory for tradition had been hard won, and behind the serene, majestic tower there lies an epic struggle. I witnessed it, as each week my friend Warwick and I would talk on the telephone, or meet in Cambridge over a coffee, and he would relate to me the latest developments. The battles that took place between the powers that be at the Cathedral and Warwick, raged as the tower rose. However, the extraordinary outcome of these battles was that in all matters that counted, Pethers was victorious; the tower was built to his design using the traditional methods he had stipulated. It would be difficult to find a building that owes more to one man than the tower of St Edmundsbury Cathedral. It is Warwick Pether's masterpiece. Now he is the last remaining master of Gothic architecture, and the sixth in a direct line from the reviver of the tradition, August Pugin.

Yet when the tower was all but finished, Warwick was sacked. Another architect was brought in who spoilt the little that was left to do. The Cathedral authorities basked in the praise and congratulations that were heaped upon them for the building of a magnificent tower, claiming all the glory for themselves, and at the same time slamming the door firmly shut on anything like it ever happening again.

With the fire at Tonbridge School Chapel, I was taken on an extraordinary journey. The last two great masters of Gothic architecture became my friends. They had guided me through two planning battles; the first, pitched the modern against the traditional, and the second, the fusion of traditional and modern against the traditional. My understanding of the principles that separate the traditional from the modern, and the impossibility of a fusion between them, was further clarified. For ten years I was privileged to follow week-by-week and step-by-step the process by which Warwick Pethers was able to build his Tower.

The two and a half years of the Chapel Campaign put me back in the saddle. I was fully functioning and ready to engage in whatever lay ahead.

II

FROM 50 TO 70 YEARS

12

CAMBRIDGE

THE MOVE TO CAMBRIDGE opened a new chapter in our lives. We were not sorry to leave Tonbridge. The Chapel Campaign had come to an end and left behind bitterness and division. With our having left the Maryamiyya, our reason for being in Tonbridge, close to Martin Ling's cottage in the woods, had gone.

We needed a new beginning and it was through Annabel that the opportunity came about. She had done well at SOAS, gaining a first and being awarded a prize for 'an outstanding performance in honours' and was encouraged to take the next step and do her doctorate. She decided that she wanted to study the Sufi Rashid al-Din Maybudi's Persian commentary on the Qur'an, which required both Persian and Arabic. She found that the only person in the UK who was qualified to supervise her thesis was John Cooper who was a lecturer at Cambridge University. He was very happy to enrol her, and her application for a grant was successful. Our departure from Tonbridge and move to Cambridge could begin. Annabel started her course in October 1992 and took up rooms in Wolfson College.

I stayed in Tonbridge arranging the sale of our house. By the summer of 1993, the house had been sold and we were once again living in rented accommodation owing to the depletion of our funds, with no immediate prospect of money coming in to support us.

The first few months in Cambridge were exhilarating. We had landed in possibly the most important institution in the formation of the modern world; it was the university of William Harvey, Isaac Newton, Charles Darwin, Alan Turing, Francis Crick and Stephen Hawking. I studied the structure of the University. It reminded me of Charlie Chaplin's *The Gold Rush*. The various academic disciplines were like the holes the individual miners had dug, and each shaft was ferociously defended. It was a vertical world, with the scholars digging for their own treasure and every so often putting their findings on display. There was almost no connection between the disciplines. CP Snow had tried to bridge the chasm that separated the Humanities and the Sciences in his Rede Lecture, 'The Two Cultures and the Scientific Revolution', delivered at Cambridge in 1959. When we arrived in 1993, inter-disciplinary studies were all the rage. It was clear to me that the lack of a holistic understanding was keenly felt. But attempts to remedy the problem were clearly failing.

What excited me most at this time was the contact with brilliant young students from every part of the Muslim world. Cambridge attracted the brightest, and over the years they have contributed hugely to my understanding of Islam and its vast heritage. But their own worlds were changing. A Sudanese student intrigued me with his stories about the valley he came from in Darfur, and I fell in love with the Swat Valley in Pakistan when I saw it through the eyes of a friend, whom I only knew as Swati. Both of these places were now overwhelmed by conflict, and the peace that had been so vividly described to me, had been destroyed. My wife was a member of Wolfson College, which drew graduate students from all over the world. Our first Ramadan was memorable; tarawih prayers were held in the college, and the iftars were a feast of cuisines from different parts of Dar al-Islam.

An important presence in Cambridge during the 1980s was Syed Ali Ashraf. He was born in Dhaka, Bangladesh in 1925. After obtaining his Master's degree in English from the University of Dhaka, he came to Cambridge where he completed his Honours and a PhD. He had been the principal organizer of the Conference on Muslim Education held in Mecca in 1977, where I first encountered him. Afterwards he became the Director-General of the World Centre for Islamic Education, set up by the newly-formed Organization of Islamic Conferences. He was in the vanguard of Muslim thinkers addressing the problem of educating Muslims in a modern, secular society. His faith-based approach put him in touch with educators facing the same problems in other religions, and he was able to make common cause with them, without compromising the uniqueness and integrity of Islam. He settled in Cambridge in 1980 and established the Islamic Academy. As well as carrying out an academic programme, the Academy was the focus for Cambridge's Bangladeshi community. I would often attend Friday prayers at the Academy. His sermons were short, learned, easily accessible and inspiring. The congregation, which was always packed, consisted of students and many Bangladeshis working in Cambridge. I felt very much at home in their company. I came to realize that the young Bangladeshis knew very little of their history. This led to the only lecture I gave at the university until the launch of my slide lecture 'Reflections of an English Muslim' in 2014.

GOLDEN BENGAL

The lecture was entitled 'Golden Bengal'. I wanted to show how Bengal had gone from being one of the richest and most successful societies on earth in the 18th century, to a symbol of the direst poverty two hundred years later. My interest in Bengal had been sparked by Will Durant's *The Case for India,* whose dramatic entry into my life I related in Chapter 3. I had come to realize that it was the pillage and destruction of Bengal that had been one of the key factors that had made possible the Industrial Revolution, with the forced transfer of the cotton industry from Bengal to Manchester. This was the beginning of the change from a craft-based world, which worked at every level, to the insanity of the industrial/commercial mono-culture that is drowning us in pollution, and is the engine of global warming.

I was able to present the whole case through the British parliamentary records. The debates regarding Robert Clive's tenure as first Governor General in Bengal exposed the horrors of his rule, which caused the terrible famines of 1769-1773, when it is estimated a third of the population died. Reflecting on his suicide in 1774 at the age of 49, Samuel Johnson wrote that he 'had acquired his fortune by such crimes that his consciousness of them impelled him to cut his own throat'. The second Governor General, Warren Hastings, was impeached by parliament and the hearings took place between 1788 and 1795. Those on the prosecution side were able to present in fine detail the full catastrophe of the East India Company's rule and the plunder that its officers had taken away from the country. Edmund Burke and the playwright Sheridan led the charge, Sheridan delivering what is considered to be one of the greatest parliamentary speeches. However, the power of the East India Company meant that both governor generals were in the end exonerated and turned into heroes of the British Empire. As a school boy this is how I perceived them!

General Sir Charles Napier (1782-1853) was a hero of the Napoleonic Wars. The respect and honour he was accorded is evident in the statue of him that was paid for by his soldiers, which still graces Trafalgar Square. The cache of parliamentary papers surrounding his resignation as Commander-in-Chief in India is a treasure trove. His letter of resignation castigated the East India Company's rule, and in his posthumously published *Defects, Civil and Military of the Indian Government* (Westerton, 1853), he condemned the growing superciliousness of the British in India towards the Indians; 'The younger race of Europeans keeps aloof from native officers' he wrote. He proposed that British officers should learn the language of the natives, and that native officers be appointed as ADCs and Companions of the Bath. 'The Eastern intellect is great, and… the native officers have a full share of Eastern daring, genius and ambition; but to nourish these qualities, they must be placed on a par with European officers.' When revolt broke out in 1857, resulting in the blood bath known as the Indian Mutiny, Napier's *Defects, Civil and Military of the Indian Government* was hailed as a prophetic work which correctly identified many of the seething tensions in the sub-continent.

Every twenty years the East India Company had to renew its charter and these took place in 1813, 1833 and 1853. Once again, they are a mine of information regarding the Company's misrule. One of the great speeches opposing renewal was given by the eminent MP John Bright. Each time, however, Parliament renewed the East India Company charter.

The corruption and injustice continued until it reached a tipping point in 1857. After the British quelled what is now viewed by Indians as the first attempt at freedom from their yoke, they released a terrible vengeance upon the population, particularly the Muslims, whose ruling and educated elites were decimated. Long after the demise of the British Empire, the story is finally becoming known, but back in 1993 when I gave my talk, it was only beginning to appear. I found it sobering to discover that all the evidence required to condemn us for our misrule in India was to be found in our own parliamentary records.

After the lecture, I met Shah Faiez, a post graduate from Malaysia, who would become a great companion on my journey. He was the first of several students who became my friends, and who, over the years, have contributed to my understanding of the various parts of Dar al-Islam whence they hailed.

13

THE TRADITIONS OF MANKIND PART I

A NEW PROJECT

BY THE TIME WE had arrived in Cambridge, I had already formulated a plan for my next project, which would combine a world festival and a great exhibition! With the growing terrorist attacks and the fury surrounding the publication of the *Satanic Verses* by Salman Rushdie, any attempt to present Islam was becoming increasingly problematic. I decided to propose a celebration of the traditions of mankind. This would provide a framework in which Islam and its civilization could be fully explored, without drawing attention to it in the title. To explain the proposition, I cannot do better than place before you the paper I produced and circulated at the beginning of 1993.

> Plans for celebrating the new millennium are now being discussed. The Government has established the Millennium Commission which will be responsible for allocating the considerable funds earmarked for the occasion. Ideas so far have called for: a renewal of our national

life, the refurbishment of existing monuments, the building of new landmarks, such as opera houses, and the holding of international expos celebrating advances in science, technology and industry. We believe, however, there is an over-riding case for this most significant of transitions to be marked by another kind of international event which Great Britain is ideally placed to organize.

The millennium provides us with a unique and timely opportunity to reflect upon the thousand years that have passed and to focus upon all that is of lasting value. A thousand years ago many cultures and civilizations inhabited a world abounding in flora and fauna. Today we are facing a future in which a global mono-culture threatens to cover the earth, replacing the many ways of life and the eco-systems that support them.

There is, therefore, no more appropriate way of marking the millennium than by mounting a great festival that celebrates the diversity of the heritage of mankind, and seeks a new understanding of the world's cultures and civilizations. This new understanding is not a luxury but a necessity. In a world where everyone has been brought closer together, it is of paramount importance that we learn to respect beliefs and accommodate ways of life that are different from our own. We are encountering new problems in many areas of life, and a great debate is taking place concerning the future. However, for this re-evaluation to have meaning it must include the reservoir of wisdom and experience contained within the myriad traditions that have existed for millennia. The importance of conserving the diversity of the much-depleted natural world is now universally accepted; this new awareness needs to be extended to include mankind's diverse cultures.

Whilst such a festival will involve Europe, there are pressing reasons why Great Britain should take the initiative: Great Britain had the largest, richest and the most far-reaching of the European empires; the Industrial Revolution, which has wrought the greatest global change since the Agricultural Revolution ten thousand years ago, was born here; since the war, we have become a multi-cultural society; the first international exhibition ever held took place in London in 1851, and since then, our record for successfully holding international cultural events is second to none.

Although the festival could be placed almost anywhere in the United Kingdom, the transformation of one of the abandoned industrial or mining locations in the heart of the world's first industrial region would be a powerful symbol of renewal and provide an ideal site for the festival. Often close to urban centres, such sites have excellent rail and road access and, served by either Manchester, Leeds or the East Midland airports, have all the national and international connections necessary for mounting such an event. The creation of employment and the boost to tourism and international investment which such projects inevitably bring, will make a major contribution to the regeneration of such an area.

It is proposed that a Festival City should be built on the chosen site. This Festival City will be a walled enclosure, covering some 30 acres, with four gates. Within the walls, cloistered courtyard gardens and covered courts will be linked by arcades, providing pleasant access to the exhibitions, auditoria, craft areas, shops, restaurants and other facilities. Garden festivals have demonstrated how areas blighted by industry and mining can be restored to their former beauty, and typical English countryside, with meadows, woodland, orchards and gardens, will be created around the City, providing an ideal setting for the presentation of folklore and the rural crafts, as well as a living demonstration of sustainable systems of organic farming.

A major theme of the Festival will be the relationship between mankind and the natural world, showing how traditional societies, governed by their belief systems, whether dwelling in cities or villages, in desert, forest or the arctic waste, have developed ways of life that co-exist in harmony with nature.

Great attention will be given to showing the principles that have ordered traditional societies and their development through the millennium. However, an essential part of the Festival will be the presentation of the living arts and sciences, including many forms of music, dance, and drama; poetry, literature and recitation; calligraphy, painting and architecture; the crafts of weaving, pottery, metalwork, glasswork, woodwork and carving; technologies; the medical sciences; and the growing, preparation and cooking of food.

The immense scholarship that is to be found in our museums, universities and learned societies, and within similar institutions throughout the world, will be harnessed to provide the necessary knowledge for the production of the exhibitions, films and publications associated with the event. The Festival will represent that moment when the fruits of specialist research become accessible to the general public and a new understanding is born.

The exhibitions and auditoria will include the most advanced technologies in displays, models, audio-visual presentations, computer graphics and sound production systems. The finest documentary film-makers, exhibition designers, graphic artists, model makers, and craftsmen and women will be commissioned to create multi-media productions, presenting and exploring the many themes of the Festival.

Governments and institutions will be invited to provide individual items or contribute larger elements to the Festival, from single displays to whole exhibitions, from individual performers and craftsmen, to theatrical and folklore troupes. Sponsorship will be sought from governments, foundations and commercial companies across the globe.

The Festival City, with its surrounding park will be built to last. Once the Festival is over, and the exhibits have returned to their countries of origin, their places will be filled from the immense collections of the world's heritage held in the storerooms of our national museums and galleries that have seldom, if ever, been seen by the public. This permanent centre, with all its facilities, will become a major all-year international attraction, and will continue to provide employment and act as a focus for tourism and education.

The Festival should be the culmination of the cultural exhibitions and festivals held during the last 150 years, giving birth to a new national institution, a permanent monument to mark the millennium, which will carry on the work of presenting our global heritage, and continue to contribute towards the survival and perpetuation of the precious and irreplaceable traditions of mankind.

Shortly after circulating the paper, I received a telephone call from Canon Wyatt. He invited me to come up to Salford to look at a site that he thought would be perfect for my project.

THE IRWELL VALLEY

The next day Canon Wyatt was shepherding me through a row of drab houses in Pendlebury, leading me to an unforgettable experience. We arrived at the top of a valley, and looking directly down into it, I beheld a scene of such natural beauty that it could have graced a landscape by Constable. A small river wound its way through the valley, with on its banks, a profusion of wildflowers, shrubs and trees. But when the eyes turned to the right, a massive power station with its cooling towers loomed up, and to the left in the distance, was a scene of dereliction where chemical and other factories lay abandoned. Canon Wyatt informed me that the power station was going to be demolished. Here was the perfect site for our project. This is where the Industrial Revolution began, and the Irwell was the first river to be polluted by modern industry. We could now restore the valley and place the great celebration of the Traditions of Mankind in a wonderful setting that was redolent with meaning.

I spent the summer of 1993 exploring the Irwell valley and meeting various groups engaged in different aspects of its restoration. Most memorable were the enthusiasts working to revive the extensive canal system that had linked up the region. I followed the Irwell River back to its source in the South Pennines. A farmer pointed to a boulder in his field which covered the spring. I stood there, contemplating the trickle of water which, by the time it reached the valley, had grown into the river that had powered the first phase of the terrible change in the way humanity makes things. I read *Dark River* by Cyril Bracegirdle, which tells the story of how this beautiful valley with its picturesque river became the most polluted stretch of water on earth. Salford was the world's centre of industry in the 19th century, and cotton mills, coal mines, dye works, paint manufacturers, chemical works and many other factories were discharging their effluent into the river. Now the river was being cleaned and fish were returning. The mills and factories had been in Salford, and the warehouses and shops in Manchester. The Victorian centre of Manchester with its fine civic buildings was also being refurbished. By the end of the summer, I had developed my proposal to fit neatly into the recovery that was already taking place.

I needed a platform on which I could present my proposal to the right people. I put my case to David Bellamy, and he suggested we organize a field trip. He had set up the Conservation Foundation with David Shreeve, and they agreed to invite a group of around 40 influential people whose support would enable the project to be launched. I worked closely with Canon Wyatt regarding the local councillors and planning officials to be put on the list, whose involvement would be essential if we were to gain any traction for the project. The list was completed, and on a beautiful autumn day the group, brought together by the charisma of David Bellamy, were standing in the place that Canon Wyatt had first taken me to, looking down into the Irwell Valley. Our companions for the day were made up of environmentalists, politicians, museum curators, journalists, local councillors and planning officers. In the morning we walked beside the Irwell River, and then took a short trip on the Manchester, Bolton and Bury Canal, which was being restored. David Bellamy was fully abreast of the history and present plans for the area, and provided an entertaining commentary. We arrived at the hotel for lunch, and before launching into the buffet, I gave my slide presentation of the Traditions of Mankind proposal. After lunch we walked to Canon Wyatt's church past the tower blocks. Canon Wyatt then gave an illuminating talk on how the church had been restored, and how the new clergy house and church hall had been built in the Gothic tradition, after which we had tea in the walled garden, with the tower blocks looming over us.

The party then broke up. Everyone appeared to have enjoyed themselves and the preservation and restoration initiatives for the Irwell Valley were met with enthusiasm. However, my presentation had gone down like a lead balloon. I cannot remember ever having had such a vacant response to any idea I have ever tried to float. They simply could not see that there was any connection between the restoration of the Irwell Valley and what I was proposing. My attempt at launching my Millennium project in the Irwell Valley had come to an end.

There is a sad addendum to this episode. Several years later Canon Wyatt took me to the spot where we had at first surveyed the little river meandering through the valley. But we could not see the river. The view was blocked by a refuse mountain that had been grassed over. Funnels were poking out of the grass, releasing methane gas. It was like a scene out of Dante's Inferno. I looked to the right. The power station had gone, and in its place was a prison.

Although our day in the Irwell Valley did not deliver my expectations, it did bring about very fruitful meetings for the future, between Canon Wyatt, Anthony Milroy and David Bellamy.

ANTHONY MILROY

I was introduced to Anthony Milroy by Anderson Bakewell whom we will meet later in this chapter. Tony became my gateway into an understanding of traditional husbandry and farming in Dar al-Islam. Our research into Polebrook Farm and the experience of the landscape had given me some idea of what a traditional agricultural environment was like. But Tony Milroy had lived for years in a traditional farming world that was fully alive and functioning. I was enthralled by the story of his sojourn with the farmers of Yemen and his response to the task he had been set.

Tony was one of the first graduates to emerge from the pioneering agricultural engineering course at Newcastle University. He was then selected as one of the first HMG Overseas Development Administration (ODA) 'advisors' to be sent to the newly-established government of the Yemen Arab Republic, which was only just emerging from a decade of civil war after the British retreated from its imperial, 'Protectorate' role in Aden. In the south of Yemen, a brutal communist regime had filled the vacuum left by the British withdrawal. Keen to establish a political and commercial presence in Yemen's north, ODA's brief to Tony Milroy was to create an agricultural engineering programme to help 'modernize' Yemen's agriculture, hopefully leading to exports of British agricultural machinery, scholarships etc. and 'renewed friendship' with this now independent Arab state.

After several months living with the farmers of North Yemen, the land of the mountain terraces, he realized that he had nothing to teach them. They were masters of their environment. He became their student and began studying their traditions. The mountain terraces were an incredibly challenging environment. The walls containing them had to be continually maintained to protect the precious fertile soil, that had been nurtured by generations of farmers. They were at the head of a system that led down into the naturally rich and fertile wadis. When the monsoon arrived, the rain would cascade upon the mountain tops, watering the trees, and then was channeled through the terraces, and by the time it arrived in the valley below, it had become a controlled flow, ready to enter the fields of the lowland farmers. Ridges separated the fields, and when the water had been held for a sufficient period, the ridges were breached and the water flowed into the next field. For the children it was a time of high excitement as they played in these seasonal lakes and were carried by the flows. By the time the water had reached the end of the wadi, the community had secured its crop. The whole operation needed the engagement and collaboration of the entire community for a successful outcome, and no one was more important than the local 'water master', who ensured that everyone had their fair share. Tony Milroy was in awe at the sophistication and wealth of this traditional system of husbandry, which was transmitted through poetry, song and 'learning by doing', as son followed father, and daughter followed mother in the field. Here was a living tradition, increasing its knowledge as the practical experience of one generation was passed to the next, continuing as it had done for over six millennia, in an ever drier, warmer climate.

After four years, Tony Milroy was ready to submit his report. He stated that Northern Yemen was an arid land, which had been successfully farmed for thousands of years. Every inch of land that could be, had been brought into cultivation. The farmers harvested every drop of water from the monsoon for their crops. They had developed every kind of crop that grew naturally in their environment and were continually improving their seed stock. Their system of husbandry was completely integrated into their religion and way of life and was a perfect example of how to live sustainably in this fragile, arid zone. The only way we can help their farmers, he stated, was to keep out and leave them alone. The response to his report was not favourable, to put it mildly. The idea that there was any future other than the development of modern, industrial farming was untenable, and it was considered that Milroy had wasted four years of the development agency's money, studying a system that belonged in the past.

During the next decade, Milroy secured a Winston Churchill Travelling Fellowship to study semi-arid zone farming in the United States, Africa and Australia. On returning to North Yemen, he found that everything he previously predicted would happen if the West intervened, had indeed taken place. Europe, the US and Australia, through the mechanism of the World Food Programme, had flooded Yemen's local markets with their subsidized 'hard grain' wheat variety, which required the introduction of two kinds of mechanized grinding mills, 'generously donated' by the USA, to produce bread flour. This fatally undercut the staple sorghum crop, triggering the abandonment and collapse of terraces throughout Yemen's upper catchments, along with a wholesale shift to household dependency on purchased, nutrition-less white bread, considered a modern luxury. Many farmers, unable to make a living, migrated from the terraces to the oil fields of the Gulf, and as far away as the orange groves of Florida and the almond plantations of California. Without maintenance, the terrace walls crumbled and the monsoon carried the debris down the mountainside into the wadis below. Without the terraces to channel and control the flow, the water, racing down the mountain, had become a mighty torrent by the time it reached the bottom, and went on to rush through the wadis without being captured in the fields.

Western consultants had urged the drilling of deep wells to exploit ancient aquifers. Now Yemen faced an imminent water crisis; it was simply running dry. Khat, a mild stimulant which traditionally was used sparingly, had now turned into an epidemic. Grown on an industrial scale, it would become responsible for 70% of water consumed, and the chemicals used in its intensive production were causing cancers and other health problems. In the space of a few years, a once contented and self-sufficient people had been plunged into a quagmire of dependency.

In response to the crisis that was taking place in the Yemen, Tony Milroy set up the Arid Lands Initiative. There were two overriding insights that led Tony to setting up the initiative. Firstly, his survey of the arid lands of the world brought home to him the realization that the highly evolved and sophisticated Yemeni system of arid land management had a great deal to teach the other regions of arid lands he had visited. He was in the Yemen when famine was decimating Ethiopia; Yemen was suffering the same drought. However, the Yemen's more developed traditional system was able to cope with the crisis. He wanted to disseminate this knowledge as widely as possible. Secondly, he saw that the traditional systems were in crisis everywhere, and that the knowledge, which was preserved in the oral tradition, was in imminent danger of being lost.

He wanted to put across the case in as persuasive a manner as possible. This he achieved in his award-winning, hour-long, documentary film, 'The Hanging Gardens of Arabia'. In the film, he demonstrated how the hard mountain terraces and the fertile land below were inextricably linked. The crops grown by the lowland farmers depended upon the water management of the husbandmen above. The film beautifully illustrates the subtlety, depth and humanity of the way of life and belief system of the farmers through their own words. Having established the integrity and dynamism of the traditional Yemeni way of farming, Tony shows us how it is being destroyed by its encounter with the West. For me the most poignant scene is where the separation between generations with the introduction of western education is vividly exposed. There are three generations of a family sitting under the shade of a tree: grandfather, son and grandson. Grandfather and son are in the tradition, but the schoolboy grandson is being educated out of the tradition. When he is asked what he would like to be when he grows up, his eyes light up and he says he would like to be a government employee in Sanaa. The educating out of the traditional way of life, with the promise of a brighter future, is the greatest disrupter of a society, leading to migration from the countryside into the overcrowded cities and beyond. The film was released in 1990, and first shown in the UK on Channel 4's Fragile Earth Series and on the Discovery Channel in the US. It was then sold to more than 40 countries. It is a masterpiece and, as we will see later in this chapter, led to a remarkable encounter in our story.

But Tony did not want just to talk about the crisis. He wanted to affect a revival. He set about documenting the traditional practices of the farmers, and produced audio-visual material that could be used for demonstration and training purposes. He engaged all levels of Yemeni society from government to grassroots in his programme. Tony is a practical man and he worked with the social structures that had now come into existence. He encouraged the modern associations of farmers and reformed local communities to come to a new recognition that they must use their democratic, modernized structures to remobilize the renowned and ancient traditions of sustainable farming techniques, which had successfully underpinned the whole rural fabric of their society and landscape for millennia.

However, it was his close working relationship with Abdul Rahman Al-Iryani over a period of more than 25 years that allowed his work to flourish. Abdul Rahman is from a powerful Yemeni family; his grandfather had been Yemen's respected first President of the Republic, and his uncle was Chair of the Central Planning Office and later, Prime Minister and Foreign Minister.

Abdur Rahman was deeply concerned with the dangers facing Yemeni culture, and determined to address the profound challenges that Tony's film had illuminated. He resigned his government post and established a Yemeni non-governmental organization, 'Yemen Al-Khadara' (Green Yemen). By 2014 he had agreed to become Yemen's first Minister of Water and Environment, a post he insisted was fundamental if the crisis they were facing was to be averted. But then the Arab Spring arrived in Yemen, followed by civil war. Tony's work in Yemen came to a halt. However, his work elsewhere continued, and continues to this day. There are many stories I could relate regarding Anthony Milroy's incredible initiatives, but I will confine myself to the one that takes us back to Salford and Canon Wyatt's parish.

APPLE TREE COURT

The collaboration between Tony Milroy's Arid Lands Initiative and the tenants of Apple Tree Court resulted in one of the most surprising and inspiring projects that have taken place in the 'arid lands' of the inner-city tower blocks. Canon Wyatt's church was surrounded by a dozen sixteen-story flats, set in a bleak environment of grass and concrete. Peter Hook, bassist from the band New Order, grew up in the area and famously described it, in his book *Unknown Pleasures: Inside Joy Division*, as 'rotten and horrible, like a concrete wasteland'.

The remarkable story of Apple Tree Court begins in the late 1980s when a new caretaker was appointed. Mrs Betty Burton was not prepared to put up with the vandalism that plagued the tower blocks. She galvanized the tenants of Apple Tree Court into taking control of their environment. The enthusiasm that this engendered led to the formation in 1988 of a tenants' association. Betty informed Canon Wyatt that the tenants wanted a garden instead of the car park surrounding their tenement, but the

Salford Council had consistently denied them their wish. Canon Wyatt had watched 'The Hanging Gardens of Arabia' on television, and been amazed by the gardens around the high-rise buildings of Shibam. He contacted me, and I gave him Tony's number. So began the amazing creation of a beautiful, sustainable 'urban oasis' in Salford.

Tony transferred all the management and specialist skills he had been applying in the Yemen to Salford. His first task was to ensure that the oasis belonged to the community. This he achieved by engaging them at the outset in the planning of the garden. He wanted to know what they would like to see around them. He then orchestrated their ideas so that they could be realized. They wanted fresh food, a flower garden and a pond. To achieve maximum productivity, he introduced the multi-layered oasis system. In time, this urban oasis included an orchard, allotments for growing vegetables, a wildflower meadow, a Japanese garden, a water garden, a duck pond, a geodesic-domed greenhouse and a conservatory. The Urban Oasis was so successful in the production of food that a café was opened which supplied organic meals.

By the mid-1990s the Urban Oasis was receiving national and international recognition. It was awarded the top national BT/WWF Environmental Conservation Award, and received a grant of £198,000 from the National Lottery Charities Board. It was cited as one of the top 100 'Global Best Practices' by the United Nations HABITAT Programme. It was designated by the Deputy Prime Minister's Office as one of three national 'beacons of best practice' in community development and use of derelict open space.

The late Tessa Jowell came to Apple Tree Court when she was a health minister and was deeply impressed, stating that the project should be replicated elsewhere. A delegation of tenants was invited to Parliament, and the MP for Salford drew attention to the Urban Oasis in the chamber:

> At the foot of the tower block there is a wonderful community garden. The tenants grow flowers and vegetables. I am told that they even grow aubergines – in Salford! Local children learn about nature in the wildflower garden. Pensioners come to the cafe for good quality, affordable meals. There is a conservatory to catch the sun. There is even a duck pond with ducks.

David Bellamy responded to a call to arms issued by Tony, and became involved in the project. He relates:

> My small part in this story came about when one of their main open spaces came under the threat of development as a carpark, and I was asked to join them in their cause of common sense. All I really did was walk around the area with my mind wide open and say, 'Wow, if anyone is foolish enough to start to destroy this oasis of spirituality, I will come and chain myself to a tree'. Common sense did prevail and I have been asked back on a number of occasions to celebrate the opening of yet more gardens – vegetable, water, cottage, Japanese – and even a sun-room conservatory. Each one was the dream of one of these high-rise parishioners, brought into being by a hard-working band of down-to-earth angels. No wonder there is a waiting list of people hoping to move in when an apartment falls empty. My most recent visit was to take a group of bishops to see the miracle for themselves.

The Urban Oasis became the subject of academic papers. The following extract comes from The Greening of Everyday Life:

> Crime rates plummeted as neighbourly relations improved, and both gardening and the new-found availability of locally-grown vegetables have improved community health, whilst skills have been learned and a stake in the community created for youth who might otherwise struggle. (David Rudland and Nicholas Falk, 2009)

Early on in the development of the Oasis, the Tenant's Association had taken advantage of the law and established a Tenancy Management Cooperative (TMC), taking over from the Council the responsibility for the running of Apple Tree Court. When David Bellamy formally opened the Café, he stated that the Urban Oasis was an exemplar project and must be replicated throughout the tower blocks of Salford and beyond. A councillor was heard to mutter under his breath, 'This will be the only one if we have anything to do with it.' His prophesy turned out to be true. A project that had received national and international acclaim and could, if emulated throughout the country, have produced a transformation in the lives of the most disadvantaged members of our society, was snuffed out. If you visit Canon Wyatt's church today you will see all the original tower blocks surrounding the sanctuary still standing, in all their bleakness.

Three identical blocks were chosen in 2014 for demolition, Pear Tree, Peach and Apple Tree. All the blocks had been named by the developers after fruits which, given the total absence of flora, is nothing but a sick joke. However, the tenants of Apple Tree Court had given meaning to the name and turned it into a reality, and for a short time they were a beacon of light for the future.

I visited Apple Tree Court with Tony, shortly before it was demolished. The last tenant, an American academic, was getting ready to leave. I asked her what it had been like living there. She said it had been wonderful. She told me how her daughter had grown up with the gardens and become so involved with nature, that she was now studying botany at university.

14

THE TRADITIONS OF MANKIND PART II

A NEW PROJECT

MY SECOND ATTEMPT at launching the Traditions of Mankind Millennium Project fared a little better. I had a partner with whom I was able to share the endeavour.

ANDERSON BAKEWELL

Anderson Bakewell was born in St Louis, the capital of African-American Blues. He fell in love with the Blues at an early age, and after leaving university departed from America and embarked on a life of adventure. He spent several years in India where he learnt Sanskrit, and by the mid-1970s, was living in Sanaa, Yemen, where he learnt Arabic. It was there that Anderson and Francine Stone, a fellow American, got married. Francine went on to have a lifelong interest in the Yemen. They made a formidable couple. While Anderson was recording and documenting the traditional music of the Yemen, Francine was researching and writing about the history and culture of the area. Anderson was spurred on by the realization that across Africa and Asia the music traditions were being threatened by the marginalization of traditional musicians, under the rising tide of imported pop music. For some 25 years he worked with a number of organizations, including the Ford Foundation, the BBC, The Greek and Near Eastern Music Society and the Maqam Society, to preserve, document and promote the traditional music of these disappearing worlds.

In 1978, Anderson and Francine came to settle in the UK. They took up residence just outside Oxford in a farmhouse with a smallholding, which they farmed organically. In 1995 Anderson bought the uninhabited Island of Scarp, which is in the Outer Hebrides of Scotland, west of Hushinish on Harris. With his life balanced between his travels, his work, his family, mountain climbing and withdrawing to his island, where sheep grazed and there was no electricity, he represented a unique figure amongst my friends with his calm and healing presence.

It was shortly after his arrival in England that I met Anderson at one of Mahmud's concerts. Although we only worked closely together on the Millennium Project, we have, over the years, kept up a dialogue regarding what each of us was doing at the time. He was one of those companions on my journey who stirred my imagination and from whom I gained valuable insights. He was the only person I could telephone before breakfast to have an in-depth conversation. This suited me because that is the best part of my day! In the 1990s Anderson branched out from his musical activities and produced two remarkable projects which have affected my understanding and contributed to my knowledge of Tradition.

OTTOMAN GARDEN

The first was the creation of an Ottoman garden. Anderson's father died in 1993 and left a bequest to the Missouri Botanical Garden in St Louis. Anderson and his brother had to decide what to do with the bequest, and because of a family legend which linked an ancestor to the Ottoman sultans, they settled on the creation of an Ottoman garden. This was well received, as the Botanic Garden already featured a number of international gardens, including a Chinese 'scholars' garden, a Japanese garden and an English 'woodland' garden.

However, he and his brother were immediately faced with a major problem. At the Anglo-Turkish Society/Royal Anthropological Institute Lecture that he gave on the creation of the garden on 22 November 2018, Anderson related that if they had known the extent of the challenge that they faced and the time it would take to realize the project, it was unlikely that they would have gone ahead. The problem was that for several centuries the Ottoman gardens were being influenced by European garden designs, and by the 19th century had, more or less, lost their distinct character and traditional role in Ottoman life. By the 20th, they were for all intents and purposes extinct. There were no examples of the Ottoman garden for them to follow.

Fortunately, they did go ahead and were happy that they had done so, as Anderson described in his lecture:

> ... the rewards were great in the end, and amongst them was the opportunity to gather together and work with a large number of very interesting and knowledgeable people, authorities in the fields of horticulture, botany, architecture and landscape architecture, crafts, history and calligraphy.

Although the gardens no longer existed, he goes on to describe the sources that were available:

> Fortunately for us, however, what was preserved were historical sources, in the form of archived documents; they included agricultural treatises, royal garden registers and account books containing plant lists, as well as orders by the sultans for plants for palace gardens; horticultural treatises such as the *Revnak'i Bostan*, with sections on soils, tree planting, pruning and grafting, diseases and their treatment; kitchen and flower gardens, and fruit orchards, were particularly revealing, as was surviving visual material in the form of paintings, particularly Ottoman miniatures, depictions of garden layouts and individual plant species on carpets, tiles, textiles and pottery. Descriptions and drawings by European travellers were interesting in that they highlighted the contrasts with contemporary Western gardens, and provided plans and sections of no longer existing gardens and parks. There are also fragments - in the form of forgotten corners, flower-bed shapes, fountain elements, pools and canals - from old garden sites around Anatolia.

Anderson then goes on to describe their research findings and the discovery of a unique tradition:

> It didn't take long in such company to learn that indeed there had been a rich, even great, Ottoman garden tradition... Devoted to gardens to a degree perhaps unknown elsewhere before or since, the Turks brought a different sensibility altogether to them, which – long before such ideas formed any part of our European historical currency – set them apart.

He explains the difference between the formal geometric Persian and Moghul gardens, and the Ottoman preference for a more organic, naturalistic arrangement:

> This naturalistic bias keeps reasserting itself in the sources, and it found expression in a new form of garden that, with relatively informal landscapes of understated symmetry, irregular outer boundaries and loose inner arrangements, didn't conform rigidly to the straight axes dictated by the irrigation channels of the established Islamic forms. The unpredictable variety of nature was preferred to the uniformity of geometrical order, unsurprising perhaps because unlike say, the Persian *Chahar Baghs*, they were not the creation of architects, but of gardeners.

Anderson and his brother took 12 years to complete the Ottoman Garden, which was opened in 2008. Its creation has hugely increased our knowledge of this wonderful tradition. I shall tell you about Anderson's other project in Chapter 24.

MOIRA PARK MILLENNIUM BID

With Anderson beside me, my belief in the validity of the Traditions of Mankind concept was consolidated. The idea was valid and timely, it just needed the right location. We sent out a prospectus of the project to Lancashire, Yorkshire, Nottinghamshire, Derbyshire, Leicestershire, Staffordshire and Cheshire Councils. By early 1994 the search had been narrowed down to the old mining areas, and British Coal were sending us details of sites for consideration. However, it was Leicester County Council that produced the ideal site, answering all the requirements that were sought: the Crossroads Site at Moira.

The village of Moira was perfectly located for our project. It was right in the middle of England, with easy access to the country's major urban centres, and close proximity to international airports and the rail network. Surrounding the village of Moira had been five collieries which were now mostly worked out and were in the process of being sold off by the Coal Board. The Crossroads site was an open cast mine and the new owners, RJB Mining, were intending to extract the coal that remained.

For centuries, North West Leicestershire had been quarried and mined for coal, limestone, granite and brick clay. The widespread environmental damage that the region had suffered was one of the reasons why it was chosen in the 1990s as the site for the National Forest, which is part of a Government-funded programme to create more woodland. Our project would complement and accelerate this process of environmental recovery.

However, it was essential that we had the local community on our side. We began by meeting the president of the local miners' union. His reaction was very positive and he invited us to make a presentation to the next meeting of the members of the union. It was clear that they did not like open cast mining, and could see that our project would provide a better future for the community. Our next step was to see if we would be able to secure the site. The site consisted of five hundred acres, of which a hundred acres had already been mined; the rest were down to farmland waiting to be exploited. We met with Richard Budge, the owner of RJB Mining, who had been named 'King Coal' by the press, as he had hoovered up most of the remaining working sites from the Coal Board. It became clear that he would be prepared to sell if the price was right.

By 1994 the Millennium Commission had announced that it would be allocating half the money from the Lottery to a few major visionary projects of national significance; the other half would be shared out among a number of small projects. We had no doubt that our 'Traditions of Mankind Millennium Park' and 'Millennium Festival' met their criteria. The Commission were asking for projects that 'specifically celebrate the millennium' and do not wish to see 'business as usual' ideas, 'dressed up with a thin veneer of celebration'. The projects they planned to support would be 'likely to be unique in some way: they might break new ground in design or function; be of a scale to set them apart from others; make a contribution to public life or the harnessing of community endeavour'.

If they were to 'stand the test of time' they must be for 'the man and woman in the street'. They stated that they would like to see environmental applications which 'contribute to the natural world after centuries of taking away from it'. They recognized that 'festivals can have a catalytic effect on commerce and culture and have enormous potential for economic regeneration'.

By the summer of 1994 we were preparing our bid and had assembled a formidable team of consultants who were attracted by the excitement that was growing around our endeavour. We had curators and librarians from the British Museum, British Library, Victoria and Albert Museum and my favorite Weald and Downland Open Air Museum; we had scholars from Cambridge University and other universities and institutions. The high-powered development team included the Building and Property Group (project managers), Buro Happold (internationally renowned engineers), the Conservation Practice (architects), Roger Griffiths Associates (landscape architects), ILM (management and operations consultants), and Jasper Jacob Associates (exhibition design consultants). The London estate agents Chestertons had agreed to act for us in the purchase of the land if the bid was successful, and solicitors, specializing in charities, had set up the foundation that would own the project.

The bid was supported by Leicestershire County Council, North West Leicestershire District Council, South Derbyshire District Council, Leicestershire Training and Enterprise Council and the Rural Development Commission. Leicester County Council contributed £10,000 to the bid, which included a detailed description of the project with an artist's impression of the site before and after development, a geotechnical desk study by Buro Happold, a site appraisal by Roger Griffiths Associates, a usage estimate by ILM, and a budget forecast for both the building and running of the Park prepared by the Building and Property Group.

Our bid was completed in April 1995 and submitted to the Commission in May of that year. It passed the first hurdle of projects to be considered, and fell at the second. No reason was given for its rejection. We were of course all very disappointed; the bid had been a tremendous collaborative effort. However, by this time I was so steeled in failure that I accepted this new set back with equanimity. I would make one more attempt to realize the Traditions of Mankind concept.

15

THE TRADITIONS OF MANKIND PART III

DEPTFORD CREEK & GREENWICH REACH

OUR FINAL ATTEMPT at creating a project for the celebration of the new millennium took us into the heart of Maritime London. Deptford Creek is located a few hundred yards from historic Greenwich, with the Royal Observatory, the Royal Hospital, the Maritime Museum and the Cutty Sark, attracting visitors from all around the world. Between Greenwich and the Creek is Greenwich Reach. It was here that Henry VIII established the first Royal Dockyards, Sir Francis Drake was knighted after his circumnavigation of the earth in the Golden Hinde, the East India Company set up its first dock, and Peter the Great, Tsar of Russia, studied ship-building. In the 19th century, Deptford Creek and Greenwich Reach became a hive of the new industries spawned by the Industrial Revolution, with the first commercial power station, designed by Basil de Ferranti, located there. Now it was a wasteland of derelict factories awaiting redevelopment.

But the area was once again buzzing with activity. The Millennium Commission had decided to hold its big event in the Dome to be erected by Richard Rogers on the Greenwich Peninsular, and a new Light Railway was planned to link Greenwich to the centre of London. The Reach and the Creek were now prime development sites. In their prospectus for the development of the area, the local council had included in their bid, the creation of a Flagship Project that would be 'an introductory landmark to the Thames Gateway, positively contributing to London's status as a world city.' Surely this is where our project belonged. The docks, from where we set out to discover the world, would now become the place where we could contemplate what we encountered.

We set about converting our project from a rural setting to an urban environment. We renamed the project 'Greenwich Reach'. What follows has been extracted from the prospectus we prepared as an introduction to the proposal:

> PROJECT CONCEPT
>
> Greenwich Reach represents a new, exciting and timely concept which proposes the creation of a centre for the world's traditions within the setting of an urban tourist village. This venture will combine patronage and sponsorship with commercial investment to establish a financially viable institution, which brings together culture, tourism and regeneration to address, in an imaginative way, some of the central issues of our time.
>
> WORLD HERITAGE CENTRE
>
> There is a growing awareness that, in today's world, an understanding of other cultures and civilizations is of paramount importance… At Greenwich Reach everyone will be able to enjoy a spectacular presentation of the richness and diversity of the world's traditions and, through an expanded exhibition format, learn about the history and context of the traditional arts, sciences and crafts, whilst encountering their living practitioners. Above all, at a time when the world's traditions are increasingly threatened, the World Heritage Centre will encourage and support their conservation and renewal, and demonstrate the vital role they have to play in contemporary life and in the future well-being of mankind.

URBAN TOURIST VILLAGE

> Greenwich Reach will transpose the highly successful and proven holiday village into an urban setting, creating an environment that is permeated by the themes of world heritage and capable of providing for the daily needs of the visitor in ways that are ecologically sound. Hotels, apartments and hostels will provide accommodation for up to five thousand guests; leisure, health, conference and child-care facilities will cater for the needs of the many different kinds of temporary inhabitants of the village. The provision and marketing of organically-produced, humanely-reared food will be an essential aspect of the Project; a network will be set up of farms across the country to supply the shops, restaurants and markets.

The Greenwich Reach peninsular and the upper part of Deptford Creek provided a compact site of some fifty acres, with a wide Thames frontage, and the River Ravensbourne snaking through the site. It needed little imagination to see what a magnificent area it could become. 80% of the site had been acquired by a consortium. We approached the CEO of the consortium who welcomed our proposal and considered there should not be a problem in securing the remaining 20% of the site. The London architects Fitch joined our team and a presentation, including a first budget estimate, was put together. The plan was to approach the Millennium Commission for a third of the £200m required for the development; a third would be raised through grants and sponsorship and the remaining third would be invested by the consortium.

By the summer of 1996, it was becoming clear that the commercial possibilities of the site were overtaking our vision for the area. By the time we had prepared our approach to the Millennium Commission, the consortium had settled upon its plan to maximize profits. Our year and a half imagining the transformation of a very special and historically significant area of London had come to nothing. In the place of our beautiful vision is one of the densest high-rise developments of flats and offices to be found anywhere in the capital.

REFLECTION

Although our three attempts at launching a project to mark the new millennium failed to materialize, I gained much that contributed to my book, *Rethinking Islam and the West.* I am a Southerner, and before my visit to the Irwell Valley, I had little knowledge or experience of the North of England. The months I spent studying and trekking around the cradle of the Industrial Revolution opened my eyes to the extent of the environmental and human devastation it had wreaked. Canon Wyatt's beautiful church is at the epicentre of the catastrophe, and my visits to this sanctuary became for me a litmus test by which one could judge the state of our nation. Since my first visit thirty years ago, food banks, broken families, mental illness amongst children, drug addiction and poverty have continued to rise; and now the Coronavirus has fully exposed the scale of the crisis. Canon David and Helen Wyatt, Tony Milroy and others I was privileged to meet, live and work in the heart of this cataclysm; their courage, selflessness, and refusal to give up represents the finest in human character. I came away from the North humbled by their humanity. But what an education I had received from them!

In the Midlands, with the Moira Millennium Bid, I encountered a mining community who were attempting to recover from the wreckage visited upon them by Margaret Thatcher. It was shaming to see this closely-knit community, with the inner strength of a people who for generations have undertaken the hardest and most dangerous task imaginable, in such a depressed state. There is a chapter in George Orwell's *Wigan Pier* that hauntingly depicts the miner's life both above and below ground. It is beyond my understanding how people could have endured such hardship. I left Moira with a heavy heart, feeling that I had built up their expectations only for them to be dashed. But they had become used to being let down.

During the four years of my millennium endeavour, I suffered the loss that comes to us all. My father died in 1993 and my mother three years later in 1996. They had provided me with an incredibly stable background. I never suffered want in childhood, and this, I believe, enabled me to take risks and live almost continuously in a state of uncertainty as regards the income from my work. I was also blessed with the stability of my own marriage and family life. Although my grandfather and father had built a thriving business and my eldest brother inherited the mantle, the family wealth was circumscribed. My father and brother were always generous in their support of our family; however, they could never bail me out from my projects when they failed.

By 1996 I had gone more than a dozen years without an income from my work. I had eaten into the money owed to the taxman on my inheritance from the sale of the family business ten years before. The Revenue had gone along with stage payments for several years but now demanded payment in full. I tried to convince them that, given time, I would be able to complete the payments, but they were not interested, and in 1997 I was bankrupted. Although we were in straitened circumstances, I was far from depressed by our situation. Something was stirring. Cambridge was proving a fertile place for Annabel and myself, and a beautiful idea was forming in my mind.

16

THE GOLDEN WEB PART I

THE BIRTH OF AN IDEA

IN THE AUTUMN of 1996, I developed the concept that would engage me for the next sixteen years. My focus had become increasingly fixed upon the traditional cultures and civilizations of Afro-Eurasia. It was clear to me that these worlds, throughout history, had been connected in many different ways. I was asking myself the question: 'But what had connected them?' The simple answer was the network of long-distance trade routes. The routes were defined on land by the passage of camel and pack-horse and, on sea, by the sailing vessel. However, I realized that this network not only made possible the trade in material goods, but was the medium for the peaceful exchange and diffusion of ideas and technologies, which facilitated the growth and flowering of countless cultures and civilizations. The more I pondered, the more I saw it as a 'golden web', that enriched its myriad participants not just materially, but culturally and spiritually. With this insight, the Golden Web became my new obsession. I believed I had found a key that could transform the way we approached the study of pre-modern Afro-Eurasia.

My companion during the first crucial months in working through the idea was my friend, Shah Faiez. He had completed his MPhil in 1994 and had returned to Cambridge in 1996 to do his PhD. Shah comes from a very 'golden web' family. He is half Indian and half Malay. His father's family were merchants who plied the sea between South India and Malaysia, and they still have links to their village in South India. Shah was part of the generation of the newly-liberated colonies, in which young scholars were trying to come to terms with what had happened to their societies. They were attempting to see beyond the mindset they had inherited from their colonial masters.

We used to meet in his rooms in Wolfson College. Our conversations ranged widely from the Golden Web, through Malay history, to encompass the growing environmental crisis. I was deeply affected when he related to me how the Malay world had been culturally divided, with Malaysia centred upon England, and Indonesia upon Holland. In his thesis he was trying to rediscover the relationships that pertained to the Malay State prior to colonization, taking as his example the kingdom of Trengganu. By using the Golden Web as a framework, the whole picture fell into place; he was able to map the multiple stories of change affecting the Trengganu Sultanate into a broader account of its transformation into becoming a modern territorial state. Shah was the first of many scholars to find the Golden Web paradigm a useful tool in the study of history. The challenge that faced me was how to realize the Golden Web as a project?

BACK TO GREENWICH REACH

My first response to the challenge was the attempt to realize the Golden Web as a heritage centre. Instead of linking it to the Millennium celebrations, I proposed to inaugurate it in 2001, the four hundredth anniversary of the first fleet belonging to the East India Company departing from Greenwich Reach for the Indies. I had retained a good relationship with the CEO of the Consortium developing Greenwich Reach, and, when we met, he was happy to explore the proposal.

I once more gathered members of my long-suffering team of participants in the three Traditions of Mankind submissions, and set to work producing a prospectus. The prospectus which was aimed at investors as well as grant giving bodies, began:

> It is proposed to establish a new kind of heritage centre...which combines a major cultural attraction with a hotel, shopping centre and craft souk, all themed to celebrate the Golden Web.

There followed a brief explanation of the main aspects of the proposal and a set of architectural plans which showed the integration of the exhibition galleries, auditoria and other cultural elements with the hotel, shopping centre and craft souk. After this came an introduction to the unfolding of the Golden Web:

> In the year 1601 a small fleet of ships, belonging to the recently founded East India Company, set sail from Greenwich Reach for the Spice Islands, and became the latest European entrants into the vast network of long-distance trade that had, for more than a thousand years, connected the Afro-Eurasian landmass.
>
> The Golden Web is an epic story. For three thousand years the Web was mostly confined to the Middle East where the foundations of trade and civilization were laid. When the pastoral nomads mounted the horse and camel, the oceans of the desert and steppe were unlocked, connecting the fertile lands of China, India, Persia and the Mediterranean. The oceans of the sea were mastered by Phoenician, Greek, Arab, Indian, Malay and Chinese seafarers.
>
> The unification of China, with thousands of miles of canals linking the two river systems, provided the Web with a huge region of craft manufacture. Indian missionaries carried Buddhism by sea to South East Asia, and by land to Central Asia, China and on to Japan, and with it went the riches of Indian civilization. The Romans unified the many and ancient cultures of the Mediterranean, creating a secure trading area which facilitated the spread of Christianity.
>
> The establishment of Islamic civilization greatly stimulated trade and city life. Baghdad became the Golden Web's largest city with a population of around half a million, at a time when Charlemagne's capital contained fewer than ten thousand inhabitants. Fifteenth

century Timbuktu, commanding the gold trade from West Africa and famed for its universities, had some hundred thousand citizens when London's population was yet to reach fifty thousand. The port of Malacca, in present day Malaysia, which controlled the straits between the Indian Ocean and the China Sea, was the most cosmopolitan of ports with representatives of many merchant communities including Syrians, Yemenis, Armenians, Jews, Gujaratis and Chinese, who traded over thousands of miles.

The greatest of the Golden Web's textile fairs was held each year in Mecca when pilgrims converged on the holy city by land and sea from every part of the Web, with the caravan from Cairo alone bringing many thousands of souls. The great emporia of the Middle East received merchandise from all quarters of the Web, and, in return, traded incense, perfumes, thoroughbred horses, gold brocade, silks, fine carpets, glassware, swords, dates, fresh and dried fruits, coffee and leather goods.

When the East India Company fleet rounded the Cape, they entered into the heart of a prosperous and flourishing trading network which had taken thousands of years to evolve, and in which commerce was carried on within the natural limits of a sustainable environment. The Europeans grew rich from their participation in the Golden Web, but, with the Industrial Revolution and the establishment of the European empires, the Golden Web was divided up and incorporated into a new and very different trading network, centred upon Europe and serving the interests of the industrialized powers.

Although the Golden Web as a trading system may have been superseded, the heritage of the Golden Web is to be found everywhere. With the commercial revival in the East and the decline of the Eurocentric view of history in the West, the time is ripe for the rediscovery of the Golden Web with a new understanding and appreciation of its place in world history.

The prospectus also included a description of the exhibition and an investment profile, containing the capital cost of the project, the running costs, and the division between grants, sponsorship and investment. The project was substantial, but a fraction of the cost and complexity of our previous proposals. It was ready to go, and eminently realizable. The prospectus was launched in February 1997, but it was clear by the autumn of that year, that the Golden Web was not going to be realized as a heritage centre. The idea was buried in millennium fever.

It was a meeting that took place in a beautiful barn conversion, in a village just outside Cambridge, that was to decide the next stage in the Golden Web story.

17

THE GOLDEN WEB PART II

JOHN COOPER

WE FIRST MET John Cooper, the supervisor for Annabel's PhD, in 1968 when, as members of the Exploding Galaxy, we were performing our happenings in Oxford. John was a member of St John's College, and was studying Psychology and Physiology. He was an imposing young man; tall with a huge shock of auburn hair. He became one of several students to take an interest in our activities and the philosophy behind our incoherent offerings. Our paths separated for more than two decades, only to converge once more when we came to Cambridge. In 1990 he had become the E.G. Browne Lecturer in Persian Studies at what was then Cambridge University's Oriental Faculty.

After graduating from Oxford in 1970, John went to Morocco, and for five years was the director of English language studies at International House, a language school in Casablanca. He then went to Iran and after initially teaching English and physiology, began learning Arabic and Persian. In 1977 he moved to the holy city of Qom, the centre of Islamic learning in Iran, where he studied with several prominent scholars. He also acted as an interpreter to Grand Ayatollah Sayyed Kazim Shariatmadari. When the Revolution took place, the Grand Ayatollah opposed the principle of the Ayatollahs taking over the State, and was placed under house arrest. John had to make a hasty exit, and returned to the UK. It was whilst John was in Iran that he embraced Islam.

On that special day, at the end of the 1997 Michaelmas term, we sat together in his lovely home, both of us now with greying hair. I had, finally, summoned up the courage to make a presentation of the Golden Web to him. I had delayed introducing him to the thesis, because I had recently clashed with him over what turned out to be my naïve understanding of the place of philosophy in Islam. It would be another twenty years before I reached an understanding of this question, and I relate how this happened in Chapter 23. But let us return to my meeting with John. I made the presentation, and he quietly listened. When I finished, he sat reflecting for a time, got up and made coffee for us both – his coffee was always excellent and took time to prepare. Finally, he returned with delicious pastries to accompany the coffee. He sat down and said, 'Academia needs a big idea to bring everything together, and this is such an idea.' He then suggested I should approach Professor Tarif Khalidi, who had recently arrived in Cambridge, and was the Sir Thomas Adam's Professor of Arabic and director of the Centre of Middle Eastern Studies.

Several days later, John came to our house for dinner, and the next day he drove to Switzerland, to spend the Christmas break in the mountains. On his way back through France, he felt ill, drew up beside the road, had a massive heart attack and died. We were all in shock. Annabel helped organize the funeral, as she knew John's friends in Iran who had to be contacted. Several weeks after the funeral there was a memorial gathering in Cambridge. John was a very special soul, full of light and laughter, who illuminated a room when he entered it. The care and generosity that he bestowed upon his students and indeed anyone who came within his orbit, meant that he was greatly missed. My wife lost the supervisor of her thesis and we both lost a friend. But the last encounter I had with him gave me the courage to tackle the rather intimidating academic community in Cambridge.

AN OFFICE IN ACADEMIA

By early March 1998, I had carefully prepared for my meeting with Tarif Khalidi and secured my appointment to see him. Tarif comes from a very distinguished family of scholars and judges who have lived in Jerusalem since the eleventh century. He was the first Arab to become the Sir Thomas Adam's Professor of Arabic at Cambridge University, since its foundation in 1632. He resided in a splendid set of rooms with a bow window, at the centre of the classical Gibbs Building of King's College, which stands adjacent to its famous Gothic Chapel. I set out before him my vision of the Golden Web, and mentioned John Cooper's response that academia needed a paradigm to bring things together. Tarif welcomed the idea, and over the next months pulled out all the stops to bring the Golden Web into the heart of the University. The first step was to organize an office for me in the Centre of Middle Eastern Studies, which was part of the Faculty of Oriental Studies. The request would have to go before the Centre's committee, and he suggested the members I needed to brief before he presented the proposal.

The first on my list was the Committee Chairman, Sir Roger Tomkys, Master of Pembroke College and a distinguished retired diplomat who had served as ambassador in Syria. Pembroke College has long been the gathering place for those engaged in Persian and Arabic Studies. He could not have been more encouraging, and I was to have several meetings with him over the next year. I then met two young lecturers who had just arrived at the University: James Montgomery from Glasgow University and Amira Bennison from Manchester University. They would both remain in Cambridge, advancing to become professors. They each responded positively, and Amira continued to be a source of encouragement and support during the life of the Golden Web. By the beginning of the Autumn Term of 1998, all had been agreed and an office allocated. I had to run the gauntlet of the office administrator, Doreen. The University still had the air of being an extension of public school, and she reminded me of my school matron. She looked after the Faculty with just two assistants. In my reflections at the end Chapter 19, I note the incredible transformation that was to take place during the following years in the way universities are run.

I was now inside one of the world's richest academic institutions, one that contained many scholars, faculties and centres that could contribute to the Golden Web. But how was the Golden Web to be manifested?

ABUL QASIM SPIKER & THE INTERNET

I was wedded to the established media of book, film and exhibition. Information Technology and the computer were anathema to me, and I wanted as little to do with them as I possibly could. I saw them as a further stage in the destruction of the human; they represented the onward march of the machine and René Guenon's 'reign of quantity'.

My introduction to the possibilities of IT came through a new arrival to Cambridge, Abul Qasim (Robert) Spiker. Abul Qasim hailed from America. He trained as an artist and sculptor and then went into publishing, working as an editor, publisher and graphic designer. In 1990 he wrote and produced the official guidebook for the Noble Sanctuary, in cooperation with the Islamic Awqaf in Jerusalem. This was followed by the production of an encyclopaedic interactive CD-ROM programme, exploring and documenting the entire complex.

He and his family became great friends with our family, and his home was a meeting point for many of the new Muslims who congregated in the area. When it was time to pray, an angelic voice floated through the house emanating from their son; little did I realize that this beautiful child would grow up to be a remarkable scholar of Arabic, who would, many years later, provide me with the final piece of the puzzle that I required to write my book.

But it was his father who would convert me to IT. I was amazed by his CD-ROM dedicated to the Noble Sanctuary. It was beautiful, and he showed me how the information was linked to plans and timelines. He then took me into the Worldwide Web and navigated through several silos rich in material relevant to the Golden Web. My resistance was beginning to weaken. I had been reading Imam Al-Ghazali's *The Ninety-nine Beautiful Names of God*, in which he states 'There is no evil in existence which does not contain some good within it'. This Worldwide Web already mirrored much of the detritus of modernity, with pornography claiming a great part of it, but there was much that was enriching. Wasn't the Web simply a great neutral connector? When I came up with the idea of the Golden Web, I had been oblivious of the existence of the Worldwide Web; surely this had to be the medium through which the Golden Web could be delivered; it would be the perfect marriage! I was soon to join the euphoria surrounding the Internet, with the zeal of a convert.

THE CD-ROM

I set to work with Abul Qasim planning a CD-ROM in which we would show how the Golden Web could be realized through the medium of IT. We needed guidance regarding mapping, which would be a key element, and a publisher who had experience in this new field, and we needed funding. One of the first people we approached with our idea was Abdal Hakim Winter. Abdal Hakim was a recent arrival and would, over the years, become an immense presence at the University and amongst the Muslim community in Cambridge.

Abdal Hakim was awarded a double first in Arabic at Cambridge University in 1983, and then departed for Cairo where he lived for three years, studying Islam under traditional teachers from Al-Azhar University. He went on to live in Jeddah for three years, where he administered a commercial translation office and maintained close contact with Habib Ahmad Mashhur al-Haddad and other scholars from the Hadramaut in Yemen. In 1989 he returned to England and spent two years at the University of London learning Turkish and Farsi. In 1992 he began his doctorate at Oxford University, which focused on Islam in the Balkans. No sooner had he begun, than the library in Sarajevo, which contained many of the manuscripts and sources he required for his thesis, was blown up by the Serbians at the outbreak of the Bosnian War. He spent the next three years accompanying aid convoys to Bosnia and acting as an interpreter for the Bosnian president Alija Izetbegović, as well as continuing his doctorate at Oxford. However, owing to the destruction of the library, he was obliged to change the subject of his thesis to the religious life of the early Ottoman Empire. In 1996, this remarkable scholar and activist was appointed the Shaykh Zayed Lecturer of Islamic Studies in the Faculty of Divinity at Cambridge University. He would go on to have a profound impact on several generations of young Muslim graduates and postgraduates, as well as becoming one of the most influential Muslim scholars in the West.

Abdul Hakim had established a charity called the Muslim Academic Trust. He invited us to apply for the funding required to produce the CD-ROM. We submitted our request and received the grant that launched us on the first stage of our journey into cyberspace. The next piece of fortune that accompanied us was meeting Andrew and Ailsa Heritage; they answered both our mapping and CD-ROM publishing requirements. They were a husband and wife team who were steeped in mapping history. They had been responsible for the production of the Times Atlas of World History. They had moved to Dorling Kindersley in 1991, where Andrew was cartographic director, and publisher for maps and atlases. On top of this, Dorling Kindersley was an early adopter of CD-ROMs, having invested heavily in their production. To cap it all, Andrew and Ailsa lived in Orwell, a village just outside Cambridge. Andrew and Ailsa helped us in assembling our CD-ROM, which was completed on 23rd November 1998.

Andrew then started introducing us to key people at Dorling Kindersley, and by the end of January 1999, he had assembled a high-powered group of DK decision makers for a presentation. Seeing this as a unique opportunity, I put my whole soul into the meeting, and I must have come across as something of a fanatic. I was by now convinced that the Golden Web would transform our approach to pre-modern history and would create a revolution within the academic community. I was therefore somewhat deflated when, having made my presentation, the senior DK executive present, asked me 'But will it be fun?' I had clearly failed to convince him that this was a product for DK. As it happened, however, Dorling Kindersley was entering rough waters; the company had overestimated the market for Star Wars books and was left with millions of unsold copies, resulting in a crippling debt. As a direct result, the company was taken over in 2000 by Pearson and became a part of the Penguin Group.

It was, nonetheless, a valuable experience. Andrew and Ailsa had become friends, and when we received the support to take the project to the next level, they played an important role in helping us set up our own mapping unit. Meanwhile, I had been casting bread upon the waters, searching for that breakthrough that I believed must happen.

THE UNIVERSITY

I was on a mission to learn, proselytize, and garner support and funding. I had entered the goldfield of Cambridge University and had access to the silos. The time left before the millennium came to an end was a great period of discovery for me. I attended lectures and seminars and had many discussions with scholars and students. I took full advantage of the University Library and its helpful librarians. It is one of the few great libraries where the books can be browsed on the shelves, and I enjoyed browsing.

One of the great Golden Web resources held in the Library is the Taylor-Schechter Cairo Genizah Collection, the world's largest and most important single collection of medieval Jewish manuscripts. For a thousand years, the Jewish community of Fustat (Old Cairo), placed their worn-out books and other writings in a storeroom (genizah) of the Ben Ezra Synagogue. There are 193,000 items in the Cambridge collection, which includes Bibles, prayer books and compendia of Jewish law. It also contains: shopping lists, marriage contracts, divorce deeds, pages from Arabic fables, works of Sufi and Shiʿite philosophy, medical books, magical amulets, business letters and accounts, and hundreds of letters, examples of practically every kind of written text produced by the Jewish communities of the Near East. It provides us with an unparalleled insight into the medieval Jewish world.

I was introduced to the Genizah collection by Professor Geoffrey Khan, who was to become deeply involved in the Golden Web, and from whom, over the years, I was to learn a great deal. He is another phenomenal linguist, working in the semitic languages (Hebrew, Aramaic, Arabic, Akkadian, and Ethiopic). Having graduated and been awarded his Ph.D. from SOAS, he moved to Cambridge in 1983, where for ten years he was employed as a researcher on the Genizah manuscripts.

Geoffrey showed me how the Genizah material paints a picture of a world which was rich in cross-cultural, linguistic and social relationships. Letters revealed the collaboration of Jews and Muslims in long distance trading enterprises, while documents like those relating to the famous occasion when the Grand Mufti of Cairo was invited to resolve a dispute between factions within the Jewish community, showed a remarkable degree of symbiosis.

I availed myself of the wealth of the Oriental Faculty and its library. I met with the Professor of Japanese, Richard Bowring and the Professor of Chinese, David McMullen. I had discussions with John Smith, University Lecturer in Sanskrit, who was an early adopter of IT and was in the process of digitizing the Hindu sacred texts, and Charles Melville, University Lecturer in Persian, who was setting up the Shahnamah (Persian Book of Kings) Project, which would use the Web to connect up various manuscripts scattered around the world, residing in a number of museums and libraries. In 2010 he organized the magnificent exhibition of Persian manuscripts and paintings of the Shahnamah at the Fitzwilliam Museum.

Beyond the Faculty of Oriental Studies there was a cornucopia of scholars and institutions that could contribute to the Golden Web, and open doors for me. The recently founded Macdonald Institute for Archaeological Research provided support for Cambridge-based researchers in the various branches of archaeology. Chris Scarre, the deputy director, was a great help in pointing me to research that was being undertaken that would be relevant to the Golden Web.

One of the very fruitful introductions was to Dr Marsha Levine. She was engaged in ground-breaking research; her study embraced the change from horse hunting to herding, and the evolution of horse husbandry and equestrian pastoral nomadism. Marsha was consumed by her subject, and gave me much food for thought. It was remarkable to learn how late the riding of the horse had taken place. The horse nomads were the last of the ways of life to appear, several millennia after the founding of cities. The horse nomads were key players in the Golden Web.

The Needham Research Institute was founded by the remarkable scholar Joseph Needham, who started out as a biochemist and ended his life as the great authority on the sciences of China. Like many initiatives in Cambridge, the Institute nestled beside the University, but remained an independent body. Christopher Cullen, the deputy director, was incredibly supportive. He was full of enthusiasm and generosity, taking time to meet with me and discuss the part China played in the Golden Web. He invited me to one of the Institute's regular text-reading sessions. A text would be chosen, and he would take the students and other participants through it, translating as he went along, and then discussing the salient points. At this memorable session a very ancient Joseph Needham attended in his wheelchair.

Christopher introduced me to Sir Geoffrey Lloyd, another remarkable polymath, and a natural 'Golden Webber' – we had begun to see everybody and everything in Golden Web terms! He began his academic life as a classicist. However, early on, he was already transcending the rigid divisions that tended to separate the different disciplines; he had a keen interest in anthropology which he allowed to enrich his reading of ancient Greek philosophy. After visiting China to give a lecture in 1987, Sir Geoffrey turned to the study of classical Chinese. This added a broad comparative scope to his work, which, following in the wake of Joseph Needham's pioneering studies, focused on how the different political cultures of ancient China and Greece influenced the forms of scientific discourse in those cultures. Sir Geoffrey was a familiar figure in Cambridge, often seen riding his bike. His enthusiasm was infectious, and he gave me long lists of people, publications and institutions that he deemed would be valuable in my quest.

I had meetings with another remarkable Cambridge scholar, the historian of the Mediterranean Sea, Professor David Abulafia, who was generous in the time he gave me, and introduced me to those of his students who could help in our research.

I have mentioned above some of the scholars and institutions that I was privileged to encounter in Cambridge. However, there were other scholars and institutions I sought out beyond Cambridge.

MUHAMMAD ISA WALEY

The British Library (BL) was at the forefront of the digital revolution. I presented the Golden Web to Dr Muhammad Isa Waley, the Library's Curator for the Persian and Turkish collections. He was an old friend, and would become an enthusiastic supporter and participant in the Golden Web as it developed over the years. He was one of the few scholars in England that specialized in Islamic mystical texts. When Annabel was working out the subject of her thesis, he advised her and pointed her in the direction of Cambridge and John Cooper. He was himself a Cambridge graduate and after graduation, went straight to the British Library, where he spent his working life. Whilst a librarian, Muhammad Isa undertook his PhD, which focused on the poetry of Jalal al-Din Rumi. He is one of those scholars who overflows with the love of their subject and brims with intelligence. Every meeting with him is an occasion. He specializes in the classical verse and prose literature of Islamic spirituality in Persian, Arabic, and Turkish. During his time at the British Library, the managers took control, and the scholar-librarians gradually became buried in administration, which meant that little time was left for their own research. In retirement, Muhammad Isa has been able to bring to fruition work that, in the old days, would have seen the light much earlier. But as I stated above, I intend to address the great administrative transformation in our institutions in the reflections at the end of Chapter 19. Muhammad Isa said that I must meet Susan Whitfield, whose work related directly to the Golden Web.

DR SUSAN WHITFIELD

Muhammad Isa was right; I was to meet an incredibly dynamic scholar who had recently obtained her PhD from SOAS and was to become a global authority on the Silk Road, authoring and editing half a dozen books and scores of papers over the years. Whitfield became the first director of the International Dunhuang Project (IDP), a position which she held for 24 years, until July 2017. Like the Geniza Collection, the IDP are engaged with another phenomenal discovery.

Little was known of the remarkable heritage of the Silk Road until explorers and archaeologists of the early twentieth century uncovered the ruins of ancient cities in the desert sands, revealing astonishing sculptures, murals and manuscripts. One of the most notable was the Buddhist cave library near the oasis town of Dunhuang on the edge of the Gobi Desert in western China. The cave had been sealed and hidden at the end of the first millennium AD and only re-discovered in 1900. Forty thousand manuscripts, paintings and printed documents on paper and silk were found in the cave itself. Tens of thousands more items were excavated from other Silk Road archaeological sites. These unique items have fascinating stories to tell of life on this great trade route from 100 BC to AD 1400. They were, however, dispersed to institutions around the world in the early 1900s, and the IDP mission was to bring them back together in cyberspace.

I gained much from my meetings with Susan Whitfield, who was generous with her time and a great communicator. I also had valuable meetings with Dr Rowena Loverance and her team, who were responsible for eLearning at the Library. However, it was the strong and indeed vehement rejection to a proposal to rename the areas of Afro-Eurasia in relation to the Golden Web that made me realize how deeply entrenched the Eurocentric vision of the world had become. Instead of the West, Middle East, Far East etc, it was clear to me that from a Golden-Web perspective the Middle East should be viewed as the Central Lands, with North, South, East and West arranged around them. England would then be the Far West and Japan the Far East. But Loverance and her team would have none of it!

There was, however, another problem that lay in our path: the Silk Road. What had begun in the 19th century as the name for the route that connected ancient China with the Roman Empire and carried the silk from the Celestial Kingdom to the end users in Rome, had, by the 20th century, morphed into an all-inclusive term to describe the multiple trade routes and everything that was carried on them, including religion, technologies and diseases. In other words, it was the Orientalist name for what we were calling the Golden Web. For the Golden Web to succeed it would have to replace the Silk Road. Given the huge academic investment in the term, it seemed a very hard nut to crack! Recently the term has been further entrenched with the publication of Peter Frankopan's bestselling book *The Silk Roads*.

The last of my encounters at the British Library during this time was with Antony Farrington, who was a perfect example of the true scholar-librarian. He was responsible for the vast India collections in the library, and specialized in the East India Company and the pre-modern trading systems. He produced works that can only be of interest to specialist scholars, such as *A Biographical Index of East India Company Maritime Service Officers, 1600–1834*, and *The English factory in Japan, 1613-1623*. However, when I met him, he was preparing an exhibition, with an accompanying book, that would provide us with the opportunity to share in his scholarship. 'Trading Places: The East India Company and Asia' was held at the British Library from 24th May until 22nd September 2002.

It was a beautifully-staged display with an excellent accompanying book, which represented a post-colonial appreciation of what took place.

The British merchants began trading with Asia in the late 1500s. They found a sophisticated and thriving network of merchant communities, where goods were manufactured and traded on a scale never seen before in Europe. The exhibits were drawn from the extensive collections of the British Library, the prime holder of the documentary legacy of the East India Company. The East India Company was founded in 1600 to consolidate and exploit the Asian markets, and over its history grew into 'the grandest society of merchants in the universe'. As a commercial enterprise it came to control half the world's trade and as political entity it administered an embryonic empire. The exhibition showed the human cost of creating this early 'global market' and how the Company's activities displayed some of the worst aspects of colonialism. It brilliantly illustrated the importance of the 400-year cultural exchange between Asia and Europe.

Whilst the British Library was at the forefront of the digital revolution, it was also proceeding apace in other museums, libraries and universities in the UK. I had valuable meetings with Oliver Watson whom I had known since the World of Islam Festival, when his first job, fresh from university, had been receiving and cataloguing the exhibits that arrived for the 'Arts of Islam' exhibition. He told me that he learnt more about Islamic art during that period than at any other time of his working life. He was now the head of the Ceramics Department at the Victoria and Albert Museum, and would go on to play an important role in the establishment of the Islamic Museum in Qatar.

I had fruitful discussions with Dr Shirin Akiner who brought to the School of Oriental and African Studies (SOAS) an amazing gift for assembling the diverse worlds of Central Asia into a coherent field of study. Shirin was a rare linguist who straddled the Slavic and Turkic worlds. I met with Dr Julian Raby in Oxford, a highly creative and broad-ranging scholar whose interests span the Asian world. In 2002 he was appointed Director of the Freer Gallery of Art, at the Smithsonian Institution in Washington.

My quest for knowledge was proceeding apace. However, there was no sign of funding materializing. And then, on an afternoon in early August 1999, my friend Dr Ricky Richardson phoned me. I introduced Ricky earlier in this story when Sarah Harding and he had just got married and were departing for Brunei, where Ricky was to set up the children's clinics for the Sultan. Ricky is one of those rare generous souls who is always supportive and encouraging, and he has been a great promoter of my projects. He phoned me to say that he had met a young shaykh from Abu Dhabi. He had spoken to him about the Golden Web, and the shaykh would like to meet me.

18

THE GOLDEN WEB PART III

MOHAMMED AHMED KHALIFA AL-SUWAIDI

THE FOLLOWING AFTERNOON I travelled up to London to meet Mohammed Al-Suwaidi. I discovered he was the eldest son of the first UAE foreign minister, who twenty-six years earlier had been responsible, with the then UAE Ambassador in London, for the initial funding that launched the World of Islam Festival. I was now in front of the person who was perhaps one of the only people on the planet who had the background, resources, knowledge and culture to enable the Golden Web to be realized. His father had set up the Cultural Foundation in Abu Dhabi in 1981, the first of its kind in the Gulf region. Mohammed was its founding Director, and for eighteen years had organized a wide-ranging programme of exhibitions, concerts, film shows, lectures, book fairs, and children's programmes. He had been an early adopter of the Internet, and his website Al-Waraq, with its highly impressive search engine, already contained thousands of volumes of Arabic literature, including many works on the travellers and geographers central to the Golden Web story.

Key to his importance as a cultural figure was that he was a poet, the poet being held in high regard in Arabic society.

The meeting went well. I showed him the Golden Web presentation, and he demonstrated Al-Waraq for me. It was an exciting moment. However, I had a difficult matter to deal with if we were to become financially involved; I informed him that I was in the last months of three years as a bankrupt. I explained my situation, but he graciously continued to discuss how we should proceed. He suggested I should go to the UAE, visit his offices in Abu Dhabi and Dubai, and meet the manager who was responsible for the team producing Al-Waraq.

Six days later, on the 9th August 1999, I was on a plane heading for Abu Dhabi, the first of many flights I would make to this city over the next twelve years. I categorize modern cities by those that you can walk in, and those you cannot. Abu Dhabi is pedestrian friendly and Dubai is a nightmare created for the car. Abu Dhabi is unique; no society on earth has passed from a frugal traditional lifestyle to become, in one generation, a modern society of wealth beyond imagination. Before oil was discovered in the late 1950s, Abu Dhabi was a fishing village with a modest Beau Geste-type fort. The frugality of their traditional way of life was exacerbated by Japan's introduction, in the early 20th century, of cultured pearls, which brought to an end the pearling industry which had augmented their austere existence. Their material life may have been frugal, but their oral, linguistic, literary and poetic heritage was immense. This was my first encounter with a Bedouin culture. My previous experience in Arabia had been in the Hejaz, the land of the sacred cities, which was very different. Jeddah and the holy cities were the melting pot of Dar al-Islam. I was now encountering a world where the tribes were clearly differentiated. Shaykh Zayed, the paramount leader of the tribes of the recently formed state, was a wise ruler, and deeply loved by his people. His wisdom was manifested in the very fabric of the newly created city of Abu Dhabi. The city was laid out on a grid system, like a tent encampment. A height limit was imposed so that no building could lord it over its neighbour; the wealthier members of society were simply able to own more plots to build on. With a corniche that ran the full length of the bay, and green areas within the city, Abu Dhabi was pleasant to wander around. After a whirlwind visit of three days, taking in Mohammed Suwaidi's offices in Abu Dhabi and Dubai, and meeting his manager and members of his team, I returned to the UK, convinced that Mohammed was the perfect patron for the Golden Web and happy that I was once again engaged with the UAE, which had played such a key role in the Festival.

THE AGREEMENT

Over the next two months I worked with Mohammed Suwaidi on establishing how we could collaborate, and on plans for the development of a website. The first step was to create a prototype which could demonstrate the structure and type of content to be included. This prototype would then form the basis for the live website that could be navigated by the end-users.

I introduced Mohammed to Dr Muhammed Isa Waley at the British Library, who took us for a tour around the building and gave us an idea of the vast holdings that were of significance to the Golden Web. We met Andrew Heritage at Dorling Kindersley to discuss our mapping programme. We also met Professor Yusuf Ibish, who had to leave Beirut when the civil war broke out, and was now director of the Al-Furqan Islamic Heritage Foundation.

The Foundation had been set up by Dr Zaki Yamani, who had come to global attention when he was the Saudi Arabian oil minister during the oil crisis. Zaki Yamani came from a distinguished family of scholars, that originally hailed from Yemen, but for several generations had lived in Mecca. Once his ministerial duties had ended, he focused his considerable intelligence, experience and wealth on creating a vehicle that would bring together the scattered Arabic and Islamic literary heritage. He began by cataloguing and then producing edited editions of this vast treasure house. The Foundation was the kind of institution that we envisioned as being part of the Golden Web sphere of activity.

Mohammed Suwaidi's IT manager came to London to meet with Abul Qasim Spiker, who was looking after the technical aspects of the project, and we discussed the team we would need to develop the prototype. This would require a research team of scholars, as well as map makers and programmers, with Abul Qasim as webmaster. A budget and timetable were drawn up, and on the 17th October 1999, I departed with Abul Qasim for Abu Dhabi to complete the arrangements.

Over the next few days, we were introduced to Mohammed Suwaidi's world. One of the permanent exhibits in the Cultural Foundation was a Bedouin tent with all its trappings; it was a magnificent work of art. Mohammed invited us into the tent, and after removing our shoes, we joined him. We sat awkwardly in our suits, whilst he was completely at home and looked splendid in his Bedouin attire. We then enjoyed the ceremony of coffee which belongs in the tent of the Bedouin. Pure coffee served in small cups, replenished by the Bedouin coffee master who dispensed the golden liquid in a beautifully-crafted bronze ewer with a long spout. A photographer appeared, and this memorable moment was captured for posterity! From the tent, we decamped to Mohammed's palatial home, and had our first taste of the hospitality for which the Arabs are famed. After a meal attended by many, we entered the majlis, a large room with low, cushioned seating around the walls. We sat in the place of honour beside Mohammed. Over several years I was to attend a number of such gatherings, where in the place of honour would be seated authors, filmmakers, artists, Sufi Shaykhs, politicians, and others of interest who were passing through Abu Dhabi. Poetry, orations and discussions would take place, accompanied by sweet tea and the cups of golden coffee.

By the 8th November, the partnership between Mohammed Suwaidi and myself had been agreed and the papers signed. The following day, Abul Qasim and I returned to Cambridge ready to set up the team that would deliver the prototype.

A FAMILY AFFAIR

I was now entering a period of my life when I would be in a much stronger position in my quest for knowledge. Members of my family were joining me after years of study, and this would both contribute to my understanding of Islam and Islamic civilization, and help me in the tasks that lay ahead.

My wife, Annabel, completed her doctorate at the end of 2001, which was published by Oxford University Press (OUP) in 2006, under the title *Sufi Hermeneutics, the Qur'an Commentary of Rashīd Al-Dīn Maybudī*. I now had beside me a scholar who was becoming increasingly recognized in her field. In the summer of 2006, Annabel organized a workshop in Cambridge, which brought together a number of leading academics in the field of the esoteric interpretation of the Qur'an. Ten years later the fruits of the workshop were published by OUP under the title, *The Spirit and The Letter, Approaches to the Esoteric Interpretation of the Qur'an.*

Our third son, Ali, was following a trajectory that would provide a whole new dimension to my appreciation of the Holy Qur'an and Islam. Ali is a musician, who studied the violin from the age of six. After school he went to the Royal Northern College of Music in Manchester, where he was a pupil of one of the great Russian teachers. However, he left the school after a year. He was being pulled between Western Classical music and Islam. From the age of fourteen he had fallen in love with the recitation of the Holy Qur'an, and had the tapes of the great Egyptian reciters, which he spent many hours listening to. He also became deeply engaged with books of the *hadith* of the Prophet, blessings and peace be upon him. So, in 1995, on quitting the Royal College, he made for Damascus. After a year, he travelled to Yemen, and was the first of the westerners to study the traditional sciences in Tarim. In 1998 he returned to Damascus, and now married, set up home and remained there for the next ten years. His focus increasingly settled on the traditional music of the area and the recitation of the Holy Qur'an. Finally, he decided to study the recitation seriously and was accepted as a student by Shaykh Abdul Razzaq Balhawan.

When making his decision to follow this course, I asked him how he thought he would get on. He answered that, since he was a musician, the mastery of recitation should not be a problem. Several years later when Shaykh Abdul Razzaq presented him with his *ijāzah*, or certificate, which gave him the authority to teach what he had learnt, I reminded him of our conversation when he was setting out on his journey with the Shaykh. I asked him how it seemed now? 'Dad I'll tell you', he replied, 'There's a great ladder and my Shaykh is right at the top, and I have put my foot on the first rung'. When I related the conversation to Ustad Mahmud Mirza, he smiled and said, 'Now he understands.' Ali had entered the fathomless ocean of the Holy Qur'an. Nothing can communicate the reality of the Revelation more than the art and science of the recitation of the Holy Qur'an. Whenever Ali stays with us, our home is bathed in the beauty of this supreme manifestation of Islam.

Annabel and Ali would go on to collaborate in the translation of the earliest of the Sufi commentaries on the Holy Qur'an; *Tafsir al-Tustari*, was published by Fons Vitae in 2011. The publication was heavily annotated and had an extensive introduction. It has become an invaluable resource.

There was, however, a third member of my family who made a considerable contribution to the Project and was my close companion along the way. Our son Joe entered this world seven years after Ali's arrival. He was nine when I had my breakdown and became housebound for a time, and with Annabel studying at SOAS, I had far more contact with him than with my other children at that age. We formed a close friendship. When Muhammed Suwaidi appeared, Joe was nineteen. He had taken a year out after finishing school to work as a chef in a high-class Thai restaurant in Cambridge. He had started as a commis chef, cutting up the vegetables, and ended up cooking the whole menu at speed and becoming fully qualified. One day he came to me with a dilemma. He told me that he had been offered a place with one of the celebrity chefs. However, he could not imagine spending his life cooking. 'What would you like to do?' I asked. His answer was that he would like to do what I was doing. Now, I had observed this son of mine very carefully whilst he was growing up. He was a grafter. Whilst at school, he would undertake jobs in the evenings, at weekends and in the holidays. He cleaned the BT offices, drove cars to their new owners for a local garage, worked in restaurants, and started cooking. He keenly observed his bosses, and discussed with me their qualities and shortcomings. He was undoubtably an organizer, and I needed help at this juncture. The first thing I suggested he should do was to enrol at the Pitman Secretarial School and do courses in touch-typing and bookkeeping. I had noticed that the American academics all knew how to touch-type, whilst the British scholars did not. In the UK, typing was for secretaries! I told Joe that in today's world every organizer had to be their own secretary. Having learnt how to touch-type, he then took a part-time course in project management and we began working together. For twelve years he was by my side, supporting me through the vicissitudes of what was to unfold.

A NEW HOME & OFFICE

Let us return to the setting up of our Project. We needed an office for the half-dozen core members of the team; others would work from home or in their own offices and come in for meetings. I had been working from home for more than twelve years, since the ending of the Travelling Exhibition; my office in the Faculty had only been for meetings. I had become set in my ways, and ideally wanted an office connected to my home. We heard on the Muslim grapevine that Suleiman and Farah, members of our Cambridge community, were moving to Egypt and had a house to let that sounded perfect. The building was a converted corner shop in a street off Mill Road. Through a small garden at the back of the house was a double garage that Suleiman had converted into a workshop. This would certainly accommodate six workstations and the shop at the front would make a perfect meeting room; with the living room and bedrooms upstairs, it seemed made for the next stage of our Project. Suleiman is a carpenter and was finishing a beautiful muqarnas mihrab for the Cambridge Mosque, and we agreed that when it was completed, we would take up residence. On the 27th February 2000 we moved into the house that was to be our home and workplace for the next seven years.

Mill Road stretches from Parker's Piece, a large open space adjacent to the centre of Cambridge, to the ring road on the outer reaches of the city. The streets around Mill Road contain modest terraced houses, which were built for the railway workers during the 19th century, when Cambridge became an important junction in the rail network that was being created. Now it was the most cosmopolitan area of the city, with many nationalities represented, and it was the heart of the Cambridge Muslim community.

THE MUSLIM COMMUNITY

This was the first time we had lived within walking distance of a mosque. The Abu Bakr Mosque was founded in 1981, and was the first of several mosques that are now in Cambridge. To reach the mosque we passed a number of shops and eateries owned by Muslims, who became our friends. Their Islam was deep inside them, and their kindness and hospitality touched my heart. The stories of their lives were incredible, and I marvelled at their courage and fortitude.

The first shop I would pass on my way to the mosque was the Yasrab Newsagent. This was owned by Parvez Malek, a tall gracious man with a long white beard. His father came from Gujarat in India and his mother from Lahore in Pakistan. They were textile weavers, and the father had kept a shop in his town in Gujarat. During the riots that took place when India was being partitioned in 1947, the father's shop was burnt down. The family had to flee to Lahore. Like millions of other victims of Partition, the family's business was ruined. After WWII, the call went out to the workers of the Commonwealth to come to the United Kingdom to help rebuild the mother country. Recruiting agents travelled around India, Pakistan and the West Indies, encouraging the young to fill vacancies in the newly formed NHS, the railways, the cotton mills, the building industry and many other industries and services. This was an opportunity to earn money that could be sent back to support their families, and many responded to the call. Parvez took up the challenge. He cut short his education, and arrived in London in 1964. For twenty-eight years he worked in a number of jobs: he was a mechanic in a garage, a guard on British Rail and on the Underground, and he worked in a bread factory. In 1992 Parvez bought the newsagents shop in Mill Road belonging to a friend who was returning to Pakistan.

Crossing the railway bridge that divides Mill Road, the next shop we encountered on our journey to the Mosque was Al-Amin. This is the domain of Abdul Kayum Arain and his family, and the shop has become a Mill Road institution. The family came to Britain from Kenya at a time when the welcome to the mother country had changed. Cotton mills and many of the old industries were closing, and unemployment was rising. Anti-immigrant marches were taking place, inflamed by Enoch Powell's infamous 'Rivers of Blood' speech. Xenophobia was raising its ugly head, and the contribution that Indians, Pakistanis, Bangladeshis and West Indians had made, and were making, to the recovery of the nation was being erased from the national memory.

However, Abdul Kayum progressed in business and for many years was in senior management, auditing for a multi-national company. But he fell out with the company on ethical grounds. Finding that he could no longer work for an organization that put profit before ethics, he resigned. A friend of the family's grocery shop in Mill Road was in trouble, and Abdul Kayum decided to help him, taking over the shop with all its debts.

He was joined by his brother Aamer, and the rest of the family took part. They decided the shop must be run ethically; out went the cigarettes, alcohol and lottery tickets. Their aim was not to sell items which were harmful to an individual or society, and they would try to promote local businesses and suppliers. They would take the environment into consideration, and put people before profits. The Al-Amin store has flourished, and provides a remarkable service to the community in many different ways.

Continuing our journey to the mosque, we would pass Arshad Malik's grocery shop and a little further on his brother Amjad's takeaway. Our son Ali, when a student, rented a room from Amjad, above the takeaway. Ali has many stories of the kindness and generosity of the brothers. We now arrive at Mawson Road where the Mosque is to be found. On the corner we pass Carlos, a Turkish Café, that provides inexpensive and wholesome food. Just beyond the turning off to the Mosque is Al-Casbah, one of the best restaurants in Cambridge, which was owned by Foudil Rerizani from Algeria. Later he would open a second restaurant on Mill Road called Bedouin, with the two restaurants he covered the full menu of tajines and grills of the Maghrebi cuisine. Whilst writing this passage, I have been informed of the death of Foudil after a long battle with cancer. I have so many memories of Foudil and seeing his five sons growing up. Each year he took them to Algeria so that they would retain their Arabic, as their mother tongue was English.

Arriving at the mosque, one would be greeted by Mahmud Dall, an imposing, caring, powerfully built man, who owned a grocery shop the other side of Cambridge. For as long as I can remember he has always served the worshippers, ensuring that everyone had a place to pray, and dealing with any problems that might arise. Ramadan was the special time of the year when the community came together, and the Mosque was fully alive. Every evening, for the breaking of the fast, the food would be provided by one of the many Muslim restaurants and eateries in Cambridge. One of our Syrian brothers, Omar Kuwaider, arranged for Qur'an reciters to come from Damascus. The Kuwaider family were famous for producing the finest Damascene sweets. Omar became a family friend and a supporter of my Golden Web at a critical moment in its development.

One of the reciters he brought to Cambridge was Shaykh Abdul Razzaq Balhawan, who became our son Ali's Shaykh, as I related above. How Shaykh Abdul Razzaq became a reciter of Qur'an is one of the most amazing stories that I have ever heard. He was a young man working in a chemical laboratory when he was arrested by the secret police. He was completely innocent, but had the misfortune of being seen talking to one of his co-workers who was being watched. His co-worker was executed and the young Abdul Razzaq spent twelve years in prison. A dozen or so prisoners were held in a cell so small that they had to take turns to sleep and pray. They were not allowed any reading material. However, among the prisoners in his cell, there happened to be one Hafiz, a man who had memorized the whole Qur'an. By the time that Abdul Razzaq was freed from prison he had learned the whole of the Qur'an by heart, and would spend the rest of his life devoted to the Holy Book, and to teaching the art of recitation. When war broke out in Syria in 2011, Shaykh Abdul Razzaq was forced to flee his beloved Damascus, and is, as I write, in Manchester, serving the Muslims of that city. Manchester's Syrian community goes back to the early 19th century when Syrian merchants arrived to engage in the cotton trade.

Another prominent member of the Mosque was Mohammed Ashraf, who would also become a close family friend and deeply involved with my work. Mohammed was born in the city of Jammu in Jammu Kashmir, and was four years old in 1947, when the Indian Subcontinent was partitioned. Jammu found itself on the Indian side of the line that had been drawn by the British. Mohammed's father was in the army, and the Muslim soldiers were disarmed. The family fled across the border in an army truck with all its members hidden under a tarpaulin. One of their uncles and his family did not make it; they were burnt alive in the conflagration of their village. After months in a refugee camp, Mohammed's family were allotted a small house in the city of Sialkot, which had been vacated by Hindus fleeing in the other direction. Only Mohammed's father had remained in Indian Jammu, as the Muslims who fled believed that they would shortly return to their homes. Three years later the father re-joined his family, as hope of a return to their homeland began to fade.

Mohammed was a good student and was awarded his Bachelor of Commerce from Punjab University in Lahore. He then went to work for Grays of Cambridge, who had a branch office in Sialkot. Grays produced cricket bats in Cambridge and hockey sticks in Sialkot. Mohammed rose to become chief accountant and became friends with one of the directors of the firm, who arranged for him to come to Cambridge so that he could obtain his Articles. This would enable him to become a Chartered

Accountant and practice in the UK. He arrived in Cambridge in 1970, and having been awarded his Articles, he struck out and established his own practice.

These are just a few of the treasures to be found amongst the Muslims who have found their way to Cambridge. Over the last thirty years, I have watched their children grow up and grandchildren appear. My life has been enriched by their company and friendship. Their presence has increased my understanding of Islam and the worlds from which they came. Their contribution to my book has been immense.

THE GOLDEN WEB TEAM

We now had our office and the funds that would enable us to produce the prototype. We could go ahead and recruit our team. We needed an accountant, and the obvious choice was Mohammed Ashraf. Abul Qasim required an assistant to work with him building the prototype. Mukhtar Sanders, the son of the well-known photographer Peter Sanders, who over the last fifty years has built a unique archive of images covering most of the Islamic world, was another natural recruit. Mukhtar inherited his father's eye, and had received his HND in Graphic Design from Amersham and Wycombe College. He was working with a firm in London as a junior designer, and leapt at the opportunity to join Abul Qasim in Cambridge.

I had been discussing the Golden Web with several scholars who intimated that they would like to become part of a research group, if the project took off. I was now in a position to bring them together. Christopher Cullen had introduced me to Dr Sally Church, a Sinologist from the USA. She had recently arrived in Cambridge, and was a junior research fellow at Wolfson College. Sally is a formidable scholar; she studied Chinese history at Middlebury College for her BA, obtained an MA in Chinese literature at the University of Chicago and a PhD, also in Chinese literature, at Harvard University, and had already co-authored *The Oxford Starter Chinese Dictionary*, which had just been published. Sally became the coordinator of our group of scholars and produced pioneering work on one of the key Golden Web subjects: the Ming Voyages. These maritime expeditions were undertaken by Ming China's huge treasure fleet between 1405 and 1435. This grand endeavour resulted in seven far-reaching ocean voyages to the coastal territories and islands in and around the South China Sea and the Indian Ocean. It was organized and led by Admiral Zheng He, one of the most powerful eunuchs in the service of the emperor. The Ming Voyages revealed the extent of the Muslim penetration of China; Zheng He was a Muslim, and so were the merchants who accompanied the fleet, and the scribes who recorded the voyages. One of the voyages included a visit to Mecca.

Other important arrivals at the Golden Web were Paul Lunde and Caroline Stone. They were a married couple, who practised very successfully as independent scholars, that is to say, scholars who are not employed by universities or other institutions, but engage in research and publications. Paul Lunde was born in the United States and brought up in Saudi Arabia. He then studied Arabic at SOAS, University of London, where he was awarded his degree. Caroline Stone received her degree from Cambridge University, and then spent three years studying at Kyoto University in Japan. The two of them specialized in producing scholarly articles that could be easily read by the general public. Many of their articles appeared in *Aramco World Magazine*, at which Paul was also a guest editor. They had already covered many aspects of the Golden Web in their features and articles, and were deeply engaged in the study of trade and travel in pre-modern Afro-Eurasia. We had met several times for discussions before the project became feasible. Now they enthusiastically joined the research team.

Dr Jane McIntosh was another independent scholar who was a valuable addition to our research group. She had obtained her PhD from Cambridge University; her thesis focusing on contacts between the Indus Valley and Mesopotamia. She then began writing books about archaeology for a wider audience; her first book, *The Practical Archaeologist* (1986), has been described as a 'key reference' and is recommended as an introduction to archaeology for beginners. Jane was living in Shropshire but made frequent visits to our office and was fully engaged in our work.

Robert Harding was completing his PhD at Cambridge University, and became a part-time member of the team, later becoming a full-time member. Robert is an Australian and was awarded his degree and MA from Melbourne University in Classical, Ancient Mediterranean and Near Eastern Studies and Archaeology. He then moved to the UK and took a further MA in Religious Studies at SOAS. His research in archaeology led him to focus increasingly on ancient India.

Sally, Paul, Caroline, Jane and Robert constituted the Golden Web's core team of scholars, and would remain working together for the next twelve years. Between them they covered key areas and periods of the Golden Web. With the appointment of Angela King, a wonderful secretary, our organization was complete, and we could start work on the prototype.

THE BUILDING OF THE PROTOTYPE

We held our first team meeting in our new office-cum-dwelling on 28th February 2000. By the end of the year, the prototype was ready. These were for me the most rewarding few months during the long existence of the Golden Web. The house was buzzing. From breakfast to the evening meal, we would be exploring our Golden Web, in our studio-workshop, in the meeting room and around the dining table, where coffee and meals accompanied the discussions. All were fully engaged in the adventure.

Andrew and Ailsa Heritage established the mapping protocols, and after much experimentation, base maps of the world and Afro-Eurasia were produced which answered to our needs. Whilst Abul Qasim devised the overall design of the website, Mukhtar began the arduous task of entering the data. Every day revealed something new, as our team of scholars produced the research that was being transformed into maps. The core of the Golden Web was a series of sixteen maps which showed the unfolding of the trade routes from 3,500 BC to 1,750 AD. We then began entering the travellers and geographers. Locating the exact position of the cities was a major task, and here we were guided by Ailsa Heritage. To see the travels of Ibn Battuta, Ibn Jubayr and other Muslims appear on the screen was wonderful, and the picture became complete when they were joined by the Chinese, Indian and European diplomatic, missionary and trade journeys. Another scholar who participated in this first stage of the Project was Adam Silverstein who was completing his PhD in Cambridge. He was engaged in a study of the pre-modern Afro-Eurasian postal system. Before migrating to Oxford, he mapped for us the Arab geographer Ibn Khordadbeh's *Book of Roads and Kingdoms*.

We then began mapping trade goods from their places of origin to their destinations. Finally, we started on what we called the Golden Web themes. These encompassed the spread of ideas, religions, technologies, crops, diseases, and whatever else could travel along the routes. We began with the unfolding of Islam. We could now illustrate the growth of Islamic civilization with the founding of many new cities and the extension of the trade routes to cover most of Afro-Eurasia.

A memorable event took place when Sally Church was entering information about the city of Hangchow in China. We were using Hangchow to demonstrate the audio aspect of the Project, with the name of the city and a poem about the celebrated lake rendered in Chinese. The agency which we had engaged to clean our home-cum-office sent us language students who came from all over the world. It so happened that at the time our cleaner was from China, so we invited her to do the recording. After she had beautifully enunciated the name of the city, Hangchow, Sally gave her the poem she had selected. She took one look at it, and handed it back to Sally saying she did not need to read it, she knew the poem by heart! It turned out that her father was a university professor of Chinese literature.

Everything we required to demonstrate our prototype was now ready. Abul Qasim had designed a beautiful home page. The main screen contained the trade maps, with, on the left, a column of the sixteen dates, which gave access to each of the maps. Above the maps, five buttons provided entry into the main categories: Cities, Routes, Travellers, Trade Goods and Themes. Above the five buttons was a banner carrying 'The Golden Web Market Place'. Here the visitor to the site would be able to purchase traditional crafts, books, videos and CDs, with tours of the heritage of the Golden Web advertised. Buttons to the left provided search and language facilities. We had devised a journey that demonstrated all the different aspects of the prototype, which took about an hour to present. On the 16th December Abul Qasim and I left for Abu Dhabi, where we gave our first presentation of the prototype to Mohammed Suwaidi and his technical manager. The presentation was well received, and it was agreed that we should go ahead with the next phase of the Project.

Over the next year we were engaged in two main tasks: presenting the prototype to a number of potential users and participants, and bringing it alive by devising an indexing and mapping tool. Meanwhile, our scholars continued their work on researching, translating relevant material, and mapping the Golden Web topics.

ROSS DUNN & WORLD HISTORY

The arrival in Cambridge of Professor Ross Dunn, who was on sabbatical from San Diego State University, California, introduced a new dynamic into our initiative. He was a life member of Clare Hall, and one of the College fellows informed him about the Golden Web. Within days of our meeting, he was opening up his vast network of contacts, and we began planning a programme.

Ross was one of the pioneers of world history studies, and had taken a special interest in the great traveller Ibn Battuta, who was a key figure in the Golden Web story. His book, *The Adventures of Ibn Battuta, a Muslim Traveler of the Fourteenth Century*, appeared in 1987 (University of California Press). It is a brilliant accompaniment to the Gibb and Beckingham translation of *The Travels* published by the Hakluyt Society. Ross beautifully describes Ibn Battuta the scholar, and the world he traversed in a memorable passage in his introduction:

> First, he was a pilgrim, joining the march of pious believers to the spiritual shrines of Mecca and Medina at least four times in his career. Second, he was a devotee of Sufism, or mystical Islam, travelling, as thousands did, to the hermitages and lodges of venerable holy men to receive their blessing and wisdom. Third, he was a juridical scholar, seeking knowledge and erudite company in the great cities of the Islamic heartland. And finally, he was a member of the literate, mobile, world-minded elite, an educated adventurer as it were, looking for hospitality, honours, and profitable employment in the more newly established centres of Islamic civilization in the further regions of Asia and Africa. In any of these travelling roles, however, he regarded himself as a citizen, not of a country called Morocco, but of Dar al-Islam, to whose universalist spiritual, moral and social values he was loyal above any other allegiance.

Shortly after his arrival in Cambridge, Ross gave a lecture at the Oriental Faculty on Ibn Battuta. During questions, a professor in the department made the claim that the travels of Marco Polo were far more interesting than those of Ibn Battuta, and that he (Marco Polo) was a far more interesting man. Sitting behind me and my wife was Tim MacIntosh Smith who took up the case for Ibn Battuta, and his great erudition and formidable knowledge carried the day. It was hardly surprising; Tim's award-winning *Travels with a Tangerine; a journey in the footnotes of Ibn Battuta* was about to be published, and would appear as a BBC documentary series later in the decade.

Ibn Battuta had become a major focus for our project, and Mohammed Suwaidi was leading the way in commissioning a photographer to capture the places, buildings and any other artifacts that still existed, that were mentioned in the account of his travels. I am writing this whilst the Covid 19 pandemic is ravaging the world. It seems fitting to mention the passage in the *Travels*, which describes what happened when Ibn Battuta approached Damascus at a time when an outbreak of the plague had just preceded him. Emerging from the city gate came a great procession of the inhabitants: the Muslims led by their shaykhs and imams, the Christians by their bishops and priests, and the Jews by their rabbis, all carrying their Holy Books. Together they visited a place which all three religions held sacred, and prayed to God to lift the pandemic. How different from our time!

The first meeting Ross organized for me was with Christine Counsell. Christine had arrived in Cambridge in 1997, and over a period of twenty years would establish Cambridge University as the country's leader in history education. He then arranged for me to present the Golden Web at the World History Association 2001 Annual Conference, which was to be held in Salt Lake City. I left for the Conference on the 27th June and returned to Cambridge on 3rd July. I gave my presentation of the Golden Web, which was very well received. History teachers came up to me afterwards, keen to know when the website would be available. During those five days Ross introduced me to all the leading figures in the World History movement who were present at the Conference. I had a memorable meeting with David Christian, who had developed the concept of Big History. This covered the timespan from the Big Bang to the present, and engaged a multidisciplinary approach. His major work on the subject, *Maps of Time: An Introduction to Big History*, was published by University of California Press in 2005.

My collaboration with Ross and World History culminated in a symposium entitled 'World History and the Golden Web', held in Cambridge in June 2008, which brought together some sixty scholars from around the world, for two days of talks and discussions.

BACK IN CAMBRIDGE

But let us return to 2001. On my arrival back in Cambridge from the World History Conference in Salt Lake City, I had meetings with Sir Alec Broer, Vice Chancellor of the University, and officers of the Cambridge University Press. I also gave a presentation to members of the Oriental Faculty. I introduced the Golden Web to Dr Zaki Badawi, the principal and founder of the Muslim College in London, an eminent scholar and a leading figure in the Muslim community of the UK. I then travelled to Portugal for the opening of the Gulbenkian Museum's refurbished Islamic Galleries, where I was able to introduce the project to several scholars.

By the beginning of 2002 we were well equipped with feedback from the many meetings that had taken place, and were encouraged by the positive and, indeed, enthusiastic response the Golden Web Prototype had received. However, the other challenge we faced, that of developing the indexing and mapping tool, was making slower progress.

BRINGING IT ALIVE

One of the people on my journey who provided me with a haven and a refuge from the intensity and growing stresses of my visits to Abu Dhabi, was Khalid Osman. He had a small office in the Cultural Foundation where he looked after the IT needs of the institution. After meetings, I would seek him out and discuss developments with him. His wisdom and common-sense responses were always helpful in my understanding of what was actually taking place. He loved the Golden Web and was busy working on ideas for how to deal with our indexing and mapping problems. It was therefore a great delight when Mohammed Suwaidi decided to send Khalid to Cambridge to work with us. He arrived on the 23rd January 2001 and would make extended visits to Cambridge over the next year.

The system he devised required a 'chunking' of the texts, so that when a city or subject was clicked on, only the data relating to it appeared. It sounds simple, but it was not. It engaged the team in many discussions concerning semantics and how to chunk the material, with the overlaps which were bound to occur. By the summer of that year, the system was set up and the team spent part of their time over the following years chunking their material. It was at the beginning of this process that we were joined by Ayman Haleem.

AYMAN HALEEM

Ayman is the son of Dr Muhammad Abdel Haleem, the long serving and distinguished Professor of Qur'anic Arabic at SOAS. It can be said that the professor's working life has been defined by the Holy Qur'an; first as a teacher, then as the editor of the *Journal of Qur'anic Studies* and the author of numerous articles and two books on the language and style of the Qur'an, and finally with his translation of the Holy Qur'an into English, published by Oxford University Press.

Ayman arrived in Cambridge in 1999 to take his M.Phil. in Theology at the Divinity Faculty, having gained his BA in Arabic with first class honours at SOAS, where he had received an award for outstanding academic performance, achieving the highest results in the entire university for his final year. A gentle giant, with a lovely sense of humour, he became a prominent figure amongst the Muslims of the university. He was our Imam at Wolfson College during the Ramadan of 2000, and as soon as he completed his M.Phil., he joined the Golden Web Project.

Ayman performed two roles during the life of the Golden Web. He began by employing his considerable language skills, in researching, translating, collating and chunking the accounts of Arabic travellers and geographers, taking on the awesome task of *The Travels of Ibn Battuta*. In the second phase, when the organization expanded dramatically and became a Foundation, Ayman moved across to an administrative role and supported me in overseeing the Project. For six years, Ayman was intimately involved with everything I was engaged with, and had a direct overview of almost all aspects of the Foundation's work. He was also Secretary to the Board of Trustees, and was responsible for ensuring the correct governance of the Foundation. My role required me to visit a number of Muslim countries during this second phase, and Ayman's companionship, knowledge and 'adab' in dealing with scholars, politicians and other VIPs was key to my being able to function, and indeed enjoy the experience. Let us, however, once again return to 2001.

THE PROSPECTUS

On 26th February 2001 I flew out to Abu Dhabi, and spent the next few days working on a prospectus with Mohammed Suwaidi's IT Manager. In this prospectus we can see how the ambitions for the Golden Web were beginning to expand. The following encapsulated our vision:

> A NEW WAY OF USING THE INTERNET
>
> The usual way of using the Internet is to gather together a body of related information into a website, attach a search engine to it, and link to other websites for more information. In order to create the Golden Web, a far more sophisticated deployment of the Internet is required. The information first has to be gathered from institutions and individuals in many parts of the world on a continuous basis. For this, a remote access of entry for data is essential. This data then has to be indexed, geo-referenced and mapped. Only then does it become the Golden Web.
>
> This operation involves a tremendous collaboration between the different individuals and institutions involved in the process of research and discovery, and necessitates the establishment of a network of builder-users.

The prospectus included the development costs, and a timetable which envisioned the launch of the Golden Web in cyberspace within two and a half years. With a large budget to raise and an unrealistic timetable, Mohammed Suwaidi and I set out on what became a two-year tour of governments, foundations, institutions and individuals that could help build or fund our Golden Web.

However, I cannot leave 2001 without referring to 9/11. Abul Qasim had organized the filming of the restoration of a dhow on the Syrian coast, and had arranged for a team to film a group of the last of the traditional craftsmen at work. We were in our meeting room which had been turned into an editing suite, when the planes crashed into the buildings. The TV happened to be on for the news; the newscaster switched to New York, and we watched the drama unfold. Looking back, it was somehow appropriate that we were engaged with the restoration of a ship; the Golden Web was like an ark which, for ten years, was to carry us across the turbulent waters that followed 9/11, as Islam became the big issue and the war on 'Islamic terrorism' raged.

SEEKING SUPPORT

Mohammed Suwaidi now set about opening up all the contacts that he deemed could advance our cause. Over the next two and a half years, from January 2002 to June 2004, he arranged ten trips, which we either went on together, or which I made alone. We began by introducing the Golden Web to senior figures in the government of the UAE, and the Emirates of Abu Dhabi, Dubai and Sharjah.

Our next trip found us in Egypt and Algeria. In Cairo we made a presentation to the Secretary General of the Arab League, and Mohammed gave a dinner for a group of poets, literati and artists. We then travelled to Algiers and were accommodated in a government guest house, surrounded by a beautiful wood. After a visit to the casbah, which was familiar to me from the 1960s film 'The Battle for Algiers', we met with the Prime Minister and then the President. The latter had sought refuge in Abu Dhabi during the war with France, and become a close friend of Mohammed's father and his family. The presidential jet flew us down into the desert, close by the Moroccan border, and we travelled by car along an incredible oasis which stretched for some seventy miles above an underground river. The trees and vegetation were only a few hundred metres wide, and on one side there were black granite hills rising up, and on the other side, sand dunes rippling into the distance. We arrived at a desert town on the old trade route through to the Sahel. Here we visited a large zawiya, in the process of being restored, with accommodation for many visitors, which had been created in the 19th century by a merchant who carried Islam wherever he went. I remember Uthman, my friend from Darfur, telling me that the people of his area had received their Islam very recently from the Maghreb, and not from Egypt. Perhaps this was the merchant who had brought Islam with him on one of his trading ventures. This excursion into the desert concluded our memorable visit to Algeria.

The third trip took us to Kuwait, Oman and Saudi Arabia. In Kuwait we met with Shaykha Hussa al-Sabah, co-founder of Dar al-Athar al-

Islamiyah with her husband Shaykh Nasser Al-Sabah. They had created one of the first major collections of Islamic art to have been made after the World of Islam Festival, and their centre was to become an important showcase for the dissemination of Islamic art and culture. In Oman we met the cultural advisor to the Sultan. In my presentation I mentioned Imam al-Ghazali, and it was as though I had trodden on a landmine; the advisor exploded, stating that he, Imam Al-Ghazali, had been responsible for the stagnation and decline of Islam after the Golden Age. I trod gingerly through the rest of my presentation! This critical question of the Golden Age of Islam and the hold it has over the Muslim imagination is a matter that I address in Part Three of this book. In Saudi Arabia we met the Governor of Asir Province, and visited the Faisal Foundation where we made a presentation to the Director and his staff.

Trip number four took us to Tehran to make a presentation to the Director and members of the Dialogue Among Civilizations team. This visionary project was initiated by the former Iranian President, Mohammed Khatami, as a response to Samuel P Huntingdon's theory of a 'clash of civilizations'.

In trips five and six I visited the Hariri Foundation in Lebanon, the Gulbenkian Foundation in Lisbon, and UNESCO in Paris. We then began to focus on Abu Dhabi for the funding that was becoming increasingly urgent. Trips seven to ten were taken up with meetings with various government personnel and agencies. But before I address these, we need to return to Cambridge where, in between the trips, I was being caught up in the technology fever that was sweeping the country.

TECHNOLOGY TO THE FORE

Cambridge University was at the centre of developments in IT and was brimming with excitement and activity during the early 2000s. We had a meeting with one of the pioneers of computing, Professor Roger Needham, who had been Head of the Computer Laboratory and Professor of Computer Systems, and was now the Managing Director of the Cambridge Microsoft Research Centre, the first to be set up outside the USA. Cambridge was selected to take advantage both of the University and Roger Needham's formidable brain.

One of the Cambridge academics who had embraced the new technology was Alan Macfarlane, Professor of Anthropological Science in the Department of Social Anthropology. His areas of research covered England, Nepal, Japan and China, and focused on a comparative study of the origins of the modern world. Together with Mark Turin, who had been his student, the Digital Himalaya Project was established. They would go on to set up the World Oral Literature Project which Alan would chair. I will introduce you to Mark Turin later in the next chapter.

The Professor was generous with his time and gave thought to how the Golden Web could be advanced. A strong recommendation was that we should definitely meet John Snyder, one of his former students, who had successfully developed a search engine called Muscat.

JOHN SNYDER

John Snyder and his wife Sarah are a remarkable couple. They met as undergraduates during their first year at Cambridge University, and immediately engaged in one of the strands that became a life's challenge. They had both already participated in aid projects in Africa and were not happy with the monochrome picture of starving children that was being depicted through the media. In response, John set up a project, with European Union funding, that aimed to demonstrate the other side of life to European school children. It was a multimedia project that showed the multiplicity of life in Africa. I was deeply affected by one of their productions. They had spent time in Mali and studied the relationship between the settled farmers and the nomadic herders. A perfect symbiosis existed between them until the development agencies appeared. The farmers would grow and harvest their crops, and then the nomad flocks would feed off the stubble and fertilize the land. This symbiosis had existed for ever, until the agencies convinced the government of Mali that the farmers could easily grow two or even three crops with modern methods. The intensification of crop production disrupted the traditional patterns, which then led to conflict between the farmers and the nomads. This brilliant piece of work opened my eyes to the realization that many of the outbreaks of conflict in Africa and elsewhere were down to the disruption of the traditional patterns relating to the land.

The conflict they had witnessed led to another strand in Sarah and John's life's work: conflict resolution. Sarah became involved in the Cambridge University Inter-Faith Project, and became the organizer of their Scriptural Reasoning Programme, in which representatives of different faith traditions would explain and discuss passages from their sacred books. This programme increasingly engaged student and public attendance, and even began to take place in prisons. When the University decided to concentrate on research and abandon the Scriptural Reasoning Programme, Sarah took it over and it has become a part of the work of the Rose Castle Foundation which Sarah established. The vision of the Foundation is to equip a generation of leaders to engage in reconciliation, and to cross divides.

The success of this amazing venture has been partly due to John Snyder's achievements as an entrepreneur in the world of IT, where he enjoyed a brilliant partnership with Martin F Porter, the inventor of Porter Stemmer, one of the most common algorithms for stemming English. Porter was also a graduate from Cambridge University, and had been awarded his PhD at the Cambridge Computer Laboratory. I met John in the interregnum between his selling Muscat for several million pounds and his next endeavour, Grapeshot, being purchased in 2018 for several hundred million.

The Golden Web contained several of John's areas of interest. He was already well versed in the subject matter, and the technical challenge intrigued him. However, he was keen to approach the Golden Web in terms of its viability as a business model. He was at the time giving a course on entrepreneurship at the recently established Cambridge Entrepreneurship Centre. He invited me along to several one-on-one sessions. In essence, it seemed to me, the art of business was to come up with a bright idea, develop it to the point where it could be seen to be viable, and then choose the right moment for your 'exit strategy', selling it for a humongous amount of money – a far cry from my childhood memories of my father's family business! My father was concerned with the long term, now it appeared that business had become a way of making as much money as possible in the shortest possible time. My incapacity to turn the Golden Web into a viable business idea was exposed at a session where half a dozen young entrepreneurs were put through their paces and invited to deliver to John their 'elevator pitches'. This alludes to the speedy convincing of an investor, from the moment you enter the lift until you reach your floor. Depending on the height of the building, it still only gives you a very few minutes. I followed a gentleman who was proposing a new kind of radiator. I need hardly say my attempt could not compare with the crispness of his explanation. My sessions with John helped me clarify my thinking; the insight it gave me into how the modern businessman is expected to act made a valuable contribution to my understanding.

I attended a spine-chilling seminar at the Business School when a marketing chief from Coca Cola described how they entered new territories, giving as an example China. The language he used was derived from the battlefield: conquering new ground, eliminating competitors and introduction by stealth. He had a bottle of Coke beside him, and every so often he would take a sip. But the liquid did not appear to go down. During question time, I could not resist an attempt to break the mono-cultural order of the questions and discussion by asking him if he actually liked the stuff. My intervention was not well received. During the marketeer's battle briefing, all I could imagine was how, as Coke took over, thousands of vendors of pure, freshly squeezed juices would be going out of business. Already any idea that the business model could be applied to the Golden Web had disappeared. Mohammed and I had transformed our partnership into a foundation. The Golden Web Foundation was the vehicle that would now carry the Project through to its conclusion.

It was in October 2003 that John told me about a person he had in mind who could organize the IT that the Golden Web required. He knew him well and had worked with him in the past. He was presently employed; however, John was sure he would not be able to resist the lure of the Golden Web. What was special about this person was that he was not only an experienced IT manager, but he had studied history at university and was deeply interested in the subject. He would be a perfect fit for the Golden Web. Within a month a meeting had been arranged. It was exciting to be with someone who was at the cutting edge of this new world, and I was becoming enchanted. This enchantment was complete when the manager introduced the colleague with whom he was working, a brilliant physicist who had devised an advanced entity management system that appeared to be perfect for the realization of my vision for the Golden Web. I now began to work with the manager on a revised plan and budget. We would meet in the evenings and at weekends. It became clear that if we could achieve the breakthrough in Abu Dhabi, the manager and his colleague would be prepared to join the Golden Web.

Let us now return to Abu Dhabi and see what progress was being made to find a funder.

19

THE GOLDEN WEB PART IV

FROM CRISIS TO BREAKTHROUGH

THE BREAKTHROUGH that would secure the funding for the Project began in a lift in Abu Dhabi on 21st May 2003. It would, however, take another two years for it to be realized. As I entered the lift, I recognized a school friend from Lancing. Stefan Kemball had played Aaron to my Moses in *The First Born* by Christopher Fry, which had been the school play for 1959. We had not met since. After hailing each other, we retired to a coffee shop, and a rapid forty-odd years catch-up conversation ensued. I then told him about the Golden Web and our present search for funding. My friend, who was a writer, journalist and PR representative, had spent a number of years working in the Middle East, and knew his way around. He suggested we meet a colleague of his who knew the Abu Dhabi power structure extremely well. A week later a meeting had been arranged with Stefan's colleague who suggested a person whom she believed would be very interested in the Golden Web. The gentleman in question was a senior official, close to the Shaykhs, and immensely effective at getting things done. He was also interested in culture and the environment. I immediately approached Mohammed Suwaidi, who took the matter in hand. Within a week his office had organized a meeting, and I was sitting opposite a gentleman who was in a position to advance our project. He listened carefully to my exposition, and responded with grace, intelligence and encouragement. Mohammed Suwaidi then met with him, and we all dined together. It was clear that we had a new ally.

The course that was suggested we follow, was to put in a formal request to Shaykh Zayed, the Emir of Abu Dhabi. I should then brief several of the influential people around the Emir. I met with his translator, who had been with him for many years, and a scholar who was one of his key advisors. I also had several meetings with the Zayed Foundation. We then met with the officials in the Shaykh's office who looked after requests to the Emir, and began the process of preparing our case. I was fired up by the vision of my newly-acquired IT experts, and we put together an ambitious plan that we believed, if realized, could transform the understanding and place of Islam in world history. There followed a protracted process of meetings, reports and further meetings. A year passed and although we were given encouraging signs, we seemed to have somehow become marooned.

Another development was now seriously threatening the Project. Mohammed Suwaidi had been funding the Golden Web personally for four and a half years, and he had made it clear he was coming to the end of what he was prepared to do. He had a number of other projects that he was seeding, and had devoted far more to the Golden Web than he had initially intended. He was also becoming nervous of the direction in which I was now taking the project, believing that it should be developed in a simpler way, more like his al-Waraq website. His funding to the Golden Web ceased in June 2004, though he continued to do everything he could to support our application to the Emir.

We then entered an interregnum during which all those employed by the Golden Web had to seek other work. The team was temporarily disbanded, whilst I continued to negotiate with Shaykh Zayed's office. This interregnum would last a year and four months.

On the 2nd November 2004, the news of the death of Shaykh Zayed was announced. It was clear that he had been ailing for some time, which explained the slowing of the pace of our application. The death of Shaykh

Zayed was profoundly felt by his people. It took several months for the new regime in Abu Dhabi to bed down. Then, seven months after this momentous event, I was invited to Abu Dhabi by the senior official who had now risen to a position that enabled him to arrange the funding for the Golden Web.

Several months were spent in developing the plan and putting together the organization capable of delivering the project. By the beginning of 2006, premises had been secured, the staff recruited, and the work began.

REORGANIZATION

With the introduction of the Advanced Entity Management System, the structure of the Golden Web Foundation underwent a major change. The Foundation would now have two principal roles. The first was that its responsibility would be solely for the IT system. All the academic work would take place where it belonged, within universities and research institutions; the role of the Foundation would be to connect up the fruits of their labour.

The Foundation's second role would be to stimulate and support key projects being developed within these external institutions. The first of these undertakings was to move our core team of academics, Sally Church, Robert Harding, Paul Lunde, Jane McIntosh and Caroline Stone, into Wolfson College, at Cambridge University. The team worked under the name of 'Civilizations in Contact', and continued the collaboration they had enjoyed within the Golden Web Foundation. Their research included trade across the Iranian plateau and through the Gulf; the movement of pilgrims and merchants across the Indian Ocean; the routes taken by diplomatic missions to and from pre-modern China; and the development and administration of emporia in Southeast Asia and Japan. The group were engaged in organizing lectures, seminars and school programmes, and the production of a number of publications. 'Civilizations in Contact' continued to exist after the Golden Web Project closed and their work is still accessible online.

A SHROUD OVER THE GOLDEN WEB PROJECT

For six years, from 2006 to 2011, the Golden Web Project had all the support that it could possibly require for a successful outcome. The funders provided the management team with everything they requested. From the Board of Trustees to everyone working on the project, a spirit of dedication and commitment prevailed, and the will to succeed was never lacking. But it was not to be.

I have drawn a shroud over the failure of the Golden Web. As you may have noticed, I have not mentioned the names of many of those who became involved in this stage of the project. This is because a blow-by-blow account of what happened would not be germane to the whole purpose of my telling my story. What I wish to tease out are the invaluable insights and knowledge that each episode of my journey has contributed to my understanding, resulting in the thesis that underlies *Rethinking Islam & the West.* It has taken me time and heartache to come to terms with, and make sense of, what happened with the Golden Web, and to draw out the fruits of this momentous period of my life. As with all failures, the end was not happy, with everyone's expectations having been shattered, and a natural scattering of those who had been involved taking place. Having been the instigator and leader of the Project, its demise left me isolated and deeply saddened. However, before embarking on my reflections regarding the benefits which came out of this stage of the Golden Web, I need to look at the reasons for what happened, and place our failure within the context of the time.

REFLECTIONS

The demise of the Golden Web could be put down to the failure of the technology. We were certainly involved in ground-breaking work. It was a period in the evolution and application of innovative IT systems when there were more casualties than success stories. The NHS had to abandon a large part of its programme after spending many billions, the UK border Agency cancelled their project having spent several hundred million, and the BBC theirs, after a hundred million had been dispersed. Nearer home, Cambridge University Library had got into difficulties with its cataloguing system. One could put down the eventual demise of the Golden Web to the inevitable process of expectations outstripping the actual capabilities of what was, at the time, possible in IT.

But maybe there is a simpler reason why our Advanced Entity Management System could not be realized: it required active engagement from the participants who were entering the data, and the academics did not have a sufficient incentive to undertake the work required. Ross Dunn had explained to me that academics fall into two groups: the truffle hunters and the parachutists. Most academics and historians were truffle hunters, interested in going deep into their limited area of interest. Parachutists who endeavoured to understand the picture across time and space were rare. Our system required a mass uptake by the truffle hunters for it to be successful in its aim of to discover a multitude of hitherto unrealized connections. It was not suited to the academics with whom we wished to engage. Maybe the system could have been successful if it had been placed in an environment where the incentives to make the connections already existed. This, I believe explains why the system failed to be realized.

But Golden Web also failed to be realized as a cultural phenomenon, and this was due to certain fundamental errors of judgement I made along the way. What were these errors of judgement? The first was that I had not understood the true nature of the Web. You will recall that right at the beginning of my engagement with the internet, I embraced the idea that the good to be found within it was that it was a great connector. I envisaged a perfect marriage between the World Wide Web and the Golden Web. With the emergence of Myspace in 2003 and Facebook in 2004, the true nature of the Web began to be revealed. Far from being the great connector for humanity, it was manifesting itself as the great disintegrator, the perfect vehicle for the post-modern world: isolated users in front of their screens were encouraged and empowered to exist in their own little bubbles. When our IT team came up with Mygoldenweb, the divorce between my original concept and what was logically unfolding, following the trajectory of the technology, was complete. We had two Golden Webs: an IT System that had no boundaries and would be controlled by the user, and a cultural concept that was intended to deliver a particular way of looking at the past. By 2010 the problem had reached crisis point, and a charette was organized in Abu Dhabi to try and break the deadlock. The key players from the Golden Web were joined by outside experts and spent two days wrestling with the problem. The conclusion drawn was that there were, indeed, two Golden Webs! The tension between them was never resolved.

My second error was that, having become mesmerized by the medium, I had allowed the concept of the Golden Web to be stretched beyond its natural limits. The Golden Web was an historical concept bound by time and space. I had tried to turn it into an all-encompassing system that would be like another World Wide Web. Mohammed Suwaidi attempted to draw me away from this approach, and our scholars were also unhappy with the direction the project was taking. However, wild horses could not have diverted me from the inexorable path on which I was bound. Muhammed Suwaidi's love was with the content, and he went on to create a suite of websites under the title of the Electronic Village, in which a great wealth of literary, historical and poetic material resides, and some of the content from the Golden Web has found a home. Otherwise, the research papers and publications we produced are scattered amongst academic journals and various publishers. The good that had to exist in the Web was not in the system, but in certain silos that contained valuable information. The Golden Web should have been developed as a website, which could, over time, have grown into a major resource.

GOLDEN WEB ACHIEVEMENTS

Let us now turn our minds to the benefits that this stage of the Golden Web delivered. Several projects that we placed within the institutions yielded valuable research and publications, and a programme devoted to the Living Traditions also garnered rich rewards. Let us begin with some of the researchers and their projects.

ANTHONY MILROY

Most people in the pre-modern world worked on the land, and the understanding of traditional husbandry had become an important part of the Golden Web. Tony Milroy's brilliant work in Yemen, captured in the documentary film 'Hanging Gardens of Arabia', and his other projects were brought together in a website which we sponsored. Tony then began a collaboration with Dr Karim Lahham, who produced several research papers, documenting the attempts made to recover the traditional systems of husbandry, after the assault of modern agribusiness. I will introduce Karim to you in Part 3 when he played a key role in my story.

SIMON FITZWILLIAM-HALL

Simon Fitzwilliam-Hall was one of the first group of Golden Web scholars who came together in 2000, and was to make an important contribution to our study of traditional husbandry. He joined us after having spent fifteen years in Saudi Arabia, where he was the head of geography at the Manarat International School in Jeddah. He was the exception to our rule, and was our only in-house researcher. He developed two very valuable initiatives. The first was 'The Filaha Texts Project', which was realized as a website, and is still accessible online. The project has undertaken the translation, elucidation and publishing of the *Kutub al-Filaha* or 'Books of Husbandry', compiled by Arab, especially Andalusi, agronomists mainly between the 10th and 14th centuries. They not only provide primary source material for the understanding of what has been called the 'Islamic Green Revolution', but also constitute a rich body of knowledge concerning a traditional system of husbandry which is as valid today as it was a thousand years ago and has much relevance to future sustainable agriculture.

Simon's other major project was the result of a field trip to Southern Morocco, where he studied the water systems *(khettaras)* which feed the desert oasis cities along the ancient trade routes to the Sahel, and are now threatened with extinction. The oasis gardens, fed by the underground khettaras, which draw their water from distant mountains, developed an incredibly productive multi-layered system that made maximum use of the terrain in a sustainable manner. Several articles and a rich pictorial documentation came out of the study. Tony Milroy had explained to me how many of the oasis settlements were man-made. By bringing the water into the desert, these remarkable farmer-gardeners had made the desert bloom. Simon's work had brought this alive for me. Some of the articles documenting his work are available online.

KIRTI NARAYAN CHAUDHURI

The next scholar who played an important part in my education is Kirti Narayan Chaudhuri. Ranked 57 on the Daily Telegraph's list of the 'Top 100 Living Geniuses', he is a historian, writer, graphic artist and film-maker. He is the author of several historical monographs, over thirty artist's books, and the director of twelve feature films.

Chaudhuri was deeply affected by the historical approach of Fernand Braudel, brilliantly illustrated in Braudel's magnus opus *The Mediterranean and the Mediterranean World in the Age of Philip II.* Braudel had approached the Mediterranean Sea and its people as a unity. Chaudhuri followed the same approach in his magnificent, *Trade and Civilization in the Indian Ocean; an Economic History from the Rise of Islam to 1750.* This book is one of a handful of academic works that deeply affected my understanding. In a meticulous feat of analysis, he showed how the great pre-modern trading system was maintained through a process of collaboration. When the Europeans arrived in the Indian Ocean it became a theatre for competition, conflict and conquest. The great change that took place is stark, a seminal moment being the conquest of Bengal by the British.

It reminded me of an incident during another dramatic time of change which I witnessed in Jeddah at the end of the 1970s. I was sitting with a group of merchants who until recently had been modest traders with their small shops in the souk; now they were becoming mega-rich merchants controlling car, cement and other lucrative franchises. I asked them, 'Was it better before or is it better now?'. After a pregnant silence, as the question filtered through, an elderly member of the group spoke. 'It was better before', he said, and then went on to give an illustration of why it was better. 'We were all grouped together in our various trades. The first sale of the day had a particular *baraka.* If we had made our first sale, and noticed that a neighbour had not, we would direct the next customer who approached us, to go to our neighbour's stall. Today,' he stated emphatically – 'impossible!' The other merchants nodded their heads in agreement. Then another of the company related how if a merchant fell on hard times, they would club together to put him back on his feet. And so, the floodgates were opened and I sat transfixed as the stories continued, bringing back to life a world governed by criteria that emanated from Islam and the practice of the Prophet, blessings and peace be upon him. These merchants were experiencing the abrupt change from a collaborative way of life to one determined by rivalry and the 'survival of the fittest'.

We were very fortunate in that Chaudhuri visited the Golden Web on several occasions, giving a workshop and producing an overview paper for us. I also made a memorable visit to his home in Avignon, where he was beginning his period as a graphic artist and fine book publisher. I was glad that we encountered him when we did.

THE MARES PROJECT

Professor Dionysius Agius was another active participant in the Golden Web. I first met him when he was Professor of Arabic at Leeds University, after which he moved to Exeter University and we embarked on a very productive collaboration. Dionysius belongs to a rare group of academics who engage with several disciplines in order to capture the traditional knowledge of worlds that are fast disappearing.

From 2008 to 2011, the Golden Web Foundation jointly funded with the Seven Pillars of Wisdom Trust, the Mares Project. Dionysius had gathered a small group of postgraduate researchers and embarked on an ambitious multi-disciplinary, multi-period project, focusing on the maritime traditions of the peoples of the Red Sea. Drawing on ethnography, archaeology, history and linguistics, it sought to understand how people inhabited and navigated these seascapes in late antiquity and the medieval period, and how they continue to do so today. Meetings were held in Exeter and Cambridge, and it was fascinating to witness the way the project evolved, and to watch the skill with which Dionysius guided and inspired his team.

LANGUAGES IN CONTACT

Professor Geoffrey Khan, who had introduced me to the Genizah Texts, was a great supporter of the Golden Web, and we developed the idea of a programme entitled 'Languages in Contact'. He chaired, in Cambridge, the first of what was hoped would be a continuing series of seminars which would bring together scholars engaged in the field. This inaugural gathering included Professor Clive Holes from Oxford University, who specializes in the Arabic language and its dialects, and Professor Janet Watson from Salford University whose work includes the Yemeni Arabic dialects. Janet went on to found, with Professor Jon Lovett, 'The Centre for Endangered Languages, Cultures and Ecosystems' at Leeds University. There was a keen sense that just as there was a mass extinction of flora and fauna taking place, the same thing was happening with languages. The scholars were engaged in a race against time, as the vast knowledge contained within these linguistic universes was vanishing. Our primary interest was the rich tapestry of connections that had grown up between them over time.

The Golden Web Foundation jointly funded with the Newton Trust a research project which focused on the endangered dialects of Aramaic. Geoffrey Khan was the principal investigator, supported by Dr Alinda Damsma, research fellow. Aramaic, which was the language spoken by Jesus Christ, had been the lingua franca across the Middle East before the rise of Islam. With the political upheavals of the 20th century, the remaining Aramaic-speaking communities had been scattered across the world. The language contained within it a rich history of the settled populations of the Middle East's engagement with Islam. One of the major outcomes from the research was the linguistic evidence that Islam, for the most part, spread gradually amongst them over centuries.

MARK TURIN

It is at this juncture I would like to introduce Mark Turin. After establishing the Digital Himalaya Project with Alan Macfarlane at Cambridge University, he went on in 2009 to set up the World Oral Literature Project, for the documentation and preservation of oral literatures and endangered cultural traditions. Passing from Cambridge to Yale and then to the University of British Columbia, where he now resides, Mark has continued to build support for this project. For over twenty years, Mark's own research focus has been the languages of the Himalayan region, and, more recently, the Pacific Northwest of North America. Mark has carried his mission beyond academia to the general public through publications, radio, television, and social media.

Mark was closely involved in 'Communities in Symbiosis', a project we were seeding shortly before the demise of the Golden Web.

COMMUNITIES IN SYMBIOSIS

What sparked my interest in this project was a reporter's interview with a Kosovan farmer in a BBC documentary about the war. The farmer was lamenting the ripping apart of his village community. He related how Muslims and Christians had lived peacefully side by side for generations. He then went on to describe a remarkable ceremony that bound them together. When a baby is born in a Muslim home, one of the first acts is to cut a piece of hair from the child's head. The farmer related how they would invite a member from the Christian community to perform this ceremony. There happened to be a scholar from Bosnia at Cambridge at the time, and I told him about this extraordinary practice. He was not surprised, and said that they had the same tradition in Bosnia. He went on to tell me about other examples of symbiosis between the communities. I already knew of many examples of the way the communities in India were bound together, before divide and rule poisoned their world. This was surely a really important theme for the Golden Web to pursue. We prepared a proposal that outlined the critical need to explore the many ways in which different faith communities, ethnic groups and ways of life have peacefully co-existed and collaborated with each other, rather than focusing on the tensions and divisions that push communities apart.

The following projects had been identified and summaries prepared by the scholars wishing to undertake the research; 'Living in Balance: Himalayan Partnerships', by Dr Mark Turin; 'The Case of Bosnia', by Dr Asim Zubevic; 'Abd Al-Ghani Al-Nabulusi: Understanding the religious other', by Dr Lejla Demiri; and 'Arab-Jewish Communities: Within and Outside Arab Lands', by Dr Merav Rosenfeld Haddad. It was a great sadness that this initiative was buried in the closure that took place shortly after we had completed the proposal.

SUPPORTING PHDS

An effective way of engaging young scholars in the Golden Web was to support Golden Web themed PhDs. Our first and only venture in this area was with Samir Mahmud, a remarkable young scholar, who was born in Lebanon, and whose family then moved to Australia. Samir's wide interests had already garnered diplomas and degrees in Economics, Sociology & Anthropology, Politics & Development Studies, Architectural History & Theory, and Urban Design, when, in 2005, he arrived in Cambridge. Samir was awarded his Master of Philosophy in Comparative Philosophy in 2006, and his PhD in Theology & Religious Studies, in 2012. His thesis was supervised by Abdal Hakim Winter, and part funded by the Golden Web Foundation. The title of his thesis was 'The Art of Remembrance, and the Aesthetic of Unity'. He focused his research on the relationship between the mystical philosophy of Ibn Arabi and beauty. It was rare to see beauty and the intellect brought together.

Samir became a close family friend and companion on my journey. Annabel and Samir shared their love of Sufism and with another colleague began a Sufi Texts reading group, which attracted the handful of scholars in Cambridge engaged in the subject. He was one of those with whom I could allow my thoughts to roam and crystallize, and we would meet on Sundays in the upper room in Nero's coffee house. Fortunately, we (the Golden Web) were able to complete our part of the funding for his PhD and contribute to the launching of a very special scholar.

We now come to what I came to realize was at the very heart of the Golden Web.

THE LIVING TRADITIONS PROGRAMME

The many traditional cultures and civilizations of the Golden Web have been disappearing at an escalating rate since the European conquests. What remains are isolated islands in a sea of modernity. Our attempt to understand the Golden Web, a world that was very different in practically every way from our modern existence, engaged many academic disciplines. The written, material and living evidence was studied, researched and analysed by a host of academics, including anthropologists and ethnographers, language and literature specialists, archaeologists, historians and geographers, sociologists and psychologists, and those engaged in religious studies. All of these contributed to our field of study.

However, these multiple ways of studying the other depend for their veracity upon the perspective of the scholar. Where the scholar is coming from will inevitably colour his or her understanding. Modern academia prizes what is seen as an objective outsider viewpoint, and, depending upon the character and empathy of the scholar, valuable insights can be garnered. As you will have seen from my journey, I have received so much from the many scholars I have encountered. However, their knowledge is of a different order from the living and experienced knowledge of the practitioners who are inside a culture. It was to explore this living dimension of the Golden Web that I established the Living Traditions Programme. I began by bringing together the traditional practitioners, scholars and friends who had informed my understanding over decades. A circle of some twenty participants came together several times during the final years of the Golden Web.

OPENING EVENT

With the project entering a new phase, we moved to a larger house in one of the villages, where we could entertain and hold small gatherings. The first of the Living Tradition circles took place in our new home. It was a beautiful summer day. Warwick Pethers gave an inspiring lecture about the building of the tower of St Edmundsbury Cathedral, and in the evening, Mahmud Mirza gave a wonderful concert. Mahmud's tradition is a perfect example of the Golden Web. He traces his musical ancestry back to the great 13th century Turkish poet, musician, scholar and courtier, Amir Khosrow. The court music of the Delhi Sultans and after them the Mughal emperors, assembled Turkish, Arab, Persian and Hindu musicians, and a synthesis was formed that perfectly manifested the Indian Islamic aesthetic; what was produced in sound is the equivalent of the Taj Mahal in architecture.

CANON WYATT'S CHURCH

The second of our gatherings took place at Canon Wyatt's church in Salford. Once again, it was a beautiful day. We lunched in the walled garden, overlooked by the tower blocks. Canon Wyatt gave a talk in the church about its restoration. He then invited my son Ali to recite the Holy Qur'an. After Ali's recitation of the Verse of Light, his eldest son, who was just emerging from childhood, recited a few verses. On a second visit to Salford, Canon Wyatt took us to another church for which he had been handed responsibility. This great Victorian Gothic edifice stood alone surrounded by a whole district that had been bulldozed to make way for a new housing estate. Once again, Canon Wyatt had stepped in to save the demolition of the church. A wonderful project was taking place on the land around the building. Anthony Milroy had designed a Paradise Garden which was in the process of being planted. Tony had already galvanized volunteers in the community and young people on work experience to join in.

One of the members of our Living Traditions circle was the Golden Web Foundation's Chairman of Trustees, George Windsor, Earl of St Andrews. George is a scholar and resident of Cambridge. He received his MA in history from Cambridge University, and then served for a time in the Diplomatic Service. George's knowledge and experience were a tremendous support in steering the Golden Web along its eventful path. The Foundation had contributed a small grant to the Paradise Garden, and George was with us to see the progress that was being made. It was heartening to witness another of the fine Gothic churches being brought back to life under the wing of Canon Wyatt. But they were small shoots in an otherwise bleak picture for the traditional architecture of the Church of England.

TRADITIONAL ENGLISH MOSQUE

St Edmundsbury Cathedral had just sacked the last remaining master of the Gothic tradition, at the point when most of the work had been completed, and, no doubt, they imagined they could dispense with his services. Warwick had produced his masterpiece, but the Church seemed determined that this would be the last in the Gothic tradition. From now on, modernity would reign supreme. I invited Warwick into the Living Traditions Programme with the idea of exploring the creation of the traditional English mosque. Here was the opportunity to do what had naturally taken place whenever Islam arrived in a new land and engaged with the existing culture. My imagination envisaged a flowering of Islamic architecture, that would demonstrate that Islam belonged in our green and pleasant land, and was not a foreign visitor.

ENTER THE MACHINE

Meanwhile, something terrible was striking at the very heart of both the Gothic and Islamic traditions of architecture. The machine was taking over the role of the craftsman and woman. The final act that was required to complete the work at Bury St Edmunds was the creation of the vault of heaven or ceiling of the interior of the tower. This was a wooden structure that had to be drawn up by pulleys into its position. It should have been a beautifully crafted, painted and gilded work of art. Instead, it is a laser-produced facsimile, finished with gold paint instead of gold leaf.

My first experience of this phenomenon in Islamic architecture was in the Gulf, where a group from the Golden Web were being shown around a recently-built mosque. Our guide excitedly drew our attention to the great doors, and said that they had been made with the latest laser technology. 'What would have taken months to produce by hand', he proudly stated, 'was done in weeks, at a fraction of the cost.' The doors were made from the finest hard wood. However, the machine-made transfer that had been laminated upon them, gave the wood the appearance of plastic. The doors were dead, bereft of the *baraka* of the hand and soul of the craftsman. This iniquitous process has now become standard. Designers formulate the pattern, and the machine does the rest. Even calligraphy is being produced in the same way. A famous calligrapher traditionally would have a workshop full of apprentices. Now he has machines that take his pieces and blow them up to the required size for whatever mosque or palace he may be working on. The machine is draining away the connection with heaven that we need and yearn for in our places of worship.

RETURN TO MY BIRTH TRADITION

I was keen to understand what was taking place in my birth tradition and I had the perfect teacher. I went with Warwick to Windsor. I wanted to show him the beautiful little church of my childhood. As we approached, the building appeared abandoned. On entering, we found the main aisle and choir had been cleared to provide a space for netball and other games. The marks where the altar had been ripped out from the wall were clearly visible. The beauty that informed my childhood was no more.

I had not been back to Lancing College since I had left the school, and I wanted to see the Chapel through Warwick's eyes. After all, it was his master, Dykes Bower, who had produced the designs for the completion of the West End. We met the chaplain, who explained the way the Chapel was now used, and it became clear that the place of worship in the life of the school had gone through a radical change. No longer did the school gather for morning and evening prayers each day, and three times on Sundays. Now they assembled as a body once a week on a Thursday. He took us into the Crypt which was clearly the most active part of the building. Here, each house would have a weekly service, and other services were held for those who wished to attend. It seemed that Christianity had retreated back into the catacombs. This loss of confidence was clearly manifested in the new plans for the completion of the West End. After Dykes Bower's magnificent rose window was completed, his plans for the narthex or entrance area to the Chapel were abandoned. This would have provided a suitably spacious antechamber to such a magnificent building. Nathanial Woodard, the founder of the school, made sure his vision would not be reduced after his death, by first building the East End to its full height, as high as Westminster Abbey. With the reduced new design for the entrance to the West End now being built, it is clear that the founder's vision has finally run out of steam. When I was at Lancing, there was a covered wooden cloister that connected the Chapel with the main school. Now the area between the Chapel and the school is the domain of the car. The Chapel stands alone and pupils have to brave the elements to gain access. The Chapel, having been at the centre of the life of the school, now finds itself, in all its magnificence, on the periphery.

EL-WAKIL & THE OXFORD ISLAMIC CENTRE

One of the most memorable of our Living Traditions events was a visit to the Oxford Islamic Centre. The Centre was founded in 1985, and came to national attention in 1993 when the Prince of Wales, who had become its Patron, gave his lecture, 'Islam and the West'. Our visit was to the site, where a new complex, designed by Abdel-Wahed El-Wakil, was being built.

Several years before, I had seen the plans for the complex. El-Wakil had maintained an apartment in Folkstone since 1982, and it was on one of my many visits to see him that I was privileged to have the plans explained to me. El-Wakil's apartment was in one of those massive, Edwardian hotels that had commanded the sea front when Folkstone had been a fashionable resort, and had now been turned into flats. He was on the third floor and a number of corridors had to be navigated before arriving at his front door. I was always on high alert when awaiting his response to my knocking, as every meeting with him was an occasion to be savoured. On this particular occasion, when showing me the plans for the Oxford Islamic Centre, he explained how the use of brick and stone had to be modulated. Stone should only appear at important moments, such as the main entrance gate and the mosque. On the walls of the room in which we sat and talked, were hung beautiful water colours of his buildings by the artist Ed Venn. From the balcony adjoining the room we could enjoy the view of the sea, and on a clear day, the outline of the French coast. It was in this room that I imbibed so much of my understanding of traditional architecture and much more besides. I was in the presence of a great artist and human being. Few visits would take place without him disappearing into the kitchen and producing a delicious meal, with its centrepiece, a freshly-caught fish.

Let us return to our visit to the building site. The main structures had been erected, and it was clear that what we were seeing differed from the plans I had seen in El-Wakil's studio. Stone seemed to predominate over the brick, and the subtle play between brick and stone in the drawings had been lost. The minaret, which was beautifully proportioned in the drawings, had been truncated; there had been objections to the height of the minaret, and so it had been cut down. El-Wakil's discomfort with these changes was evident; they had been made over his head. When I finally visited the Centre, after it had been completed, the craft finishing of the project seemed a mess. It was a far cry from the interiors of El-Wakil's mosques in Saudi Arabia, where he orchestrated the various crafts into a symphony of beauty and unity. Those running the Centre had decided to do their own thing and give the different parts of the complex to the areas of the Islamic world that sponsored them.

I had seen the Tower at Bury St Edmunds, the completion of the West End of Lancing Chapel and now the Oxford Islamic Centre, all spoiled by the authorities over-riding the wisdom and knowledge of the traditional master architects. Despite this, all three buildings still stand as beacons of beauty in the growing desert of modernity.

SPAIN

Another of our Living Traditions Circles took place in Spain. Our son Ali had moved with his family from Damascus to Granada. He arranged for our party to stay in one of the traditional Arab houses of the city, and organized a ten-day programme for us. We visited the Alhambra, with its glorious gardens, and went on a day trip to Cordoba, where we stood in awe before the mihrab of the great mosque, which El-Wakil had described to me as one of the wonders of Islamic architecture.

The high point of the visit was a lecture prepared by Anthony Milroy. He showed how the farmers of Yemen and Syria had brought their knowledge and techniques to southern Spain and turned it into a Garden of Eden, which later decayed after the expulsion of the Muslims. Derelict water systems illustrated this sad demise. But the really significant aspect of his talk was to demonstrate the superiority of traditional husbandry over the modern systems now taking over the world. He showed how in terms of sustainability, the health of communities, the environment, and long-term productivity, the traditional methods of farming far outshone the modern. The great difference was that the traditional systems needed people, lots of people, to perform the tasks, whereas the modern was increasingly dependent on the machine for its commercial viability. The propaganda that props up this sick modern system of chemical farming is, of course, so massive and powerfully funded that it is difficult to counter the myths that have been spun. But in time, the work of people like Tony must break through if we are not to end up poisoning the earth irrevocably. It was instructive to have seen the remains of the civilization that Islam had left behind in Spain, and learn about the high farming culture that supported this magnificent manifestation.

It was also in Spain that Mahmud Mirza gave a series of recitals at different times of the day at the Azzagra Cultural Foundation, which we recorded. He also gave a rare interview describing the master musician's understanding of the history of his tradition. The Foundation was an inspiring and wonderful setting for the occasion: the 117-hectare farm is set in the foothills of the Sierra de La Sagra. Abdus Samad Romero's family turned the farm into a charitable trust in 1993, and since then, Abdus Samad has transformed the holding into a beautiful and thriving cultural and religious centre, where courses, retreats, seminars and other events take place.

UTHMAN SAYYID AHMAD ISMAIL AL-BILI

Another of the remarkable men I encountered during this phase of the Golden Web was Professor Uthman Sayyid Ahmad Ismail al-Bili, the director of the Centre for Muslim Contribution to Civilization in Doha, Qatar. I met Al-Bili through Ayman Haleem who was part of the team of scholars who translated *The Perfect Guide to the Sciences of the Qur'an, (Al-itqan fi 'ulum al-Qur'an)*, by Imam Jalal al-Din al-Suyuti, which was the first volume in the Centre's series, 'The Great Books of Islamic Civilization.' Al-Bili had been Professor of Islamic and Middle East History at Ahmadu Bello University in Nigeria, before moving to Qatar. He had a refreshing perspective, and his book *Some Aspects of Islam in Africa* was part of an effort to establish an independent and indigenous school of African history that sees history through African eyes, and presents it in such a way as to include internal written and oral traditions. I would pass by Doha on my frequent visits to the Gulf to visit El-Wakil, who had become the Professor of Architecture at the University of Qatar, and on one of these trips, I made contact with Al-Bili. From the moment I met him, my heart was opened. I could listen to his stories for hours. But it was the description of his childhood in his ancestral village in Sudan that transfixed me.

He was born in 1930, so his childhood took place before WWII. His village was south of Khartoum beside the Nile. I asked him what was the most powerful memory of his childhood, and he said it was the feeling of security. 'You could roam anywhere around the village and you would be completely safe', he reflected. He described how the day was defined by the rhythm of the prayers. I asked him 'Wasn't the work in the fields hard?' He answered 'Yes, but we made light of it by doing it together and singing!' Disputes would be resolved by the elders, sitting in the mosque. The fertility of the land provided everything that was required to feed and clothe the community. The essential crafts of pottery, metalwork and carpentry were carried out by skilled members of the community who would be paid in products; very little money exchanged hands. Money was used for taxes paid to the government and the purchase of what could not be produced by the community. He described a happy, healthy and fulfilling way of life. 'Our village was an extended family. When I tell my children about my childhood, they imagine it's a fable, that I'm making it up,' he sadly recalled. They may well think so, for the change that has overtaken Al-Bili's village has wiped out the village of his childhood. Because of the fertility of the land, the government has turned it over to the intensive production of cash crops. The dereliction and dislocation that inevitably follows has all but wiped out what was a sustainable, God-centred, meaningful way of life.

Al-Bili had a connection to Cambridge, and I was fortunate that he visited the University shortly before he died. I asked him if I could film an interview with him. I wanted to capture his description of his childhood. He said he would be very happy to put on record his memories, for his family and future generations. Abul Qasim set up the cameras in my sitting room and I was able to capture something of this wonderful man.

THE FINAL LIVING TRADITIONS CIRCLE

The last of our Living Traditions Circle took place at Cambridge University and was part of a two-day seminar. On the first day we gathered together the various Golden Web research projects, with each giving a progress report. On the second day we held a round-table Living Traditions discussion. The event was tinged with sadness as the writing was on the wall, and it would not be long before this golden period of encounters would draw to an end.

One of those present at this final meeting was the person who had been my friend and companion during the Traditions of Mankind projects, Anderson Bakewell. One of his areas of interest had been the ships of the Indian Ocean. Not, however, being satisfied with just studying them, he had gone about actually constructing a great ocean-going dhow, probably the last of its kind to be built.

SANJEEDA

The construction of the dhow, named Sanjeeda, began in January 2000 in Mandvi under the supervision of Ibrahim Mistry, a master shipwright who had served as apprentice in the 1950s to his father. She was built by hand, without power tools, by an average of 25 men working over 16 months. The ship was spared during a severe earthquake in January 2001, and despite the interruption, was launched on the 8th of May, later that year, just in time to avoid the arrival of the southwest monsoon winds which annually force the closing of the ports of western India. Fitted out in Dubai, and later adorned with fine wood-carving in Mangalore, South India, Sanjeeda was operated until 2007 as a charter and expedition vessel in the western Indian Ocean, sailing between India, Sri Lanka, the Maldives, the Persian Gulf, Oman, Aden, the Seychelles and East Africa. Anderson then sold the vessel, and proceeded to engage with his next project.

His love of the Scottish Islands had resulted, as I described earlier, in his purchasing the Isle of Scarp, a small uninhabited island off Harris, in the 1990s. Alarmed by the exodus of young people from the islands, and wishing to give something back, he set up the Isle of Harris Distillery. The water and ingredients, mostly sourced locally, produce the finest whisky. The distillery is already the largest employer on the island and has won several awards.

Anderson explained in a letter to me how his projects had linked together:

> The inspiration for constructing Sanjeeda was my musical work around the coasts of the Indian Ocean, and particularly the difficulty of access to various remote places. I was also being drawn into the cultural and trading sphere that it represented (which we had so often discussed with Kirti Chaudhury) and wanted to get to know this 'from the inside', as it were. It's an interesting coincidence that the 18th century house we're restoring on the Isle of Harris was built by Capt. Alexander MacLeod, a servant of the East India Company who sailed in the Indian Ocean throughout his career. A day spent at the British Library with his journals and ships' logs was a revelation, as they recounted such similar experiences and challenges to mine, in many cases at the same ports.

THE HEART OF THE WORLD

It was Anderson Bakewell who had made an introduction that would lead me to another seminal moment in my education. It took place back in 1991 when he invited me to accompany him to a summer fair in a village outside Oxford. He wanted me to meet a filmmaker who was appearing at the event along with his latest production. The filmmaker was Alan Eriera and the film *From the Heart of the World – the Elder Brother's Warning*. What I was to see was a revelation. The film begins with the description of what can only be described as a microcosm of the earth:

> Imagine a pyramid standing alone by the sea, each side a hundred miles long. It's a mountain nearly four miles high. In its folds, imagine every different climate on earth. This is the Sierra Nevada de Santa Marta and the people hidden here call the Sierra the Heart of the World and themselves the Elder Brothers.

The twenty thousand or so members of this remarkable community are the descendants of the Tairona civilization which inhabited cities in the valleys and by the sea in what is now Columbia. For a time, when the Spanish arrived, they held their territory. However, they realized they were going to be overwhelmed, so they withdrew into the mountain fastness. There, for four hundred years, forgotten to history, they have continued their way of life. They are the only high civilization of the Americas that survived the Iberian holocaust.

It was when the Kogi, as they are now known, realized their mountain was dying, that they decided to send a message to those who they knew were responsible for what was happening. They call us, the ones who with our machines are destroying the earth, the 'Younger Brothers'. Serendipity was at work! It so happened that at the same time, Alan Eriera was making a film for the BBC about the Tairona cities which had recently been discovered. For hundreds of years, they had been lost to view in the tropical forest. Alan had heard about the people in the mountain and wanted to engage with them. An emissary, who spoke Spanish, was sent by the Kogi to meet with Alan, and it was agreed that he could make one visit to the Kogi so that they could deliver their message to the world.

Alan entered the realm of a people who were spiritually advanced and clearly had a far deeper understanding of the natural world than we can ever discover through our material sciences. Their stark message was that if Younger Brother did not start behaving properly, our world would be destroyed. They allowed Alan to see into their world, and took the trouble to explain everything to him. Their intelligence, generosity and humility shines through, and by the time Alan was ready to leave, he had clearly become passionate about their message. The film is a treasure, which reveals fresh insights every time I view it.

Needless to say, their message was lost in the noise of the modern media. Troubled by the lack of response and seeing the destruction intensifying around the base of their mountain and on the coast, the Kogi invited Alan Ereira back. It was twenty years since the first film, and the Kogi were moved to make another attempt to try and get through the gravity of the situation to Younger Brother. It was in 2008, when Alan was putting together support for this new film, that I invited him to Cambridge as part of the Living Traditions Programme. After a viewing of *From the Heart of the World – the Elder Brother's Warning*, Alan introduced the subject of the latest Kogi initiative. The Kogi were making one last attempt to save the world. This time they would try to show how their sacred environment is connected up, and how Younger Brother is destroying the links which hold everything together. With a golden thread, spun out from a spindle, they would take us on a journey, laying a trail along the coast which links the sacred sites. They would then explain the significance of these sites for the health of the whole mountain, and why the destruction of the sites is affecting the cycle of water, from the sea, into the clouds, which then falls as snow on top of the mountain. The sacred and the materially intelligible are perfectly combined. Once again Alan Eriera has produced a masterpiece; *Aluna: a Journey to Save the World,* beautifully and hauntingly articulates the profound message the Kogi have for us.

My encounter with some of the last remaining masters of the traditional arts has made me acutely conscious of the speed with which all traces of a tradition can disappear. In my childhood, the Gothic tradition of architecture in the Church was everywhere intact, and was the norm. Now only one architect, who has been fully trained in the system and who has reached the degree of master, remains: Warwick Pethers.

USTAD MAHMUD MIRZA

It was in 1997 that it was brought home to me just how rare Ustad Mahmud Mirza had become. He was in Delhi during the 50th Anniversary of Indian Independence. There were a number of musical events taking place, engaging all of the leading musicians of the time. It was a perfect moment to assess the health of the great tradition of North Indian Classical music. The prevailing atmosphere was of a new world of entertainment with its accompanying adulation of the stars. Kuldeep Kumar, a leading critic from the prestigious The Hindu newspaper, bemoaned the poor fare that was on offer, and went on to say:

> Against the gloomy backdrop of culture turning into crass commerce came a very heartening sitar recital, which assured that all the good old-world values had not been lost. Mahmud Mirza, an exceptionally gifted musician, offered a wonderful evening of classical music. A true votary of tradition, Mirza abhors gimmickry and media hype. He has been living in the United Kingdom for more than three decades, but this has not affected his art in any adverse manner. He showed how beautiful music could be created by taking a plunge into the unknown terrain of creative expression. Perhaps I will be able to tell you more about him some other time.

It would, however, be another nine years before Kuldeep Kumar would have the opportunity of hearing Mahmud play again in Delhi. Always inspired by the city where he was born and grew up, and never losing his Indian roots, Mahmud's visits to Delhi were an essential part of his musical life. But lack of funds had denied his return until 1996, when the Golden Web took off.

For the next nine years, until his eightieth birthday, Mahmud made annual visits, to the delight of Kuldeep Kumar and other music critics. The first review began 'After a long gap, Mahmud Mirza enthralled the discerning audiences of the capital.' Kuldeep Kumar noted that when Mahmud performed, the front rows would be taken up by well-known musicians. It was, he commented, an unusual occurrence, 'in an era when musicians have stopped attending other musicians' performances.' The reviews are full of praise for Mahmud's mastery, and his choice of difficult ragas that are seldom attempted nowadays. The critics made it clear that his music was for the connoisseur.

It was my close association with Mahmud Mirza, Abdel-Wahed El-Wakil, Warwick Pethers, Anthony Milroy and the others mentioned above, that gave me glimpses into the traditional world of the Golden Web, which, through the Living Traditions Programme, I was able to share with our circle and beyond. They are amongst the last surviving examples of the world of the Golden Web, and are the heroes of my story. To hold on to tradition in our time of virulent and aggressive modernism is the most difficult task imaginable.

The Academic and Living Traditions Programmes provided me with a treasure trove of knowledge, however, it was an insight into the West, derived through the experience of organizing the Golden Web, that would lead to the discovery of the narrative that made sense for me of our Age of Crises.

THE THREE WORLDS

The realization that the West was not one world but consisted of three quite separate worlds took time to form in my mind. It was during the Golden Web project that I began to experience and recognize the changes that were taking place, which led to this understanding.

As I mentioned above, when we arrived in Cambridge in 1992, what was then the Oriental Faculty had a secretary and two assistants running the department, and the academic staff had little to do with administration. The Oriental Faculty, which was renamed the Faculty of Asian and Middle Eastern Studies, now has a bevy of specialist administrators, and the teachers are also burdened with administration. The corporate business ethos has taken over; everything has to be planned, supervised and controlled; there is no trust in the modern corporate world. A university, where the humanities were king, has mutated into a very different place, where science and business studies rule the roost. The civilizing of the individual has been replaced by the creation of a powerhouse where innovation and entrepreneurship are cultivated. To create something new and be able to sell it is the goal of the modern university. So that there can be no misunderstanding of the new role expected of universities, Higher Education is now under the Department of Business and Innovation.

I wanted to understand the changes that had taken place within the universities since they were founded, so I initiated a research project. We took Oxford and Cambridge and plotted the establishment of the Professorships and Chairs. What emerged was a clear picture of three quite separate educational systems. The Medieval university was there to educate a Christian, and the sacred texts were at the centre. With the Renaissance, ancient Latin and Greek replaced the sacred texts and became the core subjects, being christened 'the Classics', and the humanities began to unfold; the purpose of education was now to produce a civilized human being. With the emergence of the modern sciences in the 19th century and Business Studies in the late 20th century, the stage was set for the modern university to announce itself, and deliver modern man and modern woman.

In our project the three worlds were present. The Living Traditions programme embodied the religious perspective, the academics were engaged with the humanities, and the modern was fully manifested in the medium of IT. This was the medium that took over the project and dictated its terms; the Living Traditions and Academic programmes became peripheral.

By the time the Golden Web was terminated, I had most of the pieces of the puzzle, but it wasn't until I began to reflect upon them as I began writing, that everything fell into place. When it came, the decision to bring the Golden Web Project to an end was a huge relief. I had been riding the tiger for several years, as it gradually dawned on me that the Project was heading for failure. But the end was accompanied by all the usual disappointments which generally accompany failure. Friendships that had formed were broken as we were, as I observed earlier, scattered. I withdrew into a period of isolation. I wanted to leave the past behind. But it was not to be, and the story of how I was enabled to embark on a period of my life that made sense of all that came before forms the next and final part of this chronicle.

III

FROM 70 TO MY 80TH YEAR

20

A NEW BEGINNING

KARIM LAHHAM

IT WAS THE BEGINNING of May 2012, and we had just returned from visiting our son Ali and his family in Spain, when I received a phone call from Karim Lahham. After inquiries about the health of our families, he came around to the point of his call. The launch of his book *Muhammad Shahrur's Cargo Cult* was to take place in Oxford in ten days' time, and he was asking me to chair the meeting. I categorically refused, saying that I knew nothing about philosophy, and I could name a dozen people who would be far more suitable for such an undertaking. However, Karim would not take no for an answer. I remonstrated for about half an hour, but in the end, I had to capitulate. Reluctantly, I asked him to send me the book so I could prepare myself as best I could. When the book arrived, I had a week to get myself ready.

It was a slim volume of some seventy-three pages with copious footnotes. With dictionary beside me I started to read. My first reading produced a sizable glossary of unfamiliar words and terms, and had taken me three days to complete. During the second reading, light began to penetrate the dense fog of my mind. By the time I had completed the third reading I was elated. I had not felt such a thrill since I had learnt to ride a bike. Karim had brilliantly destroyed the shallow and derivative ideas of an engineer, posing as a philosopher, who, with his attacks upon traditional Islam, was causing havoc amongst Muslims. I was so grateful to Karim for insisting I chair the meeting, otherwise I would never have had the patience to read the book properly. It brought home to me the power of the reasoning mind and the dangers it could create. The book was published by the Tabah Foundation. It was the way that secular modern ideas were seeping into the intellectual and cultural world of the Muslims that had moved Shaykh Habib Ali to set up the Tabah Foundation in 2003. Tabah Foundation Research was established to counter this trend; Karim Lahham was appointed a Senior Fellow and his book was one of their first publications.

The time has come for me to introduce this remarkable man to you properly. Dr Karim Lahham is a true polymath: he was awarded a Masters from the Royal College of Art, read law at St Edmund Hall, Oxford, and completed a doctorate in Islamic Studies at Pembroke College, Cambridge. He was called to the London Bar in 1999 as an Inner Temple Major Scholar and continues to practise. In between, he completed an apprenticeship in stone carving in Paris and at York Minster. One of the great influences in his life is his uncle, Abdel-Wahed El-Wakil, the master traditional architect. His publications for Tabah have included: *The Roman Catholic Church's Position on Islam After Vatican II; Muhammad Shahrur's Cargo Cult; Response to Cardinal Scola's House of Lords Speech; The Intelligibility of the Islamic Tradition in the Context of Modern Thought; The Vocational Society;* and he is working on a critical edition of Ibn 'Arabi's *al-Tanazzulat al-Mawsiliyya.* Karim Lahham is both a scholar and a craftsman, and straddles the worlds of Islam and the West. I first encountered him, as you may recall, during the Golden Web Project. I was unaware that during the next stage of my journey, Karim's friendship, support and wisdom would play a key role in its unfolding. I was just happy to see there was an organization that was taking on modernity and presenting traditional Islam as I had endeavoured to do through my projects. But this was an institution headed by a hugely respected and influential Shaykh who was gathering a brilliant team of scholars around him. Surely it would succeed where I considered I had failed.

MY SEVENTIETH BIRTHDAY

It was a day in two halves. The rain came down in torrents in the morning, and the sun broke through after lunch to give us a fine early July afternoon. My mood was better expressed by the morning. As all the members of my immediate family, some from my extended family and a few close friends gathered for tea, I was encompassed by the feeling of the failure of my working life. The inevitable speech that has to take place on such occasions allowed me to make an apology to my family for my failure as a parent to provide the security that is incumbent upon this role in life. And yet the very gathering spoke of a community that was full of love and laughter. Some things must have gone right, and I could count my many blessings.

However, I felt that the Golden Web would be my last project. My credibility would not sustain another venture and, in any case, I was bereft of ideas. I had now to face a very different future. The grandchildren would become the focus of my attention, and I was determined to make a success of this role. And then it happened: I received the missive from my friend with the inquiry as to how my book was going.

This was the spark that transformed my seventies into the decade that made sense of my working life. But let us return to my response to my friend's coaxing me to write a book. My first problem was my overwhelming sense of failure. My confidence was at a very low ebb. Anyway, I was not a writer, and as I related in my Prologue, I did not like looking back, and was not a hoarder. And yet, something inside me tingled with the idea. There was clearly nothing else on offer, and maybe this was what I had to do. It was Karim Lahham who encouraged me to see my past in a more positive light. He kept telling me that my projects had not been failures because people had benefitted hugely from them. His generation had grown up with the publications and films produced by the World of Islam Festival, and they had been deeply influential. The Golden Web, he insisted, had been remarkable in the people it brought together, and the perspective it opened up. He would not allow me to languish in my slough of despond.

Somewhat reluctantly, I started the process of trying to reconstruct my past. As the picture of my journey through life began to emerge, I became increasingly astonished. I began to see patterns unfolding. I seem to have been placed in worlds, introduced to people and read books which would enable me to see the false nature of modernity and the beauty of traditional Islam and Islamic civilization.

I was now embarking on a nine-year journey, during which I would encounter further remarkable people and situations, resulting in the publication of not one but three books. However, my attempt to become a writer was not going well. Each morning I would rise early and write for two hours before breakfast, and then another two hours after breakfast. The next morning, I would read what I had written the previous day, screw it into a ball and throw it in the wastepaper basket. This went on for several months, and then I had a brainwave: why not do it as a slide presentation? My subject was eminently illustratable, and I enjoyed talking about it. I contacted Nabeel, the son of my friend Mohammed Ashraf. Nabeel is a graphic designer who had worked under Abul Qasim Spiker in the Golden Web, and who lived in Cambridge. He generously agreed to help me and we set to work.

21
REFLECTIONS OF AN ENGLISH MUSLIM

THERE FOLLOWED TWENTY happy and creative months as we put our slide presentation together. Nabeel has a wonderful eye, was brilliant at finding the images, and could produce arresting graphics. I assembled photos that illustrated my early life, mainly from my brother Richard, and set about devising the story we were going to tell. By the spring of 2014 our slide presentation was ready.

The presentation, which we called 'Reflections of An English Muslim', was in two halves. The first half was devoted to my journey to Islam, and the second, my reflections on how we had arrived at the chaos and ugliness of our present world. The first two chapters of this current book came from my slide presentation. I told the story of how my halcyon childhood was brought to an end by ten years of boarding school, where I was educated to serve an empire which no longer existed, and how, during the sixties, I was immersed in modern theatre, modern art and the counterculture of the hippies, all of which were attacking the establishment that had nurtured me. I then went on to introduce the two people who changed my life; the first being Annabel who would become my wife, companion and the partner in my work, and then, together, our meeting with Ustad Mahmud Mirza, who would take us into the traditional arts, and the culture and civilization of Islam. With a much shorter sequence than is contained in this book I told the story of the World of Islam Festivals, and my finally embracing Islam. I was at pains to show that I became a Muslim because of the beauty, truth and goodness I was surrounded by whilst assembling the exhibits and events for the Festival, and in particular the understanding of the traditional arts that I had gleaned from Ustad Mahmud Mirza and the other traditional practitioners that I would encounter on my journey into Islam.

I ended the first half of my presentation by looking back at the cultural revolution of the sixties, and reflecting on what had happened to those worlds that I had been immersed in. The revolutionary playwrights were now the revered members of an establishment which embraced the angst that had been unleashed in our theatres, cinemas and TV screens; the breakdown of society with all its suffering was now our daily fare. Modern Art had conquered the establishment in no uncertain terms. The works of the contemporary artists were commanding astronomical prices. However, it was clear to me, there had been a dramatic deterioration in the content of the art. Ugliness and self-obsession had reached rock bottom with Tracy Emine's Bed. The musical raves of the hippies, which horrified the establishment, were now the norm. The one that took place around Queen Victoria's monument in front of Buckingham palace, for Her Majesty's Diamond Jubilee, was equal to anything that was mounted during the sixties. Her Majesty was reported to be wearing ear plugs, but the Archbishop of Canterbury beside her, was rocking to the beat. The next day he was officiating at a service in St Paul's Cathedral, with Her Majesty, members of the Royal Family and the cream of the British establishment joining together to celebrate, before God, her long reign.

The contradictions and confusions that were now at the heart of our society, culture, civilization, call it what you will, alarmed me. You must remember, I was now seeing everything from a very different point of view. It was, however, a perspective which had far more in common with the values of my childhood. I was engaged in the return to a moral code governed by religion. This code had been breached by the cultural revolution of the sixties, and was producing a very different kind of social order. In the second half of my presentation, I attempted to penetrate how this descent into chaos and confusion had come about.

The more I reflected upon the three worlds that I had become aware of during the Golden Web, namely, the Christian, the Classical and the Modern, the more it became clear to me that this was where the answer lay. Modernism is propped up by the narrative of human progress, but what actually happened reveals a very different trajectory. For the West was not one world and story, it was three completely separate worlds and stories. For a thousand years Christendom had provided the culture, arts, architecture and educational system; with the Renaissance, a new culture with its own arts, architecture and educational system was born; and then the modern world emerged, quite unlike the two preceding worlds, with its own unique culture, arts, architecture and educational system. The saint was at the apex of Christendom, to be replaced, in the Renaissance, by the warrior/statesman, who would be over shadowed by the merchant in the modern. Each world had been extreme in its manifestation; from extreme spirituality, to extreme humanism to the extreme materialism that now encompasses us.

Although modernity is increasingly dominant, vestiges of the other worlds are still with us; the three worlds somehow coexist in a permanent state of conflict and contradiction. Now, seeking freedom from its Christian roots, the West is spiralling, ever more rapidly, into chaos and destruction. This was the trajectory we illustrated in the opening of the second part of the slide presentation. We continued with what I considered was one of the most compelling proofs of this trajectory: the unfolding of Modern Art.

THE CANARY IN THE MINE

I have never doubted the sincerity of the modern artist. Artists are born with a heightened sense of seeing and they need to express this by making things. The Christian artists were engaged in a vast collaborative venture in the creation of churches and cathedrals. With the Renaissance, the human body took centre stage, and the celebration of humanity through the myths of the ancients and the triumphs of the contemporary warriors became the preferred subjects, alongside, in the Catholic world, the naturalist depiction of the Bible stories.

By the nineteenth century, artists were chafing at the restrictions that the classical tradition placed upon them. The Enlightenment and the Industrial Revolutions were transforming the landscape. The art world engendered by the Renaissance had become an anachronism. A fundamental change took place as the artists sought authenticity. They became their own masters, prizing above everything their own feelings and perceptions. Instead of being at the heart of the society, providing the environment that gave it meaning, the artist became an outsider. As outsiders they became the eye witnesses and recorders of the trajectory of the modern world, mirroring its growing absurdity, with their 'works of art' becoming increasingly incomprehensible to the average person.

I saw the modern artist as 'the canary in the mine', warning us of the dangers that faced our world. But a terrible metamorphosis has taken place. From being an outsider, the modern artist has now become a pillar of the establishment. The natural instinct of the populace is to recoil from their creations, but because the establishment honours them and celebrates their work, resistance evaporates. The influence of modern art is spreading throughout society and is now playing a key role in the perpetuation of modernity. It is programming us to be able to live in a state of chaos, to love ugliness, to enjoy disequilibrium. It is normalizing the abnormal. Through this strange metamorphosis the ultimate insanity and dislocation of our modern world is fully manifested.

THE THREE WORLDS AND ISLAM

I now turned my mind to pondering how the three worlds related to Islam. They each represented a particular power base within human society: the priest, the warrior/statesman, and the merchant. In the West they created separate worlds, but in Islam they were integrated within one world. In Islam, the scholars have played the role of protector of the sacred law and knowledge; warriors have been the political rulers, and the merchants have taken care of the distribution of the material requirements of society. The stability and sustainability of this structure was based upon the person of the Prophet, blessings and peace be upon him. He was the fount of knowledge, a warrior and the ruler of his community, and a merchant living within a trading society. At the heart of Islam is unity, and this unity was manifested in the form of the civilization.

MIZAN OR BALANCE

What is the criterion by which we can understand the different unfoldings of Islam and the West? This question was resolved for me when I reflected upon verses 7-9 of Surat al-Rahman:

He raised the heavens and set up everything in balance
So that you should not transgress the balance
Therefore, maintain just measure
And do not fall short in the balance

Everything has been set up in balance, and our role as human beings is to maintain that balance. Actually, the word balance does not convey the fullness of the Arabic term *mizan* (pronounced *meezaan*), which evokes a sacred trust between God and humanity, the relationships within human society, and humanity's engagement with the natural world. Islamic civilization was structured to realize this. In the West, the balance has been broken, hence the chaos and destruction of our world.

I brought the slide presentation to an end with an attempt to show the very different perspective that what I call the 'Mizan Thesis' revealed.

LAUNCH OF THE SLIDE PRESENTATION

The date for the launch of our slide presentation was set for Sunday 27th April 2014. Mujadad Zaman and Amina Nawaz, who were doing their PhDs at Cambridge, and had become part of our circle, agreed to help organize the launch. The Old Divinity School auditorium at St John's College, which seated 160 people, was chosen as a perfect venue. I suggested three things that I thought were necessary for the event to be successful. Firstly, the auditorium must be full; to fill a 160-seater space in Cambridge, where, unless you are famous, you are lucky to get twenty to turn up, would be quite a task. But I knew that if we could fill the space our battle would be half won. Secondly, the slide presentation needed three hours for its delivery; this would be a severe test for the university audience. Thirdly, there had to be an interval in which tea and coffee and, most importantly, delicious cakes would be served.

The day of reckoning finally arrived. With the support of St John's College, The Islamic Students' Society and the Cambridge Muslim College, we were playing to a full house. Abdul Hakim Winter made the introductions and chaired the meeting. Ali Keeler then recited the opening verses of Surat al-Rahman, with Samir Mahmud reading the English translation. I then stepped up to the podium and launched into my delivery. When the interval arrived, I went backstage and nervously waited for someone to come and tell me how it was going. Two of the organizers appeared and reported that everyone was discussing my presentation, and the refreshments, particularly the cakes, were going down a treat. There was a happy buzz around the event, they said. Once I had completed the presentation, the questions flowed. After more than three hours Abdul Hakim brought the occasion to an end with the remark that I should take the presentation on tour. I then found myself surrounded by a number of people who wanted to ask more questions. Most gratifying for me was the reaction of the lawyer and novelist Hina Belitz; she said my lecture had brought many ideas that had been flying around in her head into a coherent whole. It was with a deep sense of relief and gratitude that I realized that the thesis I had presented had been well received. We were off to a good start.

CENTRE OF ISLAMIC STUDIES

My first breakthrough came when I was invited to have coffee with Yasir Suleiman, who was the Professor of Modern Arabic, and Director of the Centre of Islamic Studies (CIS). We met in Nero's coffee shop, the first of many such meetings over the next three years. He had enjoyed my lecture and was keen to engage me in the activities of the CIS. He invited me to give my lecture as part of the 2014 Cambridge University 'Festival of Ideas'. The lecture took place on 29th October in a large auditorium in Kings College. At the end of the talk, he invited me to become a CIS Visiting Fellow. There was no funding attached to the fellowship, but it would mean that I was a member of the University, and would have access to a great number of facilities, including the libraries and attendance at seminars and events. The prestige attached to Cambridge University would not go amiss in the work that lay ahead. Yasir proved to be a great support and gave me much needed encouragement as I delved ever deeper into my chosen area of exploration.

22

MALAYSIAN ODYSSEY

THE SECOND BREAKTHROUGH came when I received an invitation to tour Malaysia. This came from my old friend and first student companion in Cambridge, Shahridan Faiez. In the autumn of 2014, I arrived in Kuala Lumper and gave eleven presentations at various institutions over ten days, finally ending up at the University Sains Islam Malaysia (USIM).

The reception I received at USIM was very encouraging. After the presentation of our slide show, Tan Sri Dzulkifli Abdul Razak invited me to join him at the Faculty of Leadership, of which he was the Chair. My title would be Distinguished Scholar, and I would be required to visit USIM four times during 2015, staying several weeks on each visit. I eagerly accepted. I had met Dzul, as we came to know him, at the time of the Golden Web Project, when he was Vice Chancellor of Universiti Sains Malaysia in Penang. He had immediately grasped the concept of the Golden Web and this led to a number of very creative discussions. Now, he took on board the Mizan Thesis. And so began one of the most rewarding years of my journey, as Dzul arranged my attendance at conferences and seminars, gave me the opportunity to meet and interact with the students from a variety of disciplines, and introduced me to ministers, academics and influential people who could be helpful in propagating the Mizan Thesis. We would meet in the evenings, having dinner in restaurants open to the sky with the wonderful perfumes and sounds of the tropics, mulling over our programme and plans for the future.

USIM's philosophy was 'The integration of Naqli (revealed knowledge) and Aqli (rational knowledge)' – interpreted as the integration of Islam and modern science. Around the university there were posters with quotes from the Holy Qur'an and Hadiths side by side with statements by modern philosophers, psychologists and sociologists. They were addressing the dilemma that had faced Muslim intellectuals for more than a hundred years. It had formed the central theme of the famous educational conference, inspired by the World of Islam Festival, that was held in Mecca in 1977. The Mizan Thesis challenged the idea that such an integration was possible. Islam and modern science came from two quite different worlds and were governed by opposing criteria. I had many discussions with academics from various faculties around the topic, which only confirmed my understanding of the power held by this quest for integration. It had held me in its sway with my attempt to marry the Golden Web with the World Wide Web. We all seek unity, because unity is at the heart of our existence.

One of the seminars Dzul asked me to attend was on terrorism. This was very enlightening. There were four excellent papers, but one really affected my understanding. It was given by a brilliant Malay scholar who had interviewed seventy young Malays who had been detained at the airport attempting to travel to Syria. He stated that these young people, who were well educated and from middle-class families, were motivated by wanting to do something to alleviate the suffering of their fellow Muslims around the world. They witnessed through the media the persecution of Muslims from every corner of the globe on a daily basis. Nothing was being done about it by the governments and world bodies. They were answering the call for action, little knowing the quagmire into which they were being lured. It sounded to me very much like the spirit of those who went to fight in the Spanish Civil War.

The great insight I was given during my time at USIM concerned childhood and addiction. Dzul sent me to a class where the students were studying sociology. When I entered the room, they were busy with their mobile phones. However, they quickly settled and got out their lap tops, with their fingers at the ready to take down notes. I asked them, gently, if they could put away their laptops and mobile phones, which they duly did. Then note books and pencils began to appear. I asked them to put away their note books because I wanted to have a conversation. I began by asking them what they were studying. They answered drug addiction. I was surprised, 'You have a problem here in Malaysia?' I asked. Their answer confirmed that they had a serious problem.

I had already understood the importance of the kampung for the Malay. Wherever they lived they still identified with their ancestral neighbourhoods, in which many of the old still resided and where the communities would gather during the Eid Festivals. I asked 'how many of you live in kampungs?' All the hands shot up. We then talked about the size of their communities. One said he thought there must be five hundred in his kampung. 'Do you know everyone?' I asked. He looked at me quizzically. 'No', he said. I asked him if his grandmother knew everyone, 'O yes', he immediately replied. We then began to discuss the difference between their generation and that of their grandparents, and we reflected on how their grandparents were connected into the living community, and their generation was becoming disconnected from real life and connected through social media.

Now social media is highly addictive and I began to realize that we were producing a generation of addicts. They were studying addiction when it becomes dangerous, but the way we engage with the world is becoming addictive, whether it is obsession with our football team, pop band or latest Netflix series. This led me to study how this addictive personality was being formed in children; the children were becoming dependent on external stimuli instead of being able to foster their own imaginations and play their own games. They were being cloned by the same children's programmes, games and toys, all created by adults. Their imaginations were being taken over by adults pretending to be children. I called this process the 'dialysis of the imagination'. I worked this idea into my slide show. The next presentation I gave was to a group of Indonesian students, and when I came to this sequence I broke down in tears. When after a lecture people asked me 'what can we do? I answered, 'Reclaim childhood!'

GOTONG-ROYANG

I initially experienced *gotong-royang* when we first arrived in Cambridge and encountered Shah and his Malaysian community of students. When together, they seemed to move around as one body. I had never seen anything quite like it. They effortlessly organized, with other students, but always in the vanguard, the iftars during Ramadan at Wolfson College. The Eid celebrations were special and the food they brought amazing, and all conducted with a *baraka* that permeated their little community.

It was not until I was at USIM that I was introduced to the term *gotong-royang*, which encompasses all the ways that Malay communities traditionally came together to achieve a task, such as harvesting the rice, moving house, cleaning the communal areas, barn raising and a multitude of other activities. The work was accompanied by singing and food; they were like picnic outings with work attached. Food and laughter are two of the things I associate with my Malaysian friends, and a feeling of happiness that envelops you when in their company. Dr Ahmad Al-Dubayan, the learned Director General of the London Central Mosque and Islamic Cultural Centre, spent many years in the Malay world. He told me how the Malay language was full of different words to denote communal collaboration.

Of course, communal identity and collaboration is universal in pre-modern traditional societies, and we have already encountered Tony Milroy's example in the Yemen and Osman Bili's village in the Sudan. But it was the intensity and intactness of the Malay student group some thirty years ago, that made such an impression on me. I discovered the secret of this phenomenon on meeting Shah's parents when I arrived in Malaysia; their generation had been brought up in a traditional Malay world that was, then, still largely intact.

It began with a conversation with Shah's mother. We were talking about our childhoods, and she spoke about her life growing up in her kampung. As she described the intimate relationship that they had with the natural world around them, I began to realize that she had grown up when kampung life was still functioning. Her grandparents' family, where she had spent a great deal of time, had not had electricity until she was well into her teenage years. At night, she and other siblings would huddle around an oil lamp, with the outside world bathed in total darkness, listening to ancient Malay fables narrated by her grandfather.

Her generation in Malaysia had actually lived in a traditional society, and this explained for me why many of those I had met had a quality and depth of character that had impressed me.

DATO' DR HOOD HAJI MOHAMMED SALLEH

I now set about seeking out the elderly, so that I could listen to their stories about childhood in pre-modern Malaysia. I struck gold when I met Professor Hood Salleh. Hood studied anthropology at Oxford University, and has spent his working life engaging with the Orang Asli, the people of the forest. Early on, he became an advocate for the protection of their way of life, which has been under threat during the last fifty years with the destruction of the rain forests and the relentless spread of monocultures. He asked me if I would like to meet his grandfather. Now Hood was born in the same year that I was, and my mind was a whirl trying to work out how old his grandfather must be. Of course, I said, I would be delighted to meet his grandfather.

The next day Hood took me to his kampung which was some distance from his present residence. He then led me to the cemetery and introduced me to his grandfather, whose grave was surrounded by those of his extended family which appeared to take up a large section of the burial ground. We then proceeded to his family domain, a traditional Malay wooden house, surrounded by an unkempt garden. Looking across at what appeared to be quite a modest house, and knowing that he came from a large family, I asked 'Were you brought up here?' He replied in the affirmative and began to reminisce about his childhood. They were without electricity until he was fourteen, but the house was oriented to capture the wind and kept remarkably cool. He pointed out to me where the well had been whence they drew their water. He told me how the children would have the run of the property for their games and would go down to the river to swim.

I looked at him incredulously. 'What about the crocodiles?' I asked. 'They never bothered us,' he replied, 'They had their part of the river and we had ours; they never came into our part and we never ventured into theirs.'

Hood then told me what went on in the garden during the durian season (a fruit much loved by Malays but horrifically malodorous to the uninitiated). Tigers loved the fruit and would sit under the durian tree at night waiting for the fruit to drop, whilst bears would climb the tree, sniff out the ones about to fall and give them a pat to help them on their way. I asked him, 'Didn't you want to fence the tree in to keep out the animals?' It was his turn to look incredulously at me. 'There was enough fruit for all of us,' he replied. I then remembered the hadith, 'Never does a Muslim plant a tree or cultivate land out of which a bird or a man or a beast eats but that he is rewarded for it as an act of charity', and I felt ashamed that I could have made such a remark. My visit to Hood's kampung remains with me. Through Hood's evocation I could see how the kampung dwellers, surrounded by an incredibly powerful natural world, maintained balance in their way of life, and all of God's creatures could thrive. The rivers are now polluted and teeming with crocodiles, the forest is disappearing along with the animals, and the kampung dwellers have moved to the cities. As we drove away, there were no traditional Malay houses to be seen, only structures built out of breeze blocks surrounded by the detritus of the modern way of life.

GERARD BODEKER

Hood Salleh invited me to accompany him to a lecture which was being given by Dr Gerard Bodeker, a world-renowned public health researcher and academic, specializing in lifespan wellness and integrative healthcare. An Australian, whose doctoral studies were at Harvard, he has spent two decades in medical sciences at Oxford University, and is an adjunct professor of epidemiology at Columbia University. It was, however, a meeting with Hakim Mohammed Said at the Hamdard Institute in Pakistan that changed his life, introducing him to the traditional forms of medicine and well-being. We last encountered the remarkable Hakim in our story, when he attended the World of Islam Festival. Bodeker and the

Hakim became close friends. Bodeker then became that rare individual who encompasses both the Western and traditional forms of healing.

He was a friend of Hood's, and they had collaborated on a book entitled *Health and Beauty from the Rainforest*. The opening passage of the introduction went straight to the nub of the matter:

> A healing mixture of medicinal plants and plant parts is referred to in the Malay language as *ramuan*. The word *ramuan* also denotes ingredients used for cooking. With multiple potent properties, including use in food, *ramuan* is seen as a force for healing, beauty and vitality.

We drove to the university where Bodeker was to give his lecture. The auditorium was full and the slide presentation he gave was brilliant. He showed the gulf between the modern diet of the Malaysians and their traditional fare. The locally produced food of the kampungs had been replaced by the industrialized foods of the West. The impact upon the health of the Malaysians was dramatic; they topped the list of South East Asian countries for heart disease, cancers, diabetes and obesity. The arch villain in the story was white rice which had become the staple for the modern Malaysian, accompanying every meal. To create white rice, all the goodness was removed and what remained was pure sugar, addictive and a killer. I made the mistake of putting my hand up and asking him when this had occurred. He answered, 'A hundred years ago, and you were responsible!' As the laughter erupted, I sank back in my chair and tried to disappear. I had forgotten he was Australian. In his lecture Bodeker revealed the incredible knowledge and wisdom that the traditional Malay system embodied. Everyone, he stated, talks about the Mediterranean diet of the Italians, and this was indeed perfect for the Mediterranean dwellers. But Malaysia was in the tropics, a far more powerful and dangerous environment. Over thousands of years, an integrated health and food system had developed, which perfectly responded to the nature of the tropics. This knowledge was now in danger of being lost because it was contained within the oral tradition. He finished his lecture by exhorting us to seek out the grannies, who were the guardians of this knowledge. Once again, it was confirmed to me that I was witnessing the dramatic change from what had been a sophisticated deeply integrated world, into the flashy, dangerous world that for us in the West is all too familiar.

A SCHOOL TO FOSTER NOBEL PRIZE WINNERS

During my stay at USIM, a school was being set up in the grounds of the campus. The school embodied the philosophy of USIM, to integrate Islam and modern science, and was attracting the brightest children from around Malaysia. Their ambition was to create an environment that would foster Malaysia's Nobel Prize winners, and their first intake of pupils, some sixty boys and girls, was already installed.

One day Dzul informed me that the headmistress would like to invite me to visit her school. I imagined that I would look in on some of the classes, be introduced to members of staff and be shown the facilities. I was somewhat surprised, when the car drew up in front of the entrance, to find a delegation led by the headmistress waiting to welcome me. After the formal greetings, I was taken into the auditorium where the children had been gathered. The headmistress went on to introduce me as an eminent professor from Cambridge University! It began to dawn on me that she was expecting me to give a talk to her bright young prodigies. Panic began to envelop me. What was I to say?

Then it dawned on me that I had been learning about the wonderful childhoods of the elders in their kampungs before the great change. These children had been born into a completely different world. So, when I was invited to speak, I began by asking them when they had last seen their grandparents. I then went on to say, 'If I told you that in the woods at the back of your school there was a goldmine, you would be rushing off with your buckets and spades, wouldn't you? Well let me tell you, your grandparents have golden memories. Ask them about their childhoods.' I then suggested that the next time I visited the school they would have stories that their grandparents had related to them about how things were when they were young. After touring the school, we had lunch with the children, and I was seated with six of the boys at a round table. One of them was looking very miserable. I asked him what was the matter, he replied, 'All my grandparents are dead.' I quickly responded that he should ask his great-uncles or aunts, or some of his parents' elderly friends. This incident shook me and taught me to be ultra-cautious when dealing with children, as this little fellow was clearly distressed.

On my next visit, some of the children had been asking their grandparents or elderly members of their families about their childhoods. Sadly, all the stories they related were about the war and the Japanese occupation. It was clear that the elders did not consider that their childhood memories of the kampung had any value; they had been profoundly affected by the way that modernity has cast such ways of life as backward. Modern Malays, like moderns everywhere are looking to the future, and at best the past becomes heritage for the tourist industry. I suggested that the school should invite elders, such as Shahridan Faiez's mother, to come and talk about their childhoods, to help strengthen the links between the old and young, which modernity is insidiously dissolving.

ADI SETIA

One of the remarkable people I came to know during my year visiting Malaysia was the scholar, traditional farmer, environmentalist and activist Adi Setia. He had been a postgraduate student, junior research fellow and then a senior research fellow at the International Institute of Islamic Thought & Civilization (ISTAC) during the directorship of its founder, the great scholar of traditional Islam, Professor Dr Syed Muhammad Naquib al-Attas, whom we last met in my story, when he attended the World of Islam Festival.

Adi Setia's breadth of scholarship is astounding. I was first introduced to him through his translations of the important works of the early Muslim scholars on trade and commerce. These works ensured that the merchant in Islam remained close to the prophetic example, nurturing a pious individual who, through the way he conducted himself, carried Islam to the west, deep into Africa south of the Sahara, and to the east, into the vast worlds of India, China and South East Asia. As well as the merchants in Islam, Adi's research covers the History and Philosophy of Science, Islamic Science and the Islamic Gift Economy. I had several meetings with Adi that were broad ranging and enlightening. We met in his office at the Centre for Advanced Studies on Islam, Science & Civilization (CASIS), and he came to workshops on the Mizan Thesis which we held at USIM. But the most memorable day I spent with Adi Setia was when he invited me to visit his farm in Terengganu.

He had taken a rundown and neglected farm belonging to his family and was in the process of restoring it to its former state, reintroducing the traditional Malay husbandry that had all but been destroyed by the so-called Green Revolution, aptly re-named the Chemical Revolution by the Indian scientist and environmentalist Vandana Shiva. Adi's vision was to create a model farm where people could come and learn about, and participate in, the tradition of Malay husbandry that had sustained generations of their ancestors and been in harmony with the natural world.

By the entrance to the farm the wooden framework for a barn was being erected. This, when completed, was to serve as a meeting hall for lectures and events. We then passed a wooden structure on stilts with a ramp leading to a raised floor which contained stalls. Every evening the goats would be herded up the ramp and into the stalls to protect them from predators. We passed chickens, orchards and fields of raised beds growing root crops. But the glorious climax to the visit was the sight of the paddy fields growing rice. This really lifted my soul, and I left Adi's farm encouraged that maybe it was possible to restore the land in Malaysia to its former state.

S M MOHAMED IDRIS

No visit to Malaysia was complete without travelling to Penang Island to pay my respects and enjoy the blessing of sitting with S M Mohammed Idris, fondly known as Uncle Idris. Uncle Idris was the elder brother of Shah's father. As I noted above, Shah's family bridged the worlds of South India and Malaysia. Before independence, Georgetown, the port city of Penang, was a thriving centre of trade. Shah's family business was taking care of the port services. After the Japanese bombed Pearl Harbour, they sent bombing raids to Singapore and Georgetown. Uncle Idris' elder brother and father were killed in the first sortie. At the time, Uncle Idris was in the family home in India. A highly intelligent child, he was expected to go to Aligarh University and follow an academic vocation. However, now being the eldest son, in 1947, at the age of twenty, he travelled to Malaysia to take control of the family business.

His prodigious energy enabled him to become engaged in politics, and for a while he became a local councillor. It was when, in 1970, he was elected president of the newly-formed Consumer Association of Penang

(CAP), that his life's work began. He transformed CAP into an amazing environmental, health, social and planning NGO, which also represented the poor and wielded astonishing influence throughout Malaysia and beyond. For five decades, Uncle Idris kept alive an understanding of the values, skills and wisdom of the traditional Malay world, and fought the encroachment of the modernization which was destroying the society. He was unique in his understanding, authority and fearlessness in confronting local and national government officials and their plans to 'improve' society. Amongst CAP's achievements were the banning of toxic drugs, the labelling of expiry dates on all food products, the end of cigarette advertisements, better benefits under the Employees Provident Fund, and better legal standing for tenants and house buyers. His work led to the Malaysian Government setting up their Department of the Environment in 1975, the establishment of Friends of the Earth Malaysia in 1977, and the Third World Network in 1984. He was at the forefront of the decolonizing movement, and was invited to give the opening address at the international conference on 'Decolonizing Our Universities', which was held in Penang in 2011.

Uncle Idris died on 22nd May 2019 at the age of 93. He was one of the global pioneers of the environmental movement. But he was much more than this; his rare vision was holistic, embodying the spiritual, cultural, social and environmental dimensions of the human crises facing humanity. His passing was deeply mourned and he will be sorely missed. He contributed to my understanding in so many ways. His was an authentic voice that remained constant and deeply rooted.

WRITING A BOOK

I had agreed to write a book as part of my one year visiting fellowship at USIM. This was the first time in my life that I had been employed by an institution that I had not set up myself. It was a novel experience, and I was keen to honour this commitment. I was now faced with the task of transforming my slide lecture into a publication. What I had imagined was going to be a difficult task actually turned out to be remarkably easy. I wrote my book *Reflections of An English Muslim* in Cambridge during the month of Ramadan 2015. I had given the lecture some thirty to forty times during the previous year and a quarter, and my delivery had become pretty fluent. I had been able to hone the material by coming at it from different angles and seeking the ones that came across most clearly. I assembled the text which had accompanied each of the images in the slide presentation, into one file. What surprised me was that there were only half a dozen instances where the text did not make sense without the pictures. I was able to adapt the text in these cases, and I had a short book of twenty thousand words that stood quite happily without the need of the pictures.

My time in Malaysia had made me acutely aware of the crises that humanity was facing, and that time was running out. The speed with which Malaysian society was changing had been brought home to me in the yawning gap between grandparents and their grandchildren. They were experiencing in a few decades the changes that we had gone through in more than a hundred years. I saw the return to balance, to *mizan*, as a way forward that could bring us back to our senses. I ended the book with a clarion call for the realization of a 'Mizan Initiative':

> It is difficult to overstate the crisis facing Humanity. Separation of the spiritual and material and the consequent disequilibrium between humanity and the environment has reached dangerous levels. This crisis emerged in the West, and the West has no solution to offer, only further descent into materiality through modern science and technology. How can what has caused the crisis solve the crisis?
>
> The Muslim world has become embroiled in the cruelty and chaos that is enveloping the globe. However, Islam provided a completely different approach to how we should live on earth. Compassion and forbearance are at the heart of our Tradition, and we should turn away from this cruelty and chaos and return to the balance, justice, measure and harmony of Islam's way of *mizan*.
>
> We need to understand the principles of *mizan* that are enshrined in the Holy Qur'an and Sunnah of the Prophet, may the blessings of Almighty Allah be upon him. We need to understand how these principles were manifested intellectually through scholarship, and materially through the craftsmen and women responsible for the built and cultivated environments. We need to explore how these principles travelled and became established throughout Dar al-Islam, and we need to discover how they can be revived and reintroduced to bring humanity back to a state of *mizan*.

Reflections of An English Muslim was published by ITBM (The Malaysian Institute of Translation and Books) in collaboration with USIM Press, and the launch took place at USIM on 29th September 2015. My year was drawing to an end, and we set about studying how the Mizan Initiative could continue in Malaysia. After developing the outline of a plan with Dzul, I returned to the UK on 14th October. In mid-December I was invited back to KL for a meeting with the Bank Rakyat who had shown interest in the Project. I gave a presentation in the morning to the executives and staff of the bank. We then had lunch with the Chairman and members of the Board of Directors. Later I was to learn that the meeting had gone well, and funding had been agreed.

So ended my wonderful year visiting Malaysia. I had received so much, experienced a Muslim society in transition, and hopefully contributed to the establishment of the Mizan Initiative as a continuing programme within USIM. I had also produced my first book!

23

BACK IN ENGLAND

DURING 2015, IN BETWEEN my visits to Malaysia, and during 2016, I was promoting the Mizan Thesis, giving lectures, attending lectures and seminars, and meeting people who could advance my cause. I was seeking a breakthrough.

CAMBRIDGE

In Cambridge I started engaging with the Centre of Islamic Studies (CIS) and the University's Islamic Society (ISOC). On the 10th February, I gave my slide presentation as part of ISOC's Islamic Awareness Week. This was the start of a very fruitful relationship with the Muslim students' society. Later that month I participated in a conference which was part of the CIS project, 'Narratives of Conversion to Islam in Britain: Male Perspectives'. This followed on from the CIS highly successful project focusing on female converts. I was one of 46 male participants, and we spent two days sharing our stories. It was instructive to see how Islam had entered all the various parts of the British social structure. I have warm memories of the event. One person, however, made a deep impression on me

ADAM KELWICK

Adam Kelwick, an imam from Liverpool, stood out like a shining light. His father was Yemeni and his mother English. His father was visiting the UK and departed back to Yemen not knowing that a son was on the way. His mother married and he was brought up in a loving household with step-siblings, and enjoyed a happy childhood. His family, however, was not religious. On reaching maturity, he decided to track down his birth father in the Yemen. He succeeded in finding him and was warmly welcomed into the fold of his large Yemeni family. He entered Islam, returned to the UK, and after a while, his mother, step-father and half siblings joined him in his faith. I spent as much time as I could between sessions in Adam's company. It was, however, only later that I came to realize the awesome stature of the man, and this belongs towards the end of my story.

MUSLIMS IN THE UK AND EUROPE SYMPOSIUM

From 29-31 May I attended the 2015 'Muslims in the UK and Europe' postgraduate symposium organized by the CIS. The aim of this annual symposium is to bring together graduate students from British, European and American universities to present their research to their peers, discuss their findings and engage in debate about the issues that face Muslims in the European context. Topics vary widely, from Sufism to Salafism, from charity to burial rites, religious travel to therapy, Islamophobia to deradicalization initiatives. The papers at this symposium were of the kind expected of PhD candidates and covered a variety of disconnected subjects. During the lunch break a group of the students joined me at my table and we had a wonderful session.

I was in the middle of my study of childhood and the 'dialysis of the imagination' idea, which I shared with them. Two of the company became friends and companions along the way. Tariq Tamimi is an imposing figure whose family came from Gaza. He was clearly a leader amongst the students, and was doing his doctorate at SOAS. Elis Gievori's family is from Albania, and he was studying at Birkbeck College. They invited me up to London to meet their circle of friends, and it was agreed I should give a lecture, organized by the students during the next semester. So, on 30th

November 2015 I had the opportunity of addressing a room packed full of interested and interesting young people. They were from every corner of the Muslim world; they all had remarkable stories to tell. Elis enlightened me as to the degree of eradication of Islam achieved by the communist rulers of Albania. He told me how the Ottoman Mosque in his town had been turned into the latrines. He knew nothing of Islam in his childhood, and had only discovered his religion on coming to London as a student.

WAEL HALLAQ

2016 opened with a landmark event in my education. Tariq Tamimi invited me to join him in a workshop which was to be given by Professor Wael Hallaq from Columbia University, New York. The subject was to be his new book *The Impossible State*. Tariq emailed me a pdf of the book, and I set to preparing for the workshop. I had to read it twice and then focus on particular passages to begin to access the treasures that lay within, which were splendidly camouflaged by the academic language. The understanding of the Sharia was at the heart of Hallaq's thesis, and I was able to engage with Tariq, whose PhD addressed the Sharia, in deciphering the language. This was my first introduction to the postmodern philosopher Michel Foucault whom Hallaq used as a foil in his critique of modernity.

On 16th January 2016, I left Cambridge on an early train so that I could meet Tariq at Kings Cross station, and we could have a coffee before walking across to Birkbeck College. The workshop was scheduled to start at 9am and last until 6pm. The lecture theatre was pretty full, and I recognized several of the students who had been at my SOAS lecture. Hallaq took us through the main themes of his book, and after each theme there were questions and discussion. Until this time, I had not really taken a great interest in the Sharia. It provided the backbone of my faith, of course, but my interest lay in the arts and culture of Islam. Wael Hallaq's book opened the subject up for me and taught me to wonder at the nature of this most perfect system for the regulation of the human being.

Wael Hallaq demonstrated clearly the gulf that existed between the traditional Islamic framework of governance and that of the West. His book showed the impossibility of creating a modern Islamic State, and intelligently challenges the extreme attempts to do so. But for me, it is the light he throws upon the nature of the Sharia that makes it such an important work. With the help of my dear friend Tariq, I was able to benefit from this magnificent publication. I left Wael Hallaq's workshop hugely enriched and full of gratitude.

WORKSHOPS AND LECTURES

The Wael Hallaq workshop inspired me to see if I could take a group of students through a day's engagement. I was becoming increasingly concerned that, although I could provide a couple of hours of entertainment with my slide presentations, not a great deal seemed to remain with the recipients after my performance. Put simply, my case was not coming across strongly enough to take up residence in their minds. I decided to change my mode of operation. Because of my desperation to communicate, everything had gone into my presentation. Now I would switch to listening mode and concentrate on people's responses. I would try to understand how they were receiving the ideas. If there were barriers to their reception, what were they and how could they be overcome?

My first foray in this new initiative was a day's workshop organized by my friends at SOAS and involving 24 participants. This was a very bright group who had the freshness and enthusiasm of youth. The session went well, but I had no way of telling whether the ideas would become adopted in the longer term.

Back in Cambridge I was invited by Dr Atif Imtiaz, Academic Director at Cambridge Muslim College (CMC), to give a lecture and workshop for his students. The CMC was founded by Shaykh Abdel Hakim Murad in 2009, and was one of several educational institutions established by western converts, which included Yusuf Islam's Islamia Schools, the first of which was opened in 1983, and Zaytuna College in Berkley, California, set up by Shaykh Hamza Yusuf in 2008.

DR ATIF IMTIAZ

Atif had attended the first of my illustrated lectures back in 2014, and I had benefited from his response to the event and meetings we subsequently had in his office at the College. He had on his desk *The Hundred Letters* by

Sharafuddin Maneri, the great saint of Bihar in India. This was a work that I also treasured, and Atif explained how his family had come from Bihar, and lived in a town close to where the saint was buried. We discussed the idea of one day visiting the shrine together.

Atif is a member of the second generation of Muslims in the UK. Their understanding is particularly valuable as they were born here, and yet still retain the knowledge and language of their countries of origin. Their education has allowed them to see into both worlds. Atif was a brilliant student who had gained a PhD in Social Psychology at the London School of Economics. His dissertation was entitled *Identity and the Politics of Representation: The Case of Muslim Youth in Bradford.* His book, *Wandering Lonely in a Crowd*, contains a series of reflections on recent debates that affect the Muslim community. Atif has a deep understanding of the problems facing the Muslims in the West.

Atif fully understood what I was trying to achieve. We agreed that I should give a lecture, and then three weeks later hold a workshop to see how much of the lecture had been retained and absorbed. I ended the experiment with a workshop at the Al-Furqan Foundation in London, at which a group, who were very familiar with my work, discussed ways ahead.

The results of these meetings confirmed for me the extreme difficulty of the mizan narrative taking up residence in the mind. However, the barriers which lay in the path also became clear.

TWO MAJOR PROBLEMS

There was no question that the mizan narrative struck a deep chord. However, there were two major barriers to be overcome: the modern narrative of progress and, what I called, the 'open-plan brain' of the modern. The language of progress was deeply embedded in all cultures, East and West. Nations were categorized as being either 'developed', 'underdeveloped' or 'developing'. The Muslims were trapped in a particularly insidious aspect of this narrative; the 'Golden Age of Islam' idea. This told how Muslims enjoyed a golden age of discovery and progress, and then stagnated and declined. The initiative was passed on to the Europeans, who had awoken from their Dark Age and were forging ahead. The Muslims had fallen behind and now must wake up and catch up.

The open-plan brain of the modern is the result of the dissolution of a unitive vision. The three worlds of the Westerner: Christian, civilized and modern, were mirrored by the two worlds of the Muslim: their traditional world and the modern. Because we are unitive beings, coming from the One, we naturally seek unity. And this is especially true of Muslims. The open-plan brain accommodates both the narrative of progress and alongside it sits the newly acquired *mizan* narrative. What I now encountered was the result of the attempt to reconcile these two opposing narratives; to bring *mizan* into the modern, to have *mizan* development, join sustainable development as a way of reforming the modern.

Before the rise of modernity, every culture lived within a unitive world; the process taking place of marrying the modern and the traditional was the natural outcome of the desire for normality, for unity. However, what it was in fact doing was creating a dissonance. Islam in its manifestation embodied *mizan*, whereas the modern in its unfolding was destroying the balance. The process of destruction is at the very heart of the nature of modernity; it is ingrained in its philosophy and structure. The Mizan Thesis teaches us that Islam and the modern are quite separate worlds, and to mix them is to draw Islam into the vortex of chaos and destruction. But for those brought up and educated within a Western educational environment, and studying disciplines that would enable them to live in the modern world, the adoption of the *mizan* narrative was fraught with difficulties. The question which always arose after my talks was, 'What should we do?' How could I answer this question?

THE GOLDEN AGE OF ISLAM CONCEPT

The first step in clearing the way had to be to address the Golden Age of Islam paradigm. This concept has been with us since the middle of the 19th century, when it was fitted into the Western Progress thesis as a part of its trajectory. It appealed to radical Muslim thinkers at the time, who were trying to explain the Muslims' loss of leadership and power; it enabled them to lay claim to a key role in the development of modern science.

It was, however, after the 9/11 terrorist attack in the United States that the Golden Age idea really took off. The Golden Age of Islam was invoked to counter the savage attacks on Islam and its culture that had erupted. 'Look how much we owe to Islam and Muslim civilization in the creation of the modern world', was the response that was encapsulated in the Golden Age narrative. With the very best intentions to shed a positive light on Islam and its civilization, scholars, politicians, authors and journalists promoted the narrative.

The 1001 Inventions Exhibition was the most prominent of several exhibitions assembled to celebrate the Golden Age. It was the brain child of Dr Salim Al-Hassani, Professor of Mechanical Engineering at Manchester University. He drew together a formidable team of Muslim and Western scholars of the history of science and developed a brilliant exhibition, film and book. The third edition of the book was published by the *National Geographic.* The exhibition toured the world after its London launch at the Science Museum in January 2010, and was opened in its many venues by royalty, presidents and prime ministers. The Prince of Wales wrote an introduction to the catalogue and lent his considerable weight to the veracity of the narrative. President Obama referred to the Golden Age of Islam in his Cairo speech, receiving a rapturous response from his Egyptian audience. With such ringing and authoritative endorsements of the Golden Age narrative, and a plethora of books and encyclopaedia entries presenting the Golden Age of Islam as fact, what could be done to counter the thesis?

By moving across to the *mizan* perspective, the Golden Age of Islam appears in a totally different light. Whilst Islamic civilization undoubtably contributed to the West, modern science did not develop from it, but was born out of a complete change of perspective. The World of Islam and the modern world followed completely separate trajectories. Modern science and the Islamic sciences supported quite different ways of life. Islamic civilization manifested and maintained the *mizan*, modernity has destroyed the balance and is now facing crises that are multiplying and threatening our very existence. This is not the time for the Muslims to be claiming responsibility for the modern world! The challenge was to get across the reality of the *mizan* narrative, and the falsity of the narrative of progress.

By the summer of 2016, I was realizing that for the Mizan Initiative to succeed it would require a great deal more than myself giving talks, workshops and seminars. Funds were once again severely restricted and

I could see before me a mountain that had to be scaled. It was at this juncture I was introduced to a benefactor. He fully understood what I was attempting to achieve, and gave the project his full support. I was now able to plan a programme that would take the Mizan Initiative onto a new level.

THE PROGRAMME

The programme would take a group of Muslim students, academics, and members of the Cambridge Muslim community on a journey. I would begin with interviews to discover their present understanding of the Golden Age paradigm. I would then give a lecture introducing the Mizan Thesis. This would be followed by a seminar in which a group of scholars would be invited to speak on various aspects of *mizan*. We would then see what change in the understanding of the group had taken place. All three aspects of the programme would be filmed for further study.

My visiting fellowship at the Centre of Islamic Studies enabled me to have full access to the University. The CIS agreed to organize the seminar, and the student Islamic Society arranged to hold the lecture at Queens College auditorium. The CIS, ISOC and Cambridge Muslim College provided the students and academics for the interviews. Interview sessions were also organized by Mohammad Ashraf, who brought several older members of the Muslim community together, and Nabeel Ashraf who gathered a group of the younger ones from the community.

DR PAUL ANDERSON

One of the most valuable interviews was with Dr Paul Anderson, the deputy director of the CIS. Paul is a social anthropologist. His work encompasses the relationship between economics, morality and the religious life. With a focus on Islam and trade he is working on a monograph of Aleppo as a trading city before the outbreak of the current conflict in Syria. His research spans from the Middle East to China. His perspective enables him to appreciate the dramatic change taking place between the traditional practices of the merchant and the new world of business. It was an enlightening interview.

THE SEMINAR.

The seminar proved to be one of those key moments in my journey of discovery. 'Narratives of Islamic Civilization: Questioning the Model of the Golden Age of Islam', assembled a group of scholars researching in various fields. I had gathered together most of the Living Traditions circle from the Golden Web Project, and there were academics and students from Oxford, Cambridge and London. The seminar took place on 25th February 2017, at the Faculty of Asian and Middle East Studies, Cambridge University. Paul Anderson welcomed the participants and introduced the seminar. The day was rich in papers, interventions and discussion. Two papers made a deep impression on me.

The first was entitled '*Adab* and the Education of the Whole Person', and was delivered by Dr Talal Al-Azem, Mohammad Noah Fellow at the Oxford Centre of Islamic Studies. Dr Talal gave a brilliant description of the nature and purpose of traditional education within Islamic civilization, which showed how the system was there to produce a God-centred person, with the principle of *mizan* at the core of their being.

The second paper was given by Dr Mohamad Hammour, a scholar of Islamic economics, and showed the way in which the outrageous has become normalized in the evolution of modernity. He took as his example *The Fable of the Bees: or, Private Vices, Public Benefits*, which was first published anonymously in 1705 by the Anglo-Dutch social philosopher Bernard Mandeville.

HASAN SPIKER

However, it was a lecture entitled 'The Prophet's Way of *Mīzān*: manifestations in the Realm of Knowledge' given by Hasan Spiker, that transformed my understanding of the place of knowledge in Islam and would result in the collaboration that would enable me to complete the Mizan Thesis.

Hasan Spiker is the son of Abul Qasim Spiker, and our families have been friends since they arrived in Cambridge in the early 1990s. He was the little boy to whose angelic rendering of the call to prayer I drew your attention several chapters ago. He used to be present during my discussions with his father in the early days of the Golden Web, and selected the Golden Web as the subject for a school assignment, which he beautifully illustrated. He did not go down the usual academic route, but at the age of eighteen took off for Dar al-Islam, to seek knowledge at its source. Hasan spent twelve years studying the intellectual sciences in Morocco, Turkey and Jordan, where he also completed his memorization of the Qur'an. During this time, he studied with a number of teachers, notably the Iraqi sage Sayyid Quṣayy Abū Siʿd, one of the few remaining masters of the Ottoman and Kurdish educational curricula in their fullness, and an expert on the works of IbnʿArabī.

In 2014 Hasan was recruited by Tabah Foundation Research, to join their team, headed by Karim Lahham, that was embarking on their most ambitious undertaking to date, 'The Classification of the Sciences'. This hugely important project was re-establishing the foundations of Islam and its manifestation, at a time when post-modern ideas where eating into the very fabric of the intellectual life of Muslims. The first fruits of this great endeavour have appeared as I am in the process of finishing this book. The first two works have been published: *The Anatomy of Knowledge & The Ontological Necessity of First Principles* by Karim Laham, and *Things as they are: Nafs al-Amr & The Metaphysical Foundations of Objective Truth* by Hasan Spiker.

Although I had come to recognize the falsity of the Golden Age of Islam narrative, I had not realized that I was trapped in the flip-side of the story. In the decline and stagnation narrative, Imam al-Ghazali was the villain who, through his attack on philosophy, had brought to an end the inquiring mind of the Muslim. I followed the opposite story in which Imam al-Ghazali was the great hero who placed Sufism at the apex; it was only through the discipline and science of the purification of the soul that the believer could reach the experience of the reality of the Creator. The reasoning mind of the philosopher could not attain this supreme station; as in Christianity, the reasoning mind had to be satisfied with believing. This had been my understanding. It was now about to change.

Hasan's lecture transfixed me. I listened effortlessly to every word as the realization gradually dawned on me that the reasoning mind followed a different trajectory in Islam from that of the West. In Islam, the trajectory led to the knowledge of the reality of the Creator; it was no longer a matter of believing, it was a matter of knowing. He took us on a journey introducing us to the major thinkers and their contributions to the formation of the grand synthesis in which, by the fifteenth century, a hierarchy of knowledge had been established that took in the revealed sciences alongside all of the branches of philosophy and mysticism. This holistic knowledge system, which informed the higher education of both the Ottoman and Mughal empires, was destroyed by the British in India in 1857, and by the Turks themselves in the 1920s, to be replaced by the secular modern system. Hasan Spiker had been exposed to one of the few scholars who miraculously still retained this knowledge.

During Q&A, Hasan responded to a question which made me think that he seemed not to be fully aware of the significance of the incredible truth that he had unveiled. I brought this up with him after the lecture. It was a special moment in my long journey. I had been given the missing piece which completed the Mizan Thesis, and Hasan had found the context in which his work belonged and could thrive.

After the lecture I invited Hasan to join me in my Mizan Initiative, and in May 2017, he and his family moved back to the UK and to Cambridge, and we started our work together. I should make clear that my project was not his only reason for choosing Cambridge; his sister and family were there, and in the autumn, he would begin an MPhil in Religion at the Divinity Faculty, which would lead onto a PhD in Philosophy which he is currently pursuing; for a scholar to be taken seriously in the West, and indeed in the Muslim World, he has to have these letters after his name, and it is very important that Hasan Spiker's work is taken seriously.

REFLECTIONS ON THE PROGRAMME

The seminar brought to a conclusion a programme which had taken a cross section of Cambridge Muslims from the University and the town, on a journey from the narrative of progress to that of the Mizan Thesis. However, the programme revealed how deeply the narrative of progress had entered into the mindset of Muslims. The language of progress was fully installed in the young minds, and the students were encased in an educational process that embodied the idea of progress. Some of those who participated seemed to have benefitted, but I was keenly aware that a great deal more had to be done to get the case across. Whilst the Golden Age narrative was a natural part of the younger Muslim mindset, it had no meaning for the older group of shopkeepers from the Cambridge Muslim community. Their lives were centred upon the Prophet and his companions, and they had me spell-bound with the beautiful stories they related, with love and devotion. It was interesting to see the gap that existed between their understanding and that of the younger western-educated generation.

I needed to develop a powerful case that demonstrated the falsity of the narrative of progress. It was essential to show how the principle of *mizan* or balance underlies all existence, and that by violating this principle in its pursuit of progress, the West has led us into the chaos and danger of our present situation. I would spend the next eight months working on a slide lecture, with the idea that it would be presented in the form of a seminar in the Autumn of 2017.

Hasan Spiker took me through the 19th century philosophers who had devised the Theory of Progress, from Hegel, who believed it proceeded through conflict; Karl Marx, whose paradigm ended in a communist utopia; Comte, who celebrated the modern scientific mind as the high point of human evolution; and Spencer who believed in its biological inevitability, but that it was only open to the European superior race. It was Spencer who coined the horrendous statement 'the survival of the fittest'. What was so extraordinary was that the theory of progress had been thoroughly demolished by thinkers of the war-stricken 20th century, but this had in no way affected it remaining as an article of faith within the social, cultural and political fabric of society.

This contradiction led me to the realization of why the theory of progress was so powerful: it was modernity's only narrative, and without it the modern world could not exist. Those participating in the endeavour had to believe it had a purpose; hence the idea that we moderns are creating 'a better world' and that humanity is progressing. The fact that all the evidence is to the contrary has to date been unable to shift this fundamental pillar that props the disintegrating edifice. Having established the insanity of the theory, which was the product of a handful of 19th century thinkers, we showed how absurd it was to shoehorn Islam into the paradigm.

The next challenge was to show the reality of the *mizan* or balance. We began by demonstrating how this was a universal principle that was present in all human cultures and all natural phenomena. When the balance is broken, things fall apart. We then went on to illustrate how the manifestation of Islam as a civilization perfectly embodied the principle of *mizan*. With the introduction of Hasan's understanding of how the intellectual trajectory reached its goal, the final piece of the Mizan Thesis was in place. In Islam, the criteria for the relationship between humanity and the Creator, the society, and the domain of nature were perfectly enunciated and in balance.

We now turned to the breaking of the balance and the rise of the modern world. I had already established the three worlds of the West: Christian, Civilized and Modern, and how they had been dominated by the saint, the warrior/statesman, and the merchant, respectively. I now wanted to show the role these vocations played in the rise of Europe to global dominance, with the destruction of the traditional worlds, and the imposition of modernity.

A radical change in our understanding of the past was taking place. A generation of scholars and writers in the West, free and unencumbered by the Empire narrative that my generation was brought up with, and scholars and writers from the former colonized worlds seeking to understand what had happened to them, were producing books and documentary films that were uncovering a chilling picture of the reality of what had passed. I devoured the books and documentaries. I had already been liberated from the Empire mindset in the 1960s, however, what now came to light shook me to my core. The arrogance, cruelty and destruction that we wreaked upon the world in the name of civilization and progress went way beyond anything I had previously imagined.

GRENFELL TOWER

It was a long spring and summer of study, broken by the terrible fire at Grenfell Tower in London. My friend Tariq Tamimi lived in the area and witnessed the conflagration. He, along with many others from the community, were on site and delivering services to the stricken residents whilst the fire still raged. I visited him several days later. The burnt-out hulk of the high-rise building was like a vision from hell. Tariq introduced me to people who had lost everything and yet retained their humanity. Most memorable was a gentleman we met at the local mosque, who had returned from a business trip to Cairo, to find his wife and children had died in the fire. I will never forget his dignity and courage; although grief stricken, he trusted in his Lord. I left Tariq, who remained tending to the needs of the bereaved, and returned to Cambridge.

CHANGING THE NARRATIVE: FROM PROGRESS TO BALANCE

The seminar entitled 'Changing the Narrative: From Progress to Balance', took place on 19th November 2017 and was organized by the Centre of Islamic Studies. We chose for the occasion the Old Divinity School, where some three and a half years previously we had launched my slide presentation 'Reflections of An English Muslim'. Now it was my Mizan Thesis that was to be presented.

Dr Amina Nawaz opened the proceedings by welcoming all who were attending, and introducing what was to happen during the day. As planned, the seminar was in three parts. Part 1: 'The Myth of Progress', with Mujadad Zaman as chair and Dr Shahridan Faiez as respondent, took place during the morning. The other parts took place in the afternoon: Part 2: 'The Reality of the Balance', chaired by Hasan Spiker with Dr Karim Lahham as respondent, and Part 3: 'The Breaking of the Balance' with Dr Samir Mahmoud in the chair and Dr Mohamad Hammour as respondent.

It was an intense day. The panels had included colleagues and friends, who were already deeply engaged with my work. There was no doubt that we had reached a point of clarity, and the question now was, 'How do we proceed?'

24
THE BOOK

THE PLAN

I HAD DEVISED A PLAN which I believed could storm the ramparts and bring the *mizan* narrative to the attention of the world. A six-month programme would include: the preparation of the final draft of a book for publication and the recording of an audio book; the preparation of the 'Changing the Narrative' seminar as a documentary film; the organization of a series of lectures and seminars; the continuation of the series of filmed interviews, and the development of a draft plan for a series of television films, having identified a suitable production company.

In late December 2017, I met with our benefactor to present my plan. By now, he had come to know me well. No doubt he could see that I was reverting to my role as an organizer, and gently put his finger on the first item. He suggested I focus on the book. I had to complete my role as a writer and produce what could serve as a manifesto for the Mizan Thesis. It was wise counsel; it would take me a year and a half to finish writing the book.

DR KHALED FAHMY

January 2018 began with an important change at the Centre of Islamic Studies. Dr Khaled Fahmy succeeded Yasir Suleiman as Professor of Modern Arabic Studies and Director of the Centre. I had enjoyed an excellent relationship with Yasir, and approached my first meeting with Khaled Fahmy with concern. Would he want me to remain as a visiting scholar? After all, it was supposed to have been for three years only, and I was now entering year four. My fellowship had been very helpful in the furtherance of my work.

Our first meeting took place in late January 2018. I found myself facing a man whom I came to know as a formidable scholar and a deeply compassionate and committed human being. Khaled Fahmy is a historian of the modern Middle East, with a special interest in the social and cultural history of nineteenth-century Egypt. He received his BA in economics and his MA in political science from the American University in Cairo (AUC). He then went to the University of Oxford where he wrote his DPhil dissertation on the history of the Egyptian army during the first half of the nineteenth century, and received his doctorate in 1993. There followed seventeen years in the US, first at Princeton University, then at New York University. In 2010, he was invited back to his home country to become chair of the Department of History at his alma mater, AUC. He returned to the US in 2013, firstly as a visiting fellow at Columbia University, and then as a visiting professor at Harvard University.

Khaled gave his inaugural Cambridge lecture on 22nd February 2018 which was based on his book, *In Quest of Justice: Islamic Law and Forensic Medicine in Modern Egypt* (University of California Press, 2018). The lecture was brilliantly constructed and delivered, and the subject matter revealed a profound knowledge of the encounter between the traditional world of Egypt and the modern West.

At that first meeting with Khaled, I had given him my life story, and an outline of the book I was now endeavouring to write. He patiently listened to me, and when I asked him if he wished me to continue as a visiting fellow, he graciously said he would be very happy if I remained. There followed meetings at seminal moments during the writing of the book, and in the lead-up to the Cambridge University launch, which Khaled chaired, and which was held under the auspices of the Centre. Not being an academic in an academic environment, always meant that I was never entirely at ease; Khaled's patience, encouragement and wise counsel meant a great deal to me.

WRITING THE BOOK

2018 was a long writing year. I was now able to address the blank sheets of paper without flinching. I entered into that hermetic seal that is required of the writer. My periods of isolation were broken by meetings with Hasan Spiker, and telephone conversations with Karim Lahham. I also attended a challenging series of public lectures organized by the CIS, which included one that I found particularly enlightening.

Based on his book *The New Odyssey – the Story of the Twenty-First-Century Refugee Crisis*, the journalist Patrick Kingsley brilliantly illuminated the plight of the migrants who were fleeing the horrors taking place in the Middle East. He brought to life the humanity and courage of those seeking refuge for their families. Whilst covering the larger picture, he focused on one man's journey. Hashem al-Souki, a Syrian, left his wife Hayam and his three sons behind while he tried to make his way to Sweden, in the hope that he could later reunite his family in safety. Hashem was a civil servant with the water board, who lived in a small town outside Damascus, before political events overtook him. He was arrested during a sweep in his area, beaten, tortured and, when finally released, he returned to find his house destroyed and his country engulfed in civil war. I bought the book and became deeply engaged in his epic journey, which ended successfully with his family finally joining him in Stockholm. Patrick Kingsley's book is a welcome antidote to the way these noble and courageous victims of the crisis, which originated in our careless interventions, were being portrayed in most of the popular media, and by the new brand of nationalist politicians.

By the beginning of 2018, I had most of what I required to write the book. What I needed was a framework. While the main title for the book was established quite late in the process, the subtitle, 'A New Narrative for the Age of Crises', was there from the beginning. It provided the structure for the introduction to the Mizan Thesis, clearing the ground for the main purpose of the book. I was inspired by Pugin's great work, *Contrasts: Or, A Parallel Between the Noble Edifices of The Middle Ages and Corresponding Buildings of the Present Day*, in which the 19th century reviver of the Gothic tradition in architecture showed side by side the Classical and Gothic solutions to the built environment, making the case for the Gothic. My book would show the total contrast between Islam and the West when seen through the prism of the *mizan* perspective. Seven chapters would cover the themes of Sovereignty, Civilization, Knowledge, Commerce, Art & the Environment, Conquest and Expansion, and the Age of Crises.

By January 2019 I had completed the draft of the book. I shared this with a small circle of scholars and friends, inviting their feedback. I also worked with Abul Qasim Spiker on the design and publication of what was now entitled *Rethinking Islam & The West: A New Narrative for the Age of Crises*. We had decided to self-publish and set up Equilibra as the name under which the book would appear. By early May, just before Ramadan began, the final edit had been completed, and the book design and layout agreed. The production could now go ahead.

However, I needed to make sure the CIS would be happy with my association with the Centre appearing in the book. On the first day of Ramadan, I emailed the typescript of the book to Khaled Fahmy. I waited, on the edge of my seat, until, on the final day of Ramadan I received his response. It was a brief message in an email: 'Congratulations, your book is thought-provoking and original'. Those few words glowed in my heart, and a deep sense of relief encompassed me.

VISITING NORTHUMBERLAND

With the book now out of my hands being processed, Annabel and I took a week off. We had long wanted to visit Northumberland. It was the kingdom which was receiving Christianity from Irish monks, at the time when Islam was being revealed in Arabia. I had a great love of the flowering that took place, which was beautifully recorded by the Venerable Bede in his book *Ecclesiastical History of the English People*. Annabel was also keen to visit the Farne Islands which play host to an incredible array of seabirds. On the way up we visited Durham Cathedral and the tomb of St Cuthbert.

His resting place is one of the only tombs to have survived the orgy of destruction promulgated by Henry VIII and Oliver Cromwell.

On arriving in Northumberland, we stayed in a wooden cabin by the sea and each day visited bird sanctuaries and places associated with the life of St Cuthbert. On our journey home we stopped by Fountains Abbey, a vast ruin of one of the most important monasteries, destroyed by King Henry. It was a lovely few days and we felt refreshed and ready for what lay ahead.

THE BOOK LAUNCH

The book was published on 6th July, and was available for purchase three days later. I immediately sent copies to our circle of students, colleagues and friends. The Cambridge University launch was set for 4th November, so we had four months to prepare a core group who had already read and discussed the book. This would make for a more interesting event than is often the case, when people are confronted with the book for the first time at the launch.

The day of the launch finally arrived. The CIS administrators, Neil Cunningham and Ludmilla Applegate, pulled out all the stops, and organized a wonderful send-off for the book. The carefully planned publicity drew in around a hundred and fifty attendees. Khaled introduced the event and the speakers, who then made their brief reflections on the book. Hasan Spiker was first to the podium, followed by Professor Recep Senturk, President of Ibn Khaldoon University in Istanbul. A few questions followed, after which two postgraduate students gave their response to the book. Then more questions, with the final talk given by my dear friend Dr Samir Mahmud, who had made the hazardous journey from Beirut; because of the state of conflict in Lebanon, he had to pass through a number of roadblocks to get to the airport, especially to be present at the launch. After a final flurry of questions, and whilst there were still a number of questions pending, Khaled brought the evening to a close. *Rethinking Islam & The West: A New Narrative for the Age of Crises* had entered the arena, and I was eager to see how it would fare.

TRANSLATIONS OF *RETHINKING ISLAM & THE WEST*

After the launch I met with Professor Recep Senturk. His short talk about my book was very well constructed and it was clear that he had a deep insight into the Mizan Thesis. He is one of the few academics who had a traditional education before engaging with Western academia. He is a strong advocate of non-western sociological theories such as those by the Muslim sociologist Ibn Khaldun. He asked me if I would agree to my book being translated into Turkish and published by Ibn Haldun University Press. This made me very happy, and my joy was compounded when a Turkish student who was just completing his PhD came forward and expressed his enthusiasm for the book and his desire to undertake the translation. Mustafa Metin Basbay told me that the ideas expressed in the book were desperately needed to be communicated to the new generation growing up in modern Turkey. He has become a splendid advocate for the Mizan Thesis and a dear friend.

I met Abdus Samad Romero when he came to Cambridge for the opening of the new mosque. We encountered Abdus Samad earlier in my story, as the host when Mahmud gave a series of concerts at his beautiful Azzagra Cultural Foundation in the foothills of the Sierra de la Sagra. He asked for permission to translate and publish the book, through his foundation, into Spanish. Nothing could have made me happier. To undertake a translation requires a deep commitment, and a thorough understanding of the work.

A third request was made by another person who was moved by the book. Luca Osman Coletti asked if he could produce an Italian translation, and successfully completed the task with Claudio Abdullatif Biasotti. All three translations are now available, and I have had approaches regarding translations into Arabic, German and Malay.

THE BOOK TOUR

The next thing on the agenda was a book tour, first in the UK and then overseas to the Gulf, Malaysia and the USA. The UK Tour was being organized by Waseem Mahmood. Waseem had, over a number of years, built a phenomenal list of contacts throughout the Muslim communities of the UK. He had organized many events, most recently, the book tours of Michael Sugich's wonderful autobiographical work *Signs on the Horizons: Meetings with Men of Knowledge and Illumination*, and Peter Sanders' beautiful photographic book *Meetings with Mountains: Encounters with the Saints and Sages of the Islamic World.* Both were my contemporaries and had entered Islam around the same time, so it seemed appropriate that I should follow in their wake.

Waseem decided that we should begin our tour in Glasgow. There was, he said, no community in the UK more alive, engaged and hospitable than the Muslims of that city. Our bags were packed and, on the 16th November, Annabel and I joined Waseem and his wife at St Pancras station. We set out on the first leg of what I imagined would be at least a year and a half of travelling. Once we had got settled in our seats, Waseem handed me a poster. It was an announcement for a Mawlid (a celebration of the Prophet's birthday) to be held in Glasgow the day after our arrival. On the poster there were pictures of three venerable Shaykhs, beautifully attired in traditional dress, and myself. 'What is this?' I asked, 'I've put you down to speak at the Mawlid', Waseem replied. Now, I strongly argued that it was inappropriate for me to appear at such a function alongside the Shaykhs; they were religious scholars and were steeped in the knowledge that was expected on such occasions. But it was a fait accompli, the posters had already been distributed. So, I wracked my brains for what I might usefully share and came up with the following:

> I have been blessed and fortunate, for more than fifty years, to have been surrounded by scholars of Islam. Both in my work and my home, I have lived and engaged with those who have seriously studied Arabic and delved deeply into the Holy Qur'an and the Islamic sciences. I feed off and am continually refreshed by their knowledge which flows from an inexhaustible ocean. The gifts that Almighty Allah has given me do not include a talent for learning languages. My knowledge of Arabic is rudimentary, enough to say my prayers, alhamdulillah!
>
> I am, however, comforted by the realization that Almighty Allah provides fruit from His tree of Knowledge for all His servants, and the low-hanging fruit maybe as succulent and rewarding as that at the top of the tree. We are each provided with fruit that, with a little effort, is

> within our reach. Great scholars climb the ladder to reach the top of the tree, and we can try to hold the ladder for them. Meanwhile we can be reaching out for the low-hanging fruit. Each and every one of the fruits on the tree is destined for one of His servants. All the fruit is there to be harvested.
>
> There are three of the low-hanging fruits that I particularly love. We are told that if when we are greeted, we return the greeting more expansively, blessings will pour down on us. Thus, if someone greets you with 'Assalamu 'alaykum' you can return the greeting not just with 'Wa 'alaykum assalam', but with 'Wa 'alaykum assalam wa rahmatu'Llahi wa barakatuhu'. I try never to miss an opportunity to garner this wonderful and easy source of divine blessing.
>
> I cannot memorize the Holy Qur'an but I can memorize the 99 Names of Almighty Allah. My writing skills are also rudimentary, but I can write out and contemplate the Names, each one of which contains a saving grace. Such wealth is within my grasp.
>
> For us Muslims, marriage is half our religion. Today marriage is under attack as never before. It is very difficult to stay happily together. But for every Muslim there is a glorious passage which can help safeguard our marriages, if acted upon. Surat al-Rum, verse 21 tells us that Almighty Allah places love and mercy between husband and wife. It is only He who can grow that love and mercy. All we have to do is ask Him to do it. Thus, the third of the low-hanging fruits that I hold on to is this du'a.

I ended by wishing them good harvesting of the fruits within their grasp. I elicited from Waseem a promise that he would not land me in a similar situation again, as I was keenly aware of the dividing line that existed between the knowledge of the Shaykhs, and what I was engaged with. They represented what I was talking about.

Glasgow lived up to all that Waseem had promised. The hospitality reminded Annabel of the welcome she received on her visits to Iran. The response to the book was encouraging and we returned to Cambridge happy that our tour had begun well.

I was now beginning to receive invitations from student bodies both in Cambridge and London. A Turkish students' reading group, following the suggestion of Mustafa Metin Basbay, had selected *Rethinking Islam &*

The West, and requested a session with me to discuss the book. On 23rd November, 24 students gathered in Cambridge, mostly from London universities, and we spent the afternoon together. It was so exciting listening to the responses of those who had actually read the book. I looked forward to more of these kinds of meetings.

With the arrival of 2020, stories of a pandemic arising in China began filtering into the news. We continued our tour. Events were held at the Abdullah Quilliam Mosque lecture hall on 19th January, and the London Central Mosque and Cultural Centre on 25th January. I received a very warm welcome from the Abdullah Quilliam Society, who were in the process of restoring the first mosque to have been established in the UK. The mosque was founded in 1887, was taken over by the Liverpool City Council some twenty years later and was used for over a hundred years to house the city's records of births and marriages. The Society reclaimed a very dilapidated building a dozen years ago, and have already made great strides in bringing it back to life. They are also in the process of acquiring a large Victorian building adjoining the mosque, which will greatly enhance their capacity to deliver their ambitious cultural and educational programme. After my talk they gave me a copy of Ron Greaves' life of Abdullah Quilliam. The work of the society bearing his name, in restoring his mosque, and creating renewed interest in the life of this remarkable man, is delivering a singular service to the Muslim Community in the UK, and providing a valuable introduction to Islam in Britain for all those seeking to know more about the faith.

Liverpool was also memorable for my opportunity to meet with Shaykh Adam Kelwick again, whom you will remember had made such an impression on me when he participated in the Converts Seminar in Cambridge. Adam chaired the meeting, and we had time together on the following day. He was shortly to depart for Yemen on one of his missions as a humanitarian aid worker. Anyone who has followed on social media his remarkable reports and cries for help for the suffering and bereaved in the most devastated and dangerous areas of Syria, Lebanon and Yemen, will attest to the courage, sincerity and devotion of this wonderful man.

The London event was chaired by Dr Ahmad Al-Dubayan, Director General of the Cultural Centre. The auditorium was full, and the questions continued for some time before the event was brought to a close.

Afterwards, I continued to be engaged with members of the audience. The book was definitely making an impression.

By late January it was announced that the pandemic had arrived in the UK. Little realizing what was in store, we continued with our programme. The next event on our agenda was a study circle in Cambridge. A group of students had gathered around Hasan Spiker eager to benefit from his knowledge. They had been meeting weekly during term time. A special gathering of the circle to discuss with Hasan the aspects relating to the reasoning mind in my book was arranged for the 1st February, and was held in one of the Kings College meeting rooms.

On the 17th February I gave a lecture on 'Islam & the Environment' for the Cambridge students society as part of Islamic Awareness Week, and on 25th February I participated in a seminar on 'Climate Change and South Asia' organized by the students at Kings College London. We were now building up to our major University of London launch. This was being organized by the Centre of Islamic Studies at SOAS, and was to be held in the 300-seater Brunei Gallery auditorium on the evening of 18th March. The posters had already been circulated and a social media campaign launched. However, by early March, warnings of a possible lockdown were beginning to circulate, and by mid-March, restrictions on all but essential travel were being imposed. The University of London launch was postponed, and on 23rd March, the country went into total lockdown.

RELAUNCH IN CYBERSPACE

My response to lockdown is best described in the opening remarks of the first video I uploaded on Facebook on 2nd April 2020:

> We've been grounded. I'm sitting by myself, looking at my mobile phone, in a completely unfamiliar situation, because I'm not used to social media. I haven't engaged with it up until now. Just a few days ago I was at the beginning of the year-and-a-half-long launch of my book, *Rethinking Islam & The West.* I was having a wonderful time. When you've spent years writing a book, and are then in the situation that you are actually presenting it to the public, engaging with audiences, with the questions that inevitably come up which you have to answer, and the conversations and discussions which follow,

it's such a stimulating time for you. This is the moment when your ideas are challenged, where you gain fresh insights into them, and discover new things because people come up with their reflections and understandings. It's the moment when the whole comprehension of what you have been producing comes together, and the book is literally launched into the world, and you sit there full of excitement, and interest, and engagement, meeting new people. It's a fantastic experience, and I was so much enjoying it… and then, everything stopped. My book launch has been arrested. I can no longer go out and have that engagement, have that personal contact. So, I realized that I had to continue my book launch in cyberspace!'

Facebook contains a brilliant multimedia platform. Text with photos and videos could be easily uploaded. It seemed the perfect way of being able to introduce the remarkable people and the many projects that had informed my understanding, which had resulted in my book; to give people an idea of the rich background out of which the ideas had emerged. I could link Mahmud Mirza to his music on YouTube, create a photographic album of El-Wakil's beautiful buildings, connect Anthony Milroy to his documentary film, *The Hanging Gardens of Arabia;* I could introduce the video produced by Everyday Muslim on the fortieth anniversary of the World of Islam Festival, and carry the story of the Tonbridge School Chapel Campaign. I started posting. I felt like a journalist on a daily paper; throughout April and most of May, including the whole of Ramadan, I uploaded forty posts.

My locker was now empty, and I needed to move onto something else, some other way of getting my book across. Facebook was beginning to pall. I liked the platform; however, the medium was the quintessence of the ephemeral. The posts disappeared in a sea of chatter and opinions. I needed something more permanent to communicate my thesis. I had given my first webinar during Ramadan. Shah had invited me to give a talk on the Beautiful City for Thinkcity in Malaysia. I would give further Zoom talks and webinars, but somehow, I never felt at home in cyberspace. I missed the real-life encounters.

I had been preparing a slide lecture for my book tour, and decided to see if I could upgrade it to a video. The Cambridge launch of the book had been filmed by a locally-based production company called Dragon

Light Films. I contacted the director, Colin Ramsey, and asked if he might have the time to work with me on the project. Having also been grounded, he was in the unusual position of being free to start work immediately. There followed three wonderfully creative months. We already had a rich collection of images, and this was augmented with video sequences that Colin conjured up. I wrote the script and Colin made the best of helping me in my presentation. By the beginning of September 2020, we had completed our offering which ran for an hour and twenty minutes, and *Rethinking Islam & The West, an Illustrated Lecture* was uploaded onto YouTube.

Lockdown continued and had now become a way of life. What next for me to do? In October 2020 I began work on the book that you, dear reader, have almost finished.

EPILOGUE

SPRING HAS ARRIVED. Once again, the blackbirds are singing, the cherry trees are in bloom, and the days are lengthening. My work is almost done. I began this task a year and a half ago, and imagined it would be easy to accomplish. After all, I was simply acknowledging the sources of the understanding I had received which bore fruit in my book *Rethinking Islam & The West.* Little did I realize what lay ahead. I have passed through the fire in reliving my life, from childhood to the present.

After the success of the World of Islam Festival in 1976, my projects failed to be realized, and I experienced the bitterness of failure. But as I contemplated this unfolding, I began to see how each project had delivered up a piece of a puzzle, which only made sense when all the pieces had been assembled. Everything comes together in the Mizan Thesis. Through this perspective, the success of Islam and Islamic civilization is revealed, and we can gain an insight into the true nature of modernity. It frees us from the shackles of the narrative of progress, and enables us to face the escalating crises, which define our age, with clarity and equanimity.

As I reflect upon my journey, two themes emerge that have determined my understanding: the gulf between the traditional and modern, and the reality of the unity and universality of Islam and Islamic civilization. The momentous meeting with Ustad Mahmud Mirza in 1968 was my gateway to both of the themes. I was befriended by a traditional master musician with whom I was able to spend time, and who has remained a constant presence in my life for more than fifty years. I had come from nine years deeply immersed in modern drama, modern arts, and the counterculture, and after only a few months with Mahmud and his music, the gulf between the traditional arts and the modern became crystal clear. The beauty and clarity of his music belonged to an entirely different world from that of the chaos and angst of the modern. He was working within a form and language which allowed him to receive inspiration from above, while the modern artists had to create their own languages and were on an endless search for originality. Their products were the expressions of their own souls and what lay around them. The traditional masters did not have to seek originality. They were schooled in humility, and once they had mastered their craft, the pure originality of their being was manifested. They became perfect vehicles for divine inspiration.

My introduction to Islamic architecture was through Hasan Fathy, who, when he encountered the master masons of Nubia, became the great reviver of the tradition. However, it was his student and disciple, Abdel-Wahed El-Wakil, who fully opened my eyes. I was privileged to work with him for two years, and I also witnessed his creation of the series of beautiful mosques that were built in Saudi Arabia during the 1980s. He has remained another constant presence in my life, continually confirming the reality of the tradition of Islamic architecture.

I had grown up within the environment of the revival of Gothic architecture, and with the fire that gutted Tonbridge School Chapel, I was brought back into the heart of what remained of my birth tradition. I was to meet Stephen Dykes Bower, the last of the masters of Gothic architecture, the fifth in line to Augustus Pugin the reviver of the tradition. However, it was Warwick Pethers, his student and disciple, who became my friend and mentor. He advised me through the long planning campaign, in which we fought for the restoration of the Gothic chapel. The modern architect who had been chosen for the restoration claimed to be creating a synthesis between the modern and the traditional, when in fact, he was simply deconstructing the traditional to create his own modernist take on tradition. This was my first encounter with a phenomenon that is now beginning to plague the Islamic world. The traditional and the modern are completely separate worlds and to mix them is to destroy the traditional. I then lived through the ten years of Warwick's building of the great tower of St Edmundsbury Cathedral. Every week we would meet for coffee in Cambridge, or speak on the phone. By the time he had completed the cathedral tower, he had become the last remaining master of a tradition that had been flourishing in my childhood.

When we became the proud owners of Polebrook Farm in the early 1980s, we immersed ourselves in the history of this amazing group of completely intact medieval fields, unique in Kent and probably in South East England. We began to study how we could bring back the farm to its original use. But it was the meeting with Anthony Milroy, who had lived with the farmers of Northern Yemen, and had experienced a functioning system of husbandry, who brought alive the brilliance and reality of the tradition and demonstrated the damage that the introduction of the modern techniques was wreaking upon the land and its people. Tony became a friend, and has remained an inspiring companion in a darkening world. For the land, and the people who have tended it for millennia, are both suffering from the wanton destruction of their traditional systems which work with nature, as they are replaced by the modern systems which are destroying the natural world. My understanding of the health, intelligence and beauty of the traditional systems of husbandry and the ways of life that they supported has been further enriched by Osman Al-Bili and the description of his village in Sudan when he was a child; Professor Hood Salleh and my friends in Malaysia as they described their childhoods on the kampung; my visit to Adi Setia's family farm which he is in the process of restoring; and the research undertaken by Simon Fitzwilliam Hall which documented the remarkable multi-cropping oasis of Southern Morocco. Nothing could be clearer than the complete separation between the modern and traditional systems of farming. If the traditional is exposed to the modern, it is destroyed. There is no connector between them. They are governed by completely different principles. And this absolute separation applies to the arts, architecture and every other domain that governs human society.

It was through my desire to understand Ustad Mahmud Mirza's background that my vision of the unity and universality of Islam and Islamic civilization came about. His music belonged to the princely courts of Mughal India, and was the equivalent in music to the Taj Mahal in architecture. Now, I knew something about Moorish Spain. The kinetic artists in my Signals gallery were inspired by the geometric patterning of the Alhambra Palace. It was clear to me that the arts and architecture of Mughal India and Moorish Spain belonged to the same world, and yet only Islam connected them; their pre-Islamic languages, cultures and histories were completely separate and different. The World of Islam Festivals of 1971 and 1976 were my attempt at communicating this awesome reality.

Over the last nearly half century I have been filling in the picture of this marvellous manifestation. With my various projects, I have engaged with scores of scholars of Islamic studies from many different backgrounds, from deeply practising Muslims to atheists, from Christian monks and evangelicals to Jews and Hindus. But from whatever perspective they may have approached the World of Islam, their devotion to their particular subject would somehow shine a shaft of light on some aspect of the civilization, and their insights were invaluable in enabling me to see more of this incredible unity and universality.

The many Muslim students who came from every part of Dar al-Islam and converged upon Cambridge University, were another source that enriched my understanding. After WWII, we had invited Muslims from our collapsing empire, to come and rebuild the motherland. As prosperity returned, Muslims from many lands sought refuge in our country from the conflict, poverty and chaos overwhelming their worlds. Through these heroic newcomers to our shores, I have witnessed the reality of what exists at the centre of this unity and universality: the veneration of the Holy Qur'an and the love of the Prophet.

The constant presence of my dear friends Karim Lahham and Hasan Spiker over the stage of my journey when, with little confidence, I took pen in hand, has been critical to my understanding something of the higher reaches of Islamic thought. At a time of intellectual disintegration, their Tabah Foundation publications are a beacon of light. Finally, through my son Ali, the supreme art form that manifests the reality of the revelation, the recitation of the Holy Qur'an, has reached into my soul and allowed me to taste that unity and oneness that is at the heart of Almighty God's final revelation to humanity.

RETHINKING ISLAM & THE WEST

A New Narrative for the Age of Crises

by Ahmed Paul Keeler

ISLAM AND THE WEST have been neighbours for 1400 years. The West grew up under the shadow of Islam, and then after the Renaissance, in a dramatic reversal of roles, the West became world conquerors and subdued all other cultures and civilizations, including Islam. This transformation ushered in the modern world, a world unlike any that had existed before.

All nations are now judged according to their scientific progress, technological development and economic growth. And yet, humanity is now experiencing multiple crises that are threatening our very existence. Population explosion, financial, social and political instability, the alarming growth of mental illness, the threat of nuclear annihilation and climate change all loom over humanity like a dark cloud. Simultaneously, the world is witnessing a dangerous escalation in the polarization between Islam and the West.

In this thought-provoking book, we are invited to view the crises we are facing and the tangled relationship between Islam and the West through a different lens. Keeler proposes that the true yardstick for measuring success should be the balance achieved between the spiritual, social and material needs of humanity; a balance which makes it possible to live in harmony with nature. When the world is viewed from this perspective, a completely different picture of Islam and the West emerges.

RETHINKING ISLAM & THE WEST
A New Narrative for the Age of Crises
Ahmed Paul Keeler
ISBN: 978-1-9161738-0-4

Printed in Great Britain
by Amazon